Palgrave Studies of Marketing in Emerging Economies

Series Editors

Robert E. Hinson, Univ Ghana Bus Sch, Dept Mktg & Entr, Legon, Accra, Ghana
Ogechi Adeola, Ajah, Lagos Business School, Lagos, Nigeria

This book series focuses on contemporary themes in marketing and marketing management research in emerging markets and developing economies. Books in the series cover the BRICS (Brazil, Russia, India, China and South Africa), MINT (Mexico, Indonesia, Nigeria and Turkey), CIVETS (Colombia, Indonesia, Vietnam, Egypt, Turkey, and South Africa); EAGLE economies (those which are expected to lead growth in the next ten years, such as Brazil, China, India, Indonesia, South Korea, Mexico, Russia, Taiwan, and Turkey) and all other African countries (classified under developing countries), taking into consideration the demographic, socio-cultural and macro-economic factors influencing consumer choices in these markets. The series synthesizes key subject areas in marketing, discuss marketing issues, processes, procedures and strategies across communities, regions and continents, and also the way digital innovation is changing the business landscape in emerging economies.

Palgrave Studies of Marketing in Emerging Economies presents a unique opportunity to examine and discuss marketing strategy and its implications in emerging economies, thereby filling a gap in current marketing literature.

All chapter submissions to the series will undergo a double blind peer review and all book proposals will undergo a single blind peer review.

More information about this series at
http://www.palgrave.com/gp/series/16591

Samuelson Appau
Editor

Marketing Brands in Africa

Perspectives on the Evolution of Branding in an Emerging Market

palgrave
macmillan

Editor
Samuelson Appau
RMIT University
Melbourne, VIC, Australia

ISSN 2730-5554 ISSN 2730-5562 (electronic)
Palgrave Studies of Marketing in Emerging Economies
ISBN 978-3-030-77203-1 ISBN 978-3-030-77204-8 (eBook)
https://doi.org/10.1007/978-3-030-77204-8

This Palgrave Macmillan imprint is published by the registered company Springer Nature Switzerland AG
The registered company address is: Gewerbestrasse 11, 6330 Cham, Switzerland

For Bridget. Always.

Contents

Notes on Contributors

Samuelson Appau has a Ph.D. in Marketing from the University of Melbourne. He is a Senior Lecturer in Marketing at RMIT University in Melbourne, Australia. Samuelson's research interests include consumer culture, branding and wellbeing and have been published in leading marketing journals such as the *Journal of Consumer Research*, *Journal of Business Research*, *Marketing Theory* and the *Journal of Marketing and Public Policy*, among others. He has also co-edited a book on wellbeing and has authored many book chapters. He teaches branding, training marketing students and entrepreneurs to understand how to build and market strong brands. Prior to joining academia, Samuelson worked in market research and brand consulting for Kantar in West Africa, advising clients such as Barclays, Nestlé, Unilever and Etisalat.

Oluwadamilola Blessing Ayeni is a Ph.D. candidate at Swinburne University of Technology, Australia. Her doctoral research investigates Australians' use of Facebook and its role in influencing health messaging and communications. She is particularly interested in the way online users navigate the changing affordances of a platform to communicate key messages about childhood vaccination. Damilola holds a master's degree in Communication and Media Studies from Monash University in Australia. She is passionate about social media platforms and its widespread use in the society.

Samuel K. Bonsu is a Professor of Marketing and Consumption Studies at the Ghana Institute of Management and Public Administration (GIMPA). His works have appeared in some of the most prestigious journals in consumer culture. He serves on the editorial review boards of several quality journals and is a sought-after global speaker on African consumption and development.

Tendai Chikweche, Ph.D. is a Senior Lecturer in Marketing at Western Sydney University. He is an Experienced Academic and Researcher with more than 20 years' experience in various disciplines primarily in marketing, entrepreneurship and innovation. Tendai's research interests are in the areas of design thinking, marketing to the base of the pyramid, social entrepreneurship, small business enterprises and he has been a pioneer researcher in the area of marketing to the middle class in Africa. He has conducted research and consulting in these areas and has published in international publication outlets. Tendai is a Fellow of the Chartered Institute of Marketing and advises diaspora business councils and other agencies on issues relating to doing business in Africa.

Ebenezer Asare Effah holds a Ph.D. from London Metropolitan University and lectures at Central University, Ghana, where he is the alternate to the Head of Marketing Department. He formerly worked as Education Welfare Officer at the London Borough of Hackney, Lecturer at North London University and Senior Consultant at Ernst & Young Ghana. His research interests include services marketing, integrated marketing communications and branding.

Robert E. Hinson is a Professor of Marketing and the Head of the Department of Marketing and Entrepreneurship at the University of Ghana Business School. He is also Acting Director of Institutional Advancement at the University of Ghana and is the author of many edited books and journal publications in marketing.

Marian Makkar, Ph.D. is a Lecturer of Marketing at the College of Business, RMIT University. Her research interests cover consumer culture, the sharing economy, and market shaping and market innovations. She has published papers in international journals such as *European Journal of Marketing*, *Journal of Business Research*, *Current Issues in Tourism*, *Journal of Retailing and Consumer Services*, *Marketing Intelligence & Planning* and *Journal of Fashion Marketing & Management*.

Kobby Mensah is a Senior Lecturer at the Department of Marketing and Entrepreneurship, University of Ghana Business School. His teaching and research interests include political marketing, political communications and social media engagement. Kobby obtained his Ph.D. in Journalism from the University of Sheffield, United Kingdom. He also holds an M.Sc. in International Marketing from the Sheffield Hallam University, United Kingdom, and is a Chartered Marketer (CIM, UK). Kobby Mensah is the leading academic and advocate for political marketing teaching and practice in Africa. His analysis on political campaign management from the perspectives of political marketing is widely sought by African and global media platforms. Kobby is a member of Political Marketing Specialist Group (PMSG) of the Political Studies Association (PSA), UK, a member of the Palgrave Macmillan Board on Political Marketing Management Book Series. His recent publication is 'Political Marketing and Management in Ghana: A New Architecture' by Palgrave Macmillan, UK.

Emmanuel Mogaji is a Senior Lecturer in Advertising and Marketing Communications at the University of Greenwich, London, UK. His research interests are in artificial intelligence, digital marketing and service brand management. Emmanuel has previously worked as a marketing communication executive, responsible for creative designs and managing marketing campaigns, liaising and building relationships with a range of stakeholders. He has published peer-reviewed journal articles, book chapters and books and presented his research in many national and international conferences. His publications have appeared in *International Journal of Information Management*, *Journal of Product and Brand Management*, *Australasian Marketing Journal* and *International Journal of Bank Marketing*.

Riverson Oppong holds a Ph.D. in International Oil and Gas Management—Finance and Economics from Gubkin Russian University of Oil and Gas and a Diploma in Earth GeoScience from Stanford University. He has 11 years of global experience in the oil and gas industry with Horizon Energy Ltd, GE Energy/oil and gas (US & Ghana), PPS (Ghana and UK) and Lukoil International (Russia, Dubai, USA & Cote d'Ivoire). Riverson is currently the Commercial Manager in charge of Economic Modeling and Risk Management at Ghana National Gas Company. He is also an Adjunct Lecturer at Ghana Technology University College and the Coventry University Campus in Africa.

Sydney Scott Sam is a Brand Strategist and Serial Entrepreneur with an M.B.A. from the University of Ghana Business School. He is the Founder of Workspace Global, a Ghana-based tech-oriented brand communications company offering a boutique range of creative services with a focus on start-ups and entrepreneurs. He is on the 2019's Forbes 30 under 30 list for successful entrepreneurs in Africa. Sydney also serves as the Global curator for a growing non-profit community and conversation series for creatives, entrepreneurs and business professionals dubbed "OPENSPACE".

Slađana Starčević, Ph.D. is an Associate Professor at FEFA Faculty, Metropolitan University, Serbia. She teaches Digital Marketing, Digital Marketing Communications and Digital Marketing Analytics. Dr. Starčević is a very experienced strategic planner in marketing, as she has worked in marketing agencies for many years (Publicis, Profile South and East Europe, Ogilvy, Communis). Starčević is the author of a book and several scientific papers in the field of marketing. Particular areas of interest are marketing communications, consumer behaviour and branding. As a product of the gained experience in marketing, she has created her brand and founded the fashion company SAROSSOW.

List of Figures

List of Tables

1

On the Practice and Theory of Marketing Brands in Africa

Samuelson Appau

Why Brands and Branding in Africa?

Branding has evolved from its mundane practice of livestock differentiation in the agricultural age to become an endemic marketing element and practice. Although the practice of branding existed in different ways across multiple civilizations and cultures, at least since the Industrial Revolution, branding has evolved as trademarks of ownership, mediums of product differentiation, tools of cultural narratives, and cultural symbols (Holt, 2002). In today's globalized consumer culture, brands have become iconic, are recognised and desired in and of themselves, and unite neo-tribes from Seoul to New York City and Lagos to Copenhagen (Muniz & O'Guinn, 2001). Despite this evolution, the functional purpose of brands and branding in marketing was and is still about differentiation. Increasing marketization has heightened

S. Appau (✉)
RMIT University, Melbourne, VIC, Australia
e-mail: samuelson.appau@rmit.edu.au

S. Appau (ed.), *Marketing Brands in Africa*, Palgrave Studies of Marketing in Emerging Economies,
https://doi.org/10.1007/978-3-030-77204-8_1

the need for branding and yet paradoxically, the way differentiation is achieved through branding has evolved into a moving target. Branding has thus become increasingly critical to the success of businesses and their marketing efforts and yet vexing to achieve (Holt, 2002; Keller, 2020). Marketing research—mostly in Western contexts—has therefore burrowed over what makes certain brands and brand management decisions (un)successful, and how consumers respond, choose, use and assign meanings to brands (De Vries et al., 2017; Fournier, 1998).

There is, however, surprisingly very little research that examines brands and branding in Africa, even though Africa has been touted by Marketing Week as the "last frontier" of global brands. But more than being an attractive source of market development for foreign brands, Africa is also home to many successful brands that have also found global success such as Tusker, MTN and Dangote. With the world's youngest population and the second fastest growing economy, Africa is increasingly becoming a hotbed for the marketing and consumption of local and global brands.

Past research has mostly focused on examining the brand image of Africa and African countries in global political and philanthropical discourses (Moyo, 2010; Osei & Gbadamosi, 2011). Others have focused on branding Africa as a place for tourist consumption (Wanjiru, 2006). Whiles others have focused on branding of agricultural goods (van Biljon & van Rensburg, 2011) and corporate branding, with a focus on banking and higher education (Daffey & Abratt, 2002; Williams et al., 2012). What is missing is a comprehensive guide that discusses the theory and practice of branding and brands in and from Africa. A notable exception is Blankson and Coffie's (2019) recent work that focuses on positioning strategies for brands in Africa with a Bottom of the Pyramid perspective.

This book builds on these past research endeavours to offer a more comprehensive overview and guide to both marketing practitioners and academics seeking to do business and research in the burgeoning space of brand building and brand management in Africa. Understanding how brands are marketed in Africa is important for many reasons. First, this fills a knowledge gap for researchers seeking to understand how brands are consumed, influence and are influenced by marketing and marketplace practices and structures in Africa (Blankson & Coffie, 2019). Relatedly, understanding branding in Africa adds a much-needed diversification to the current literature on brands and branding, which is dominated by Western brands and branding theories (Bonsu, 2009). In addition, considering Africa's increasing importance for the birth and growth of local and global brands, the knowledge from this book will enable researchers and practitioners understand and negotiate the evolution, expectations, practices, opportunities and challenges that branding on the continent entails.

Rather than assuming a monolithic Africa or a one-size-fit-all branding practice, this book offers practical perspectives covering brand building learnings across different aspects of the market in different African countries. The book delivers an updated look at branding practice in traditional spaces that past research studies such as tourism (Freire, 2014), and include other traditional and emerging spaces that past research has overlooked such as religion and start-ups. By focusing on how branding is done in some industries, we inadvertently exclude others. The industries discussed in the book are not necessarily more important than the many that will not be included. However, for the purpose of this book, these industries are included because of the novel contributions they will be making as part of the book's overall narrative. In addition, the book offers critical perspectives that examine the nature, value, opportunities and challenges of branding theory and practice. These critical perspectives also examine the evolution of branding as a business and cultural practice in various African countries as it applies to local and global businesses.

This book is, therefore, a double-edged sword, speaking to both marketing practitioners and academics. The book has two parts that offer a practical perspective (aimed at practitioners) and critical perspectives (aimed at academics). To practitioners, the book brings perspectives of academics and other marketing practitioners who have found much success and lessons in their experience of studying or building brands in various sectors such as start-ups and oil and gas in different African countries. To academics, this book offers a historical, cultural, critical and political perspective about the sources, nature, value, danger, challenges and opportunities of branding at the nexus of local and global business practice and identities. In short, this book offers a satisfying balanced meal to those hungry for insights on the theory and practice of branding in and from Africa.

Summary of Chapters in This Book

The collection of chapters in this book reflects this aim. The next chapter provides a historical overview of branding in Africa. This is followed by the two parts of the book, comprised of four chapters each, that discusses practical and critical perspectives. I elaborate on the chapters below.

In Chapter 2, Slađana Starčević gives a great overview of the history of branding in Africafrom ancient Egypt to the modern day. What is evident is that prior to European colonialism, Africa developed a rich history of branding techniques which also symbolised and supported its vastly successful economy and trade. Since colonialism, the conditions increasingly became non-local, with the colonial importation of European brands and branding practices. For the most part, this spelt the flaccidity of local African brands and branding by forcefully replacing them with foreign ones, shaping local tastes and preferences for the non-local. This is a trend that has since not been reversed and today the most popular and valuable brands in Africa are non-African. Starčević suggests that the same motivation of finding external markets for European over-production that led European traders (and later colonizers) to Africa is the motivation driving American and European brands from the saturated Western markets to re-colonise African markets. Although these re-colonization attempts are not roundly successful, they pose serious threats to the emergence and success of indigenous African brands. This chapter is a useful opening act for the rest of the book.

Part I offers the practical perspective of the book and contains four chapters that cover important brand strategies in practice across different commercial contexts in Africa. Fittingly, we begin Part I with start-ups. There has been a massive upsurge in start-ups and start-up hubs and incubators in many African countries, particularly Kenya, Nigeria and South Africa, with Nairobi even being touted as the "Silicon Savannah" of Africa (Poggiali, 2016). Many global brands like Google and Facebook are investing in this space, and yet we know very little about the brand building strategies of these start-ups and how they market themselves to local and global audiences. In Chapter 3, I interview Sydney Scott Sam, a brand and creative consultant who specialises in helping start-ups and entrepreneurs with their branding strategy. Sydney is the founder of Workspace Global, a Ghana-based tech-oriented brand communications company and a 2019 Forbes 30 under 30 successful entrepreneur in Africa. In this interview, Sydney lays out the prospect of the start-up space in Africa and why branding is important in this space. He explains why African start-ups often fail to take branding seriously, highlight some successful start-up brand stories and offer practical advice that start-ups in Africa can adopt to help with their branding.

Chapter 4 provides a case study of branding strategy in the educational context of Universities. The idea that Universities—like other educational institutions—are brands is now well accepted knowledge (Mogaji, 2020). In response to growing competition and highly engaged stakeholders, many Universities have adopted marketing and customer orientations that are geared towards building sustainable brands. In Chapter 4, Ebenezer Effah and Robert E. Hinson examine how a University can build and differentiate their brand through sustainability marketing using the case study of Ghana's top University—the University of Ghana. One of the buzzwords of doing business today, sustainability has become an important basis of positioning for many brands and in this chapter the authors show its strategic value to the University of Ghana brand. While they note evidence and benefits of this brand strategy, they also note structural challenges at the nexus of University and government commitments that hamper the optimal implementation of sustainable marketing by the University. The authors believe that remedying these challenges and improving current practices can propel the University's strategic branding strategy towards greater brand equity.

Chapter 5 takes us into the very controversial market of oil and gas. For many African countries, the discovery of oil is considered a curse due to the political and sometimes violent turmoil that can result over disagreements about the dissemination of oil revenues (Obi, 2010). But the oil and gas industry itself globally has a negative brand image due the adverse effects of their business on the natural environment. Businesses that operate in this space often need to address these negative images or position themselves as part of the solution and not part of the problem. In Chapter 5, Riverson Oppong discusses how this happens in Africa. While he notes that many oil and gas businesses in Africa do not invest in branding, he notes that those who do mostly focus on corporate branding social responsibility such as providing education and health care facilities in the communities they operate. Still others engage in building better relationship with customers and engineering unique brand identities, even though this is more common with those that have retail operations. While these approaches are notable, Oppong advocates for more oil and gas companies to take branding more seriously, touting its benefit in an increasingly dynamic and controversial industry.

It is impossible to talk about Africa without talking about religion. Living in the most religious continent in the world, Africans have an "incurably religious" culture that has fostered the mass growth and marketing of religious organizations that actively brand and market themselves to a pluralistic and variety seeking religious audience (Bonsu & Belk, 2010). In many Africa countries, religion is serious business and actively compete with each other and non-religious brands for consumer spend and loyalty (Appau & Mabefam, 2020). In Chapter 6, Oluwadamilola Blessing Ayeni turns the spotlight on the use of social media by churches in Nigeria to market their brands, a practice that became even more inevitable with COVID-19 lockdowns where churches could no longer meet physically for months. She examines how various social media platforms are used by different churches and concludes that the affordances of social media are helping these churches build brand presence, salience, and engagement with their members as well as becoming easily accessible to a more global and deterritorialized audience. She premises this on her review of the literature on church marketing which problematizes declining church membership and criticism of churches' use of traditional advertising to arrest the decline. In the case of Nigeria, she suggests that social media has become a very potent media that is used in integration with traditional media to build the modern Nigerian church as both a hybridized traditional and online church.

Chapter 7 is the last of the chapters that take on issues of branding practice and takes us into the corridors of political marketing and the branding of political parties, candidates and their policies. In this chapter, Kobby Mensah takes the case of one of Ghana's two major political parties, the New Patriotic Party (NPP) and how they (re)branded themselves—while in opposition—to win the 2000 general elections. The author first provides a strong review of the body of research that has shown over the last few decades that the activities of politics is in many ways marketing, and political parties along with their candidates and policies are brands and engage in branding practices towards differentiation from opposing parties and their candidates. This is precisely the evidence that Mensah presents in this chapter with the case of NPP, which he shows engaged in a strategic (re)branding effort to position itself favourably to the Ghanaian electorate while positioning away from negative brand image tied to its historical founding and ethnic tribal leanings. The party achieved this while painting the then incumbent party as representing the undesirable undemocratic and divisive attributes that the NPP stood against—a classic case of positioning against the competition. While the author notes the inherent pitfalls of such political party branding strategies, it is nonetheless the most common approach used by many major political partiesin their branding effort in Africa and elsewhere around the world.

Part II (Critical Perspectives) contains four chapters that take on critical and theoretical perspectives of branding and reflect on their applications to the African context. We begin with Chapter 8, which turns the focus to the self as a brand. In this chapter, Samuel Bonsu takes on the practice of self-branding, where the individual self is commercialized for economic gains like a commodity. While the idea of individuals as brands has always existed with the spectacularization of rulers, conquerors, warriors and heroes, the modern practice of celebrityhood and influencers has given popular recognition and acceptance to self-branding, thanks in no small part to the sensationalism of mass and social media. While this has reached its nascent stage in many Western cultures, little is known about its global amplification in non-Western contexts. In this chapter, Bonsu examines the personal brand of Shatta Wale, one of Ghana and Africa's biggest dancehall artistes to demonstrate how this globalizing self-enterprising practice takes root and manifests locally in an African context. The author notes many areas of convergence and divergence between the local and the global and between the Shatta Wale brand and the character of the person behind the human brand.

In Chapter 9, Marian Makkar discusses the role of culture in branding. She first provides a full meal of the cultural approach to branding that locates branding within the structures, meaning systems, practices and narratives of culture. As the Makkar demonstrates, the success of modern branding and the rise of iconic brands depend on how well they are able to tell and engineer compelling stories that resonate within a certain cultural marketplace. Using evidence from Egypt, Makkar shows how this approach to branding manifest locally in a North African culture. However, she reminds us of the precarity of applying Western approaches to cultural branding such as brand activism within African contexts where the differing cultural structures and beliefs may be hostile to such imported practices. The danger then also exists for global brands that embody cultural positions which may be acceptable elsewhere but may not find root locally in some African countries. The author concludes with some suggestions for brands to negotiate these slippery surfaces.

In Chapter 10, Tendai Chikweche takes on perhaps the biggest elephant in the room of marketing brands in Africa—the informal economy. The informal economies of Africa account for most of the employment and consumption on the continent. Often, we approach branding practice and theory from the formal economy, especially in Western contexts where most of the economy is formalized. In this chapter, Chikweche poignantly reminds us that this is not the case in Africa and highlights the need for a better understanding of brands and branding in Africa's large and integral informal economies. In addition to carefully unpacking the challenges for brands and brand building in this section, he offers some very practical suggestions that businesses, informal enterprises and governments can adopt to benefit from the massive opportunities that exist in Africa's many informal economies.

The final chapter of this edited volume fittingly examines Africa as a brand. We cannot discuss brands and branding in Africa without addressing the brand that Africa is (not). In Chapter 11, Emmanuel

Mogaji takes on this important topic with comprehensive simplicity. He locates the contribution of his chapter within the common misconception that Africa is one country characterised by wars, diseases, poverty and corrupt dictators. Mogaji dispels this notion and seeks to destigmatize these perceptions by explaining their historical roots in racialized colonial misrepresentations and offering an alternative knowledge about Africa and its many countries and cultures. Building on the place branding literature, Mogaji provides specific practices that African governments, the African Union, local media and the African people can adopt to wrestle the continent's narrative from Western misrepresentations towards a truer self-presentation. He cites the use of social media by young people in this regard as evidence of the potentiality of this approach. This closing chapter is an apt reminder that to successfully market brands in Africa, we must do a better job in building and marketing the African brand. As Mogaji shows, doing this well has benefits for local brands in their own marketing efforts and also makes Africa attractive for foreign brands to market their services and/or to collaborate with local brands and peoples.

Conclusion

There is no doubt that this book is only a start, an aperitif that suggests that a fuller course of knowledge on this topic is and should be. What could be? There are so many aspects of branding in Africa that is left untouched, so many stories yet to be told. Here, we tell some, and the hope is that this will be an invitation for future volumes that can tell other stories. Easily, we can point to branding stories about media, retail, finance, mobile telecommunication, transport and migration, export, agriculture, health, craft, literature, dance, music, theatre and cinema that are yet to be told from Kenya to Mali and from Libya to Botswana. Admittedly, there is a choice paralysis that can plague telling Africa's branding stories because there is so much to tell, and one may not know where to begin. If there is any suggestion we can offer, it is this: when very little is known, starting with any story is the first step to telling every story. There is value in highlighting branding practice and theory in Africa because the branding is neither alien nor undervalued on the continent. On the contrary, as I hope this volume projects, branding is indigenous and endemic here. Wherever exchange occurs in Africa, there is likely a brand enacting its own interestingness waiting to be gazed and understood.

References

Appau, S., & Mabefam, M. G. (2020). Prosperity for the poor: Religion, poverty and development in Sub-Saharan Africa. In *Moving from the millennium to the sustainable development goals* (pp. 243–265). Palgrave Macmillan.

Blankson, C., & Coffie, S. (2019). *Branding and positioning in base of the pyramid markets in Africa: Innovative Approaches*. Routledge.

Bonsu, S. K. (2009). Colonial images in global times: Consumer interpretations of Africa and Africans in advertising. *Consumption, Markets and Culture, 12*(1), 1–25.

Bonsu, S. K., & Belk, R. W. (2010). Marketing a new African God: Pentecostalism and material salvation in Ghana. *International Journal of Nonprofit and Voluntary Sector Marketing, 15*(4), 305–323.

Daffey, A., & Abratt, R. (2002). Corporate branding in a banking environment. *Corporate Communications: An International Journal, 7*(2), 87–91.

De Vries, L., Gensler, S., & Leeflang, P. S. (2017). Effects of traditional advertising and social messages on brand-building metrics and customer acquisition. *Journal of Marketing, 81*(5), 1–15.

Fournier, S. (1998). Consumers and their brands: Developing relationship theory in consumer research. *Journal of Consumer Research, 24*(4), 343–373.

Freire, J. (2014). Place branding in Africa. *Place Brand Public Diplomacy, 10*, 32–34.

Holt, D. B. (2002). Why do brands cause trouble? A dialectical theory of consumer culture and branding. *Journal of Consumer Research, 29*(1), 70–90.

Holt, D. B. (2004). *How brands become icons: The principles of cultural branding*. Harvard Business Press.

Keller, K. L. (2020). Consumer research insights on brands and branding: A JCR curation. *Journal of Consumer Research, 46*(5), 995–1001.

Mogaji, E., Maringe, F., & Hinson, R. E. (Eds.). (2020). *Understanding the higher education market in Africa*. Routledge.
Moyo, D. (2010). *Branding Africa: Taking ownership and responsibility*. Brand Africa Forum Report.
Muniz, A. M., & O'Guinn, T. C. (2001). Brand community. *Journal of Consumer Research, 27*(4), 412–432.
Obi, C. (2010). Oil as the 'curse'of conflict in Africa: Peering through the smoke and mirrors. *Review of African Political Economy, 37*(126), 483–495.
Osei, C., & Gbadamosi, A. (2011). Re-branding Africa. *Marketing Intelligence & Planning, 29*(3), 284–304.
Poggiali, L. (2016). Seeing (from) digital peripheries: Technology and transparency in Kenya's silicon savannah. *Cultural Anthropology, 31*(3), 387–411.
van Biljon, W., & van Rensburg, M. J. (2011). Branding and packaging design: Key insights on marketing milk to low-income markets in South Africa. *African Journal of Business Management, 5*(22), 9548–9558.
Wanjiru, E. (2006). Branding African countries: A prospect for the future. *Place Branding, 2*(1), 84–95.
Williams, R., Jr., Osei, C., & Omar, M. (2012). Higher education institution branding as a component of country branding in Ghana: Renaming Kwame Nkrumah University of Science and Technology. *Journal of Marketing for Higher Education, 22*(1), 71–81.

2

The History and Evolution of Branding in Africa

Slađana Starčević

Introduction

Branding is as old as human society. The word "brand" stems from the middle ages Nordic word "brandr", meaning "burn down" (i.e., make a hot iron stamp), in order to distinguish cattle ownership (Leibtag, 2014). It is believed that Vikings imported this word into English. Dictionaries record it for the first time in 1552, as an "identifying mark made by a hot iron" (Starčević, 2015). A lot later, the word "brand" was more often associated to trade, emotions and trust, which entail the essence of contemporary branding. Although the notion of a brand per se did not emerge for quite some time, various forms of human activity can be considered as the first instances of branding. Some authors have significantly contributed to the study of history of branding in various periods

S. Starčević (✉)
Faculty of Economics, Finance and Administration, Metropolitan University, Belgrade, Serbia
e-mail: sstarcevic@fefa.edu.rs

S. Appau (ed.), *Marketing Brands in Africa*, Palgrave Studies of Marketing in Emerging Economies,
https://doi.org/10.1007/978-3-030-77204-8_2

and parts of the world (Bastos & Levy, 2012; Eckhardt & Bengtsson, 2009; Moore & Raid, 2008; Starčević, 2015).

This chapter focuses on the history of branding in Africa from its beginnings until the modern day. Such research poses many challenges, since there is very little data on the topic at any time in the past, other than in contemporary times. The aim of this chapter is to explore how much have the African countries, starting with ancient civilisations, contributed to and participated in the development of branding as we know it today. What can be claimed with certainty is that ancient civilisations of Africa were the first ones to offer to the world numerous activities that paved the way for contemporary branding. However, later, during the colonial period, there was a complete shift, when the development of Africa came to rely fully on the policies of European colonisers. Even today, it is obvious that the colonial period left a notable trace on branding in African countries.

Prehistoric Period—The First Instances of Branding on the African Continent

The first instances of branding can be traced back to the prehistoric period. Prehistoric age is generally defined by the appearance of humans (2,600,000 BCE) and it lasted until the appearance of the first-class society and written documents (4000–3000 BCE). There are few data on the life of people from this period. Archaeological excavations show certain types of activities which could be considered as the initial activities of branding. Some scientists even link the origin of branding to the late Stone Age, where hunting tools were marked with symbols for more successful hunting (Almquist & Roberts, 2008). Engraved ochres, dating back to the middle stone age, were found in the archaeological site of Blombos Cave, 300 km east of Cape Town (Henshilwood et al., 2009). More recently, other engraved objects have been excavated from archaeological sites from around South Africa. That means that the symbols and the tradition had existed in this region longer than it was previously believed (Henshilwood, 2009).

Interestingly, scientists also link the origin of visual and oral storytelling, as a contemporary means of branding, to the prehistoric period. Cave men used symbols, rock drawings and sounds to tell their hunting stories and rituals (Terrel, 1990). The oldest scientifically proven rock art in Africa dates back to the prehistoric period. It was discovered in the Apollo 11 cave in Huns Mountains in Namibia (Davis, 1984). Seven stone plates, made of brown-grey quartzite, with images of different animals, in carbon, ochre and white, date back to the middle stone age. Excavations testifying about rock art were found throughout the African continent, and mostly display local culture and life of different communities. Hunting scenes were depicted most often.

Some authors link the origin of branding to totemism, as one of the oldest forms of religion. "Brand as a religion" is the highest phase in the evolution of a brand, whereby consumers form such emotional bonds with a brand that the brand directs their behaviour (Massey, 2008). Some authors relate the origins of totemism to the Neolithic era (Anderson-Whymark and Thomas, 2012). It is now widely believed that every community celebrated its own patron saint, represented by a symbol—a totem. These were usually animals or plants (Starčević, 2015). Anthropologists claim that totems stand for a universal symbol among the first communities, overstepping the borders of a single continent. Such evidence was found in Africa, in the Arctic Polar region, Australia, east and west Europe (Makgopa, 2019). Totemism used to be the common praxis in traditional African societies which nurture such deep respect for personal and group totems (Ndubisi, 2018).

Ancient Times—Introduction to Branding

Most authors relate deep roots of branding to the early civilisations and literacy, i.e., ancient period (4000–3000 BCE), which ended with the fall of the Western Roman Empire (476 CE). It is surprising, even, to learn how progressive some of the ancient civilisations were at that time. Archaeological artefacts testify that the notion of branding dates back to ancient civilisations.

The Egyptian civilisation was one of the greatest and most progressive old civilisations of all time. It emerged around 3300 BCE. The Egyptians had a large military and cultural power in North Africa and the Mediterranean region (LaFontaine, 2002). It is related to the roots of various praxes of branding and advertising, which was not the case with other old civilisations from the same continent. Even around 2700 BC, the Egyptians used to brand their livestock. They used branding irons to imprint symbols on livestock, to mark their property and ensure it against theft (Khan & Mufti, 2007). Drawings of branded oxen were found in ancient Egyptian tombs. It is believed that this used to be the oldest practice of livestock branding in the world, which was later adopted in other regions globally. Musée Auguste Grasset in France keeps a fragment of a papyrus with three rows of hieratic characters dating as far back as the rule of Ramesses III (1187–1157 BCE). It denotes a complaint of an unknown person regarding the branding of his livestock with somebody else's symbols (Haring, 2018).

Numerous signets used to mark property, responsibility or manufacture by a single man or a group of men, date as far back as ancient Egypt. Identity and property demarcations were discovered in ceramic vases and pottery which were largely manufactured throughout the history of the Egyptian civilisation. Pottery marks are the oldest demarcation type found in the Old Egypt and the Middle East, dating back to the middle of the 4th millennium BCE (Bourbon, 2004).

What was also found were the marks of the entire teams who participated in the construction of some buildings (The Old Kingdom and the Middle Kingdom) or marks of rulers who had the building built (the time of the New Kingdom) (Harring et al., 2011; Khan & Mufti, 2007). Numerous signatures of construction workers were found in tombs in the Valley of the Kings and the Valley of the Queens. These construction workers built the tombs, while living with their families near Luxor. Such village communities were literate during the period of Egyptian New Kingdom. The bricks often contained seal of approval, i.e., a warranty of their proper production and drying process (Paster, 1969).

Furthermore, inscriptions which were used to interpret the content of the jars, the precursor of modern brand labelling, also date back to the period of the New Kingdom. Tutankhamun's tomb contained 26 wine jars with inscriptions abounding in information, in more detail than any other modern-day label—production year, the origin of grapes, winery owner's name and the winegrower in charge of the production (Lesko, 1996). VerSteeg (2018) claims that trade, legal principles and well-developed communication based on symbols in ancient Egypt paved the way for the later emergence of contemporary trademarks. Even the history of logos is related to the Egyptian civilisation. In the period between 2125 and 1991 BC, during the Eleventh Dynasty, Egyptian artists employed the system of guidelines and grids. Today, guidelines and grids are the essence of logo design, as they ensure proportion and guarantee a uniform reproduction of the same design (Novin, 2010).

The practice of personal promotion and personal branding, accompanied by storytelling, is another exemplar of ancient legacy (Starčević, 2015). Egyptian pharaohs relied heavily on personal promotion to praise their military accomplishments and the construction of facilities (Roberts, 2006). They were equal to gods and were expected to glorify their own achievements, forming their personal brands. The construction of facilities was celebrated from the start to the end of construction work. This was particularly evident during the New Kingdom and under the rule of Ramesses II (1295–1188 BCE). Reliefs, inscriptions and entire stories found on the walls of the Great Temple at Abu Simbel, south of Luxor, testify about the intensive usage of methods of personal promotion (Bourbon, 2004; Polkowski, 2020). Some authors even believe that the Battle of Kadesh, found on the Abu Simbel relief, never took place, yet that was written as a part of the ruler's campaign (Allen, 2000; Shank, 2009; Mark, 2018). War propaganda campaigns against the enemies of Egypt from the period of the father of Ramesses II (Seti I) are also well-known (Roberts, 2006). Given the number of inscriptions and drawings found, as well as their structure, it can be concluded with certainty that such activities in ancient times were well planned rather than accidental.

Another form of branding that stood the test of time is the engraving of one's face on coins. When money evolved into payment method, ancient rulers turned to the practice of engraving their image on coins to glorify themselves (personal branding). Darius the Great, the third Persian King (550–486 BCE), was the first one to engrave his image on coins. As parts of Africa used to belong to the Persian empire, this practice was soon employed in other African countries (Money Museum, n.d.). The same practice was recorded during the Ptolemaic Dynasty (305–30 BC), the Macedonian-Greek royal family ruling the Ptolemaic Kingdom in Egypt during the Hellenistic period (Bard & Shubert, 1999). This was the last dynasty of the ancient Egypt. There are coins with portraits of Ptolemy II and Arsinoe II on one side, and Ptolemy I and Berenice on the other (Fulinska, 2010). It is suggested that such money design emerged during the rule of Alexander the Great, who realised that the usage of symbols such as his image on coins, buildings, pottery and artwork, could only enhance his influence (Taylor, 1997).

The mixture of influence of various cultures in ancient period was inevitable, due to both trade and conquest of territories. The first known contact between Greece and Africa occurred in the fourteenth century BCE, when the Minoans forged trade business with Egypt. Archaeological evidence indicates that during the Middle Kingdom (2030–1640 BCE) Egyptian pottery was decorated in the Minoan style. Egyptian influence was found in Greek regions. There are remnants of jars made of ostrich eggshells, found in Santorini, together with fragments of Egypt papyrus (Jones, 2017). The first Greek mercantile colony was established in Naucratis, during the reign of pharaoh Amasis II (570–526 BC), while Alexander the Great (356–323 BC) established the city of Alexandria during his conquest of Egypt. Phoenicians established numerous colonies on the coast of North Africa, while some of them were established quite early on, such as Utica (1100 BC). On the other hand, Carthage emerged in 814 BC, in the region of modern-day Tunisia (Harden, 1971). The first territory of North Africa under the Romans was formed in 146 BCE, after the fall of Carthage and the end of the Third Punic War.

For the study of the history of branding, it is important to simultaneously observe what was happening with branding in civilisations which were in contact. There is clear evidence that mutual influence took place. Dating back to the Ancient Babylon in Mesopotamia, there is evidence on king's personal promotion (however significantly less present than in ancient Egypt), on bricks marking on public facilities, on rock monuments symbolizing land property, on the first documented evidence on the usage of outdoor advertising and trade promotion. Ancient Babylon was the cradle of hawkers who promoted goods imported via ships, to make it stand out from other goods (Starčević, 2006). This practice later spread to other civilisations, including Egypt (Danesi, 2008). Data found in ancient Ur, Mesopotamia, also testify on the employment of royal personal promotion and the usage of cylinder seals for administration purposes and property marking, while bottle caps with marks were found as well (Starčević, 2015).

Opinions differ on whether cylinder seals emerged in Mesopotamia or Egypt. Most scientists believe that they were Mesopotamian invention which spread to Egypt. These two civilisations have always been discussed regarding their mutual influence (Kantor, 1952). There are no traces of Egyptian influence in Mesopotamia, whereas there are numerous exemplars of Mesopotamian influence in Egypt, such as visual arts, products, even the possibility of writing system transfer from Mesopotamia to Egypt (Larkin, 1999). It is suggested that cylinder seals emerged around 3300–2900 BCE in Ur, as the symbol of Mesopotamian culture (Aruz & Wallenfels, 2003). They were used as seals in administration documents, as jewellery or talismans, although they were primarily meant as property demarcations and for the emphasis of the owner's reputation (Starčević, 2015). Personalised seals were used as a trademark, and as a seal of quality and the origin of goods meant for export and trade. According to Ameri et al. (2018), seals were first used in Egypt during the Naqada II period of the pre-dynasty (3500–3200 BCE). Cylinder seals were later used with the same purpose in other civilisations as well. Signet rings with personal symbols meant for stamping documents with melted wax were used in the fifteenth century BCE in Egypt (Power, 2014).

Greeks considerably marked pottery with the name of the maker or the decorator, the same way as artwork was signed by the artist. They also used to mark products meant for export. Jars with the famous Thasos wine were inscribed with the island name (origin mark), winegrower and the official who guaranteed the quality (Maniatis, 1998). The Olympic Games can be considered as the first exemplar of event branding (Starčević, 2015). Etruscans and the Romans used marks similarly. The famous cheeses and wine were marked with either names or symbols (Maniatis, 1998). They regularly marked their various types of pottery and bricks with the name of the maker and the manufacture location. Some of their products attract special attention. Such are oil lamps with a brand name sold across Europe—"Fortis" being the most famous. Another exemplar of branding with the aim of differentiation is the demarcation of ointments with the names of doctors who made them (Greenberg, 1951). Greeks, Etruscans and the Romans used signs on their shops and brand names, mostly engraved in stone, while hawkers in Rome were a legitimately paid job.

It is necessary here to mention that Egyptians invented papyrus around 3000 BCE. Around 1100 BCE, members of civilisations of West Asia started buying papyrus from Egyptians (Hornblower et al., 2012). Papyrus enabled mass communication because notes could be spread and transferred from hand to hand. The first ad on papyrus was originally made in ancient Egypt, around 3200 BCE. It was an ad for the escaped slaves' quest, offering a prize (Sandage & Fryburger, 1963). As observed today, mass communication was the prerequisite for the development of brands.

Evidently, during ancient times, advertisements and symbols performed various functions:

- ritualistic,
- property identification,
- object differentiation,
- showcasing of identity and reputation of the merchant, craftsman or the artist,
- showcasing the goods' origin, quality and value (added value),
- enforcing the reputation of kings and rulers.

Although different in forms, all branding functions that are in use today were also in use in ancient civilisations. It is a common misapprehension that brands emerged in the second half of the nineteenth century, and that goods used to be generic before that time. Even though goods during different periods were sold in bulk, from barrels, wooden boxes, and sacks, and even though there was no small size packaging, there were "surrogates" for the names and brand trademarks. Not all goods were the same even in ancient civilisations. Some merchants and craftsmen had a better reputation than others. Their name was the warranty of their goods' quality and value. Most prominent signs in shops were not fully identical, even though the same goods were being sold (Starčević, 2015). Furthermore, even though numerous trademarks were in use during ancient times, there was no legal protection, hence this was a common practice of merchants in various industries. Due to a lack of sources, it is impossible to know with certainty how this practice functioned.

Middle Ages—A New Chapter on Branding with Hidden Pages

In the middle ages, there were further developments of branding methods that emerged in ancient times, together with new discoveries. Livestock branding dates back to ancient Egypt, however in the middle ages this practice spread around Europe. After the discovery of the "new world," this practice was soon adopted in America as well (Starčević, 2016).

It is believed that Vikings were the first to start "branding" their ships (around 870 AD) by naming them after their animals and gods. Even trade ships were named after not only gods, but their owners or constructors. Numerous sources testify that trade ships around the world were named as early as thirteenth to fifteenth century, with the African continent being no exception to this practice (Jones, 2016; Uckelman, 2005).

As noted by numerous foreign authors, during the middle ages, Africa was the "continent in darkness, without history," while Europe was thriving, trading, exploring and evolving. However, according to the archaeologist François-Xavier Fauvelle, it was the period when many African cultures flourished (Fauvelle, 2018). Exploration and recording of history of Africa poses a great challenge for numerous scientists, since there are significantly fewer written sources about it than for Christian western Europe or the Islamic world. Many communities in Africa in the middle ages left no trace, unlike ancient civilisations. Explorers often rely on artefacts made outside of these communities (BBC History, 2020).

Although there are only fragments of evidence related to living in Africa in the middle ages, it is still possible to draw some general conclusions on wider trends.

Middle ages (800–1500 AD) in Africa were the period of unprecedented development and progress (Wynne-Johnes et al., 2021). Social communities from around the continent evolved into complex urban entities that were connected to their neighbours and the world in multiple ways, having in mind the widespread trade market. During the middle ages, Africa was culturally and politically under the influence of Islamisation and the Arabic Empires (Stearns et al., 2011), which was particularly evident in the north, in Sudan, and on the east coast. Prior to the Islamic conquest of Africa, the continent was a home to a plethora of societies of most various sizes and complexity. In terms of religion, pre-colonial African civilisations can be divided into Christian, Islamic and traditional communities ruled by the native African religions (Barraclough, 2003).

In sub-Saharan Africa, there were two separate trade routes. The "Trans Saharan trade" encompassed trade between west and north Africa (Konecky, 2008). Thanks to significant trade profits, great Islamic Empires were formed: Ghana, Mali and Songhay, to name just a few. East Africa was a part of the "Indian Ocean trade network," including Islamic cities on the east coast as well as traditional cities. It was this route that made it possible for Africa to develop trade with the Middle East, South and Southeast Asia. They mostly exported gold, copper and ivory. Around 1000 AD, the Bantu language-speaking people of Zimbabwe and Southern Africa developed a great overseas trade route with remote countries such as China and India, where they exported beef, steel, ivory and gold, and from where they imported porcelain, pearls and pottery (Pouwels, 2005).

This "long distance relationship" between African countries and the rest of the world at the same time signified the acceptance of ideas and goods from other communities. During trade in the middle ages, a strong influence of Chinese civilisation was recorded in African civilisations. Archaeological sites in East Africa provided numerous remnants of Chinese ceramics from different periods spanning from 800 to 1510 AD. However, there was a slight paradox: cheap Chinese ceramics traded against highly valued African commodities (Zhao, 2015). In the context of Sino-Swahili trade, the possession of Chinese ceramics (porcelain) represented a powerful social symbol. It was perceived as "exotic," while its value grew after reaching the African soil. The import of Chinese ceramics contributed to the formation of the trade elite. At the same time, this serves as evidence of the emergence of practice of conspicuous consumption, which displays the status of an individual within a society (Kumar et al., 2021).

Although there are no data which testify on further development of product demarcation in Africa in the middle ages, it is important to say what was going on with the practice of branding in Europe, having in mind that during the latter Middle ages, Africa came under the influence and, later, colonial rule of European countries. After the fall of the Western Roman Empire, there was a significant evidence of trade and handicrafts in west Europe, which lasted almost until the twelfth century. However, research shows that during the Byzantine Empire, which was spreading to the north of Africa, masonry and craftsmen marks were still in use (Diamond, 1975). In the beginning of the middle ages, the only trace of branding from west Europe comes from weapons—swords with maker's marks (Maniatis, 1998). Weakening of Europe meant the decrease in study and innovation, as well as the stagnation of trade. Illiterate and poor craftsmen with local trade had no need to mark their goods. After the decline of feudalism in Europe in the middle ages, better living conditions emerged. Numerous cities were established as a consequence of development of trade, and they constantly grew and gained wealth. City activities were well organised. In the period between thirteenth and nineteenth century, each activity had its professional unions which regulated the rules of conduct: merchant guilds and craftsmen guilds. These associations regulated quality and the price of goods, as well as who could become a new member. Guilds were quite strict due to government-imposed inspections. Marking goods with labels or symbols meant the goods were "flawless" and of good quality. There was even an exclusive usage of labels regulation for members of a certain guild or craftsmen union. Due to the regional division of trade, this made it possible to impose monopoly on the importation of goods similar to the ones they genuinely produced. Artists also labelled their work, i.e., they "reinvented" the practice of Greeks and the Romans to sign their work and mark its origin (Maniatis, 1998). Trade prosperity enabled the re-use of trademarks, to showcase the individuality of products. Personal and family symbols emerged as property demarcation.

Starting from the twelfth century, origin demarcation for a wide array of goods and geographical regions was being intensively reintroduced. Such labels in England represented superior quality. Tapestry manufacturers from central Europe labelled products with personal marks or origin marks and assured quality with a seal. That was when they started using the registries of origin trademarks, especially in cities known as great transport centres or in cities where manufacturers' and merchants' unions were established, such as Dantzig, Antwerp, or Florence (Maniatis, 1998).

In the middle ages, a plethora of formal processes related to trademarks emerged. The first law that tackled trademarks was passed in England in 1266. This law—the Bakers Marking Law—compelled bakers to mark each loaf of bread for proper weight. In the thirteenth century, trademarks became obligatory for goldsmiths, silversmiths, and knives manufacturers. Such trademarks could be registered with town administration. In 1373, a provision was made to enforce manufacturers to label their bottles and jars so as to identify their origin. Soon enough, trademarks became obligatory for bricklayers, carpenters, tiles manufacturers, and other craftsmen (Ruston, 1955). For the first time in history, the value of "intangible quality" was recognised (Starčević, 2016).

Colonial Africa and the New Rules of Branding

In 1492 Christopher Columbus made his first voyage to the New World, which is known in history as the beginning of the modern era. However, the dark side of the early modern age marks the era of slavery in South American plantations. That was when branding also turned into its dark side—human branding. The beginning of the Atlantic slave trade in the late 1400s fully changed the structure of society in Africa. Europeans infiltrated the coast of west Africa and started taking people from the heart of the continent to sell them into slavery (Beckles, 2008; da Silva, 2017). European, American and other colonial slaveholders branded millions of slaves during the period of the Atlantic slave trade. This brutal, inhumane act was exercised for commercial purposes, to mark slave as property, as well as for punishment. In 1744, geographer Joseph Randall wrote down in his travelogues that merchants used to mark slaves with red hot iron to distinguish them from other slaveholders' property because slaves were often mixed up in harbours and in ships (Hopkins, 1785). This practice was frequent until slavery was abolished. However, these were not the first instances of human branding, which in fact dates back to ancient times. Ancient Romans used to mark fugitive slaves with FGV letters (*fugitivus*) (Bradley, 1988). Another form of human branding, yet with a different purpose, is known as the "scarification." This practice was widely used in numerous tribes in west Africa to mark important milestones in the lives of men and women, such as puberty or marriage, or to showcase the social or religious role of an individual (Garve et al., 2017).

The colonisation of Africa by great European colonisers, such as England, France, Portugal, Belgium, Germany, Italy, and Spain, lasted for almost three centuries. Starting in the fifteenth century, especially since the "Scramble for Africa," the economic growth of Africa was completely subordinated to the colonisers. That is why Africa completely lacks its part in the history of branding during this period. That page in history was written by Europe and America solely. Numerous companies in Africa were directly controlled by European countries.

The colonisation of Africa changed its course of history forever. Under the influence of political structures introduced by colonialism, what completely changed was the course of thought, the development of culture and the way of life. Prior to the official division of Africa by European countries, the African economy was flourishing in every way possible. African countries had participated in international trade since ancient Egypt period, whereas west Africa developed an extensive international trade system in the middle ages, during the Ghana, Mali and Songhai Empires. These empires accumulated wealth based on the taxing of foreign trade (Settles, 1996).

It is believed that the causes of colonisation of African countries were numerous. Industrial revolution in Europe brought about an increase in manufacture. Industrial progress was faster than the advancement in agriculture, which could not supply enough raw materials for the industry nor produce enough food for the surge in population growth. Growth rate of new goods was so high that it demanded new markets where it could be sold. Africa was the ideal location for the sourcing of raw materials, exploitation of cheap labour, the placement of insufficiently used capital and the export of finished goods from Europe. Colonials completely controlled the African economy, which was subdued to the needs of Europe (Ocheni & Nwankwo, 2012). Colonies in Africa started producing raw materials exclusively while simultaneously being forced to consume European finished goods rather than their own. This one of the main reasons why even today many African countries find it impossible to industrialise and start producing finished goods. The population of African countries still consumes mostly imported goods, even food.

Considering that Africa was under European influence at this time, it is important to consider the evolution of branding Europe in that period. The development of branding in Europe was conditioned by the development of trade. With capitalism evolving in phases, there was an increase in manufacture and consumption, as well as a surge in the development of national and world markets. Mass serial production demanded for mass market, i.e., mass consumption. The 1870s and the 1880s marked the first great period of commercial branding akin to branding today (Arens et al., 1996). That was when companies such as Rowntree, Cadbury and Lever Brothers in the United Kingdom or Henkel and Liebig in Germany, were established. They quickly became international. Many of them placed their products in African countries during the colonial period, not only through export but by founding new companies or taking over majority stakes of African companies. During the colonial period, manufactured goods imported from European countries to African colonies were mostly low value products, while European countries mutually traded with high value products (El Kallab, 2018). The majority of the first brands were household items and thrived on the promotion aimed at housewives (Olins, 2005). William Lever, the founder of Lever Brothers, registered the Sunlight Trademark in South

Africa in 1887. Sunlight soap was the first packed branded product of this company sold in Africa. Lever Brothers started doing business as a company in Cape Town in 1904 (Unilever, 2020). Products of Unilever (as a merger of Lever Brothers and Margarine Unie), Pears Soap, Lux, Lifebuoy and Vaseline, which are today widely sold in African countries, have a colonial heritage (Burke, 1996). In the 1880s, advertisement of hygiene products in colonies was described as "commodity racism," the presence of which was confirmed by numerous studies (Hund et al., 2013). Based on the analysis of several advertisement databases from the colonial period, it is evident that the "Think globally, act locally" approach was promoted, including cleaning products, food, drinks and other products.

According to Preston (2009), dating as far back as 1800's, there are many exemplars of the exploitation of trademarks in Cape Colony (including American brands) such as Henry White & Co for Red Heart Rum (1877), James Crossley, Middlesex for Eno's Fruit Salt (1882), Singer Sewing Machine Manufacturing Co, New Jersey USA for Singer Sewing Machines (1880), John Johnston for Bovril (1889), Royal Baking Powder Company, New York, USA for Royal Baking Powder (1888), as well as the extraordinarily old South African brands such as Barnetts, Bradlows, All Gold and Ackermans. Ever since the British American Tobacco came to Africa in 1908, it became the predominant force in the production and consumption of tobacco in the entire continent.

The period between 1800 and 1925 was the period of the greatest brand naming in history prior to that point (Rooney, 1995). A steady inflow on new brands and a hard-sell approach to sale could not last forever (Starčević, 2007). In the beginning of the twentieth century, the key consumer markets (such as clothing, soap, and tobacco) became saturated. It was getting more difficult to increase the scope of sales and win consumers over. Some manufacturers flooded the market with hundreds of products even back then. There was demand for research in consumer psychology so as to influence consumers' behaviour. It is believed that the development of advertising in the twentieth century explains best what was going on with branding at the time (Bovee et al., 1995). In the initial stages, rational appeal was in use. However, the market saturation forced advertisers to touch the emotions of consumers and try to find the way to their hearts.

The World War I somewhat interfered with the development of brands, because funds were used in other areas (Wells et al., 1989). Several studies document the role of African countries in European wars, especially regarding mobilisation of population and the exploitation of raw goods (Olukoju, 2012). Post-war period is characterised with the creation of societies fuelled by consumption, and a steady emergence of new products and brands (Wells et al., 1989). During the 1920s and 1930s, markets abounded with numerous brands of radio machines, gas and electrical cookers, freezers, irons and various new products, all accompanied with marketing skills of manufacturers of mass consumption goods. The stage was taken over by car manufacturers, which advertised themselves quite luxuriously (Coomber, 2002). Some African countries even published car advertisements in newspapers (Pennington, 1927). In the period between the two world wars, luxurious goods were advertised a lot—scotch, wine and perfumes. Packaging was rather expensive, and the promotion was characterised by charm, style and originality (Starčević, 2016). In general, further development of branding in African colonies was a carbon copy of the development of branding methods in Europe and America. Besides, branding and advertisement in African colonies was aimed at the media. Colonial rule controlled a vast majority of media (newspapers, magazines, radio, and later TV) to additionally affirm its presence, values and ideas, which were often in contrast with the local culture and traditions (Zaghlami, 2016).

The Challenges of Branding in African Countries Today

Even in the context of brands development, it seems that colonialism left a permanent mark in African countries. According to the yearly study "Brand Africa 100: Africa's Best Brands," carried out in 27 African countries, the situation seemed optimistic for the local African brands in 2010. They were well-ranked among the most admired brands in Africa.

This was followed by a decade of public investment growth, technological advancement, growth of export to China and a fast increase of consumer class, as well as the private sector. It was estimated that the number and the popularity of local African brands was about to grow (African Business, 2020). However, in the same report for 2020, a drastic decline is evident in the popularity of African brands among African population, whereas brands from Asia, Europe and North America have only increased their market share. Nike was in the first place for three consecutive years, followed by Adidas, Samsung, Coca-Cola, Tecno, Apple, MTN (South African brand), Puma, Gucci and Airtel (Brand Africa, 2020). It is no surprise, then, that foreign brands account for 87% of the top 100 most popular brands in Africa, and also 99.3% of the most valuable (Bacon, 2017).

As the growth of the global economy is losing momentum, developed countries have started looking for possibilities to sell their brands outside of their traditional territories. Multinational companies have an insatiable appetite for the placement of their brands on the African market (Amankwah-Amonah et al., 2018). Africa is the poorest continent in the world, but it is the least taken over by global brands. Many companies still err in this sector, because they perceive Africa as a homogenous market. The African continent consists of an immense number of various cultures, traditions and ethnic groups with different values and beliefs. It is estimated that more than 2000 native languages are spoken throughout Africa. Business opportunities significantly vary from one end of the continent to the other. While some regions are devastated by wars, hunger and poverty, others record a steady economic growth, urbanisation and the growth of the middle class (Green, 2012). Namely, marketing strategies that work in one part of African market do not necessarily have to work in the other as well (Mirza, 2019). Many western brands thus continue to fail in Africa due to implementing strategies that worked in their native countries.

According to Koornneef (2018), it is crucial to take into account numerous factors so as to successfully launch a new brand in Africa. First and foremost, new products are only useful as long as their target buyers have an average income above a certain level. Poor populations can only afford the bare minimum. Secondly, brands' reputation growth is dictated by value for money, caused by low GDP per capita, even for middle-income consumers. Distribution channels vary in different markets, and their availability is key to successful product placement. The regulatory environment also significantly differs in various countries. When it comes to the traditional media, radio records the highest coverage in most African countries. TV channels coverage is improving, however only few channels have a national coverage. Outdoor media are quite popular, but only in the biggest cities. Digital marketing comes with a great potential in African countries, as long as it is mobile based, which is a great difference in comparison to Europe and America.

Conclusion

The African continent is characterised by a long history of branding. The ancient Egyptian civilisation was the inventor of numerous activities which can be inevitably linked to contemporary branding. Even during the ancient times, diverse branding functions were implemented, such as property marking, product differentiation, showcasing of product identity, reputation and origin. There was an entire set of functions that added value to the consumers' perspective, which is the entire point of contemporary branding. Little is known on the development of branding in Africa in the middle ages. During the colonial period, there is a blank page in the book of branding history when it comes to the African continent as the development of African economy was subordinated to the colonisers. Raw materials were produced, while finished goods were imported. Although there are highly ranked local brands in African countries today, non-African brands still take up the highest market share are the most admired and most valuable brands. Additionally, together with urbanisation, the growth of the middle class and digitalisation, African countries are a potential market for numerous multinational companies. What will happen next remains to be seen. Indubitably, certain African countries are ranked among the best world brands of destination due to their very own historical heritage.

References

African Business. (2020). *Africa's top 100 brands 2020*. https://african.business/2020/05/economy/africas-top-100-brands-2020/. Accessed December 24, 2020.

Almquist, E., & Roberts, K. J. (2008). A mindshare manifesto: Common misconceptions squander the power of modern brand. *Mercer Management Journal, 12*(12), 9–20.

Allen, S. (2000). *Kings and Queens of Egypt - Heilbrunn timeline of art history*. https://www.metmuseum.org/toah/hd/kqae/hd_kqae.htm. Accessed December 12, 2020.

Amankwah-Amoah, J., Boso, N., & Debrah, Y. A. (2018). Africa rising in an emerging world: An international marketing perspective. *International Marketing Review, 35*(4), 550–559.

Ameri, M., Costello, S., Jamison, G., & Scott, S. (Eds.). (2018). *Seals and sealing in the Ancient world*. Cambridge University Press.

Anderson-Whymark, H., Thomas, J. (2012). *Regional perspectives on neolithic pit deposition: Beyond the mundane*. Oxbow Books.

Arens, W. F., Weigold, M. F., Arens, C., Arens, & Bovee. (1996). *Contemporary advertising* (6th ed.). Irwin/McGraw-Hill.

Aruz, J., Wallenfels, R. (Eds.). (2003). *Art of the first cities: The third millennium B.C. from the Mediterranean to the Indus*. Metropolitan Museum of Art, New York.

Bacon, J. (2017). Why Africa is the 'final frontier' for global brands. *Marketing Week*. https://www.marketingweek.com/africa-final-frontier-global-brands/. Accesses January 5, 2021.

Bard, K. A., & Shubert, S. B. (Eds.). (1999). *Encyclopedia of the archaeology of Ancient Egypt*. Routledge.

Barraclough, G. (2003). *Harper Collins atlas of world history*. Borders Press.

Bastos, W., & Levy, S. J. (2012). A history of the concept of branding: Practice and theory. *Journal of Historical Research in Marketing, 4*(3), 347–368.

BBC History. (2020). *Africa's medieval golden age*. https://www.historyextra.com/period/what-was-africa-like-middle-ages-medieval-golden-age-culture/. Accessed January 5, 2020.

Beckles, H. M. (2008). *Slave voyages: The transatlantic trade in enslaved Africans*. Norwegian Agency for Development Cooperation.

Bourbon, F. (Ed.). (2004). *Lost civilizations: Rediscovering the great cultures of the past*. VMB Publishers.

Bovee, C. L., Thill J. V., Dovel G., & Wood, M. B. (1995). *Advertising excellence*. McGraw-Hill, Inc, New York.

Brand Africa. (2020). *Top 100 most admired brands in Africa*. https://www.brandafrica.org/Rankings.aspx. Accessed December 15, 2020.

Bradley, K. R. (1988). Roman slavery and Roman Law. *Historical Reflections, 15*(3), 477–495.

Burke, T. (1996). *Lifebuoy men, Lux women*. Duke University Press.

Coomber, S. (2002). *Branding*. Capstone Publishing, Oxford.

da Silva, F. R. (2017). The slave trade and the development of the Atlantic Africa port system, 1400s–1800s. *International Journal of Maritime History, 29*(1), 138–154.

Danesi, M. (2008). *Why it sells*. Rowman and Littlefield Publishers.

Davis, V. (1984). Representation and knowledge in the prehistoric rock art of Africa. *African Archaeological Review, 2*, 7–35.

Diamond, S. A. (1975). The historical development of trademarks. *Trademark Reporter, 65*, 265.

Eckhardt, G. M., & Bengtsson, A. (2009). A brief history of branding in China. *Journal of Macromarketing, 30*(3), 210–221.

El Kallab, T. (2018). French colonial trade patterns. *African Journal of Agricultural and Resouce Economics, 13*(1), 15–30.

Fauvelle, F. X. (2018). *The golden rhinoceros: Histories of the African middle ages*. Princeton University Press.

Fulinska, A. (2010). Iconography of the Ptolemaic queens on coins: Greek style, Egyptian ideas? *Studies in Ancient Art and Civilization, 14*, 73–92.

Garve, R., Garve, M., Turp, J. C., Fobil, J. N., & Meyer, C. G. (2017). Scarification in sub-Saharan Africa: Social skin, remedy and medical import. *A European Journal: Tropical Medicine and International Health, 22*(6), 708–715.

Greenberg, A. S. (1951). The ancient lineage of trade-marks. *Journal of the Patent Office Society., 33*, 878.

Green, E. (2012). Explaining African ethnic diversity. *International Political Science Review, 34*(3), 235–253.

Harden, D. (1971). *The Phoenicians*. Penguin.

Haring, B. (2018). Identity marks, Egyptian and other. In B. Haring (Ed.), *From single sign to pseudo-script* (pp. 39–82). Brill Publishers.

Harring, B., Kaper, O. E., Van der Moezel, K., & Soliman, D. (2011). *Symbolising identity: Identity marks and their relation to writing in New Kingdom Egypt*. Leiden University.

Henshilwood, C. S. (2009). The origins of symbolism, spirituality & shamans: Exploring Middle Stone Age material culture in South Africa. In C. Renfrew & I. Morley (Eds.), *Becoming human: Innovation in prehistoric material and spiritual culture* (pp. 29–49). Cambridge University Press.

Henshilwood, C. S., d'Errico, F., & Watts, I. (2009). Engraved ochres from the Middle Stone Age levels at Blombos Cave, South Africa. *Journal of Human Evolution, 57*(1), 27–47.

Hornblower, S., Spawforth, A., & Eidinow, E. (Eds.). (2012). *The Oxford classical dictionary*. Oxford University Press.

Hopkins, S. (1785). *A dialogue, concerning the slavery of the Africans*. Gale ECCO, UK

Hund, W. D., Pickering, M., & Ramamurthy, A. (2013). *Colonial advertising & commodity racism*. LIT Verlag.

Jones, M. (2016). Ship names. *The Oxford handbook of names and naming* (pp. 655–660). Oxford University Press.

Jones, P. (2017). *Greek and Roman perspectives from Homer to Apuleius*. Harvard University.

Kantor, H. J. (1952). Further evidence for early Mesopotamian relations with Egypt. *Journal of near Eastern Studies, 11*(4), 239–250.

Khan, S. U., & Mufti, O. (2007). The hot history and cold future of brands. *Journal of Managerial Sciencies, 1*(1), 25–87.

Konecky, S. (2008). *The chronicle of world history*. Konecky & Konecky, Old Saybrook.

Koornneef, B. (2018). *Brands & branding: Marketing across borders in Africa*. http://www.marklives.com/2018/11/brands-randing-marketing-across-borders-in-africa/. Accessed August 19, 2021

Kumar, A., Paul, J., & Starčević, S. (2021, January). Do brands make consumers happy? A masstige theory perspective. *Journal of Retailing and Consumer Services, 58*. https://doi.org/10.1016/j.jretconser.2020.102318

LaFontaine, B. (2002). *Gods of Ancient Egypt*. Dover Publication.

Larkin, M. (1999). Earliest Egyptian Glyphs. *Archaeology, 52*(2). https://archive.archaeology.org/9903/newsbriefs/egypt.html. Accessed January 10, 2020.

Leibtag, A. (2014). *The digital crown: Winning at the content on web*. Elsevier.

Lesko, L. H. (1996). Egyptian wine production during the New Kingdom. In P. E. McGovern, S. J. Fleming, S. H. Katz (Eds.), *The origins and ancient history of wine* (1st ed.). Routledge.

Makgopa, M. (2019). Totemism: A symbolic representation of a clan with specific reference to the Basotho ba Leboa – An ethnographical approach. *South African Journal of African Languages, 39*(2), 159–164.

Maniatis, S. (1998). *The communicative aspects of trade marks: A legal, functional and economic analysis*. Dissertation, University of London.

Mark, J. (2018). *Abu Simbel- Ancient History Encyclopedia*. https://www.ancient.eu/Abu_Simbel/. Accessed January 15, 2020.

Massey, G. (2008). *Totemism, tattoo and fetishism as forms of sign language*. Coismo.

Mirza, Z. (2019). *One-size-fits-all branding in Africa doesn't cut it*. https://www.businesslive.co.za/redzone/news-insights/2019-02-11-one-size-fits-all-branding-in-africa-doesnt-cut-it/. Accessed December 28, 2020.

Money Museum. (n.d.). *Features of the human face on coins: Innovations born in the Persian-Greek contact zone in Asia Minor, before 336 BC*. https://www.moneymuseum.com/en/focus/stories/innovations-in-asia-minor-before-336-bc-29?slbox=true. Accessed January 17, 2020.

Moore, K., & Reid, S. (2008). The birth of brand: 4000 years of branding. *Business History, 50*(4), 419–432.

Ndubisi, E. J. O. (2018). Totemism in Africa: A philosophical evaluation of its significance in a world of change. *Journal of African Studies and Sustainable Development, 1*(1), 25–32.

Novin, G. (2010). *A history of graphic design*. http://guity-novin.blogspot.com/2016/09/chapter-1-birth-of-graphic-design-egypt.html. Accesses January 12, 2020.

Ocheni, S., & Nwankwo, B. (2012). Analysis of colonialism and its impact in Africa. *Cross-Cultural Communication, 8*(3), 46–54. http://doi.org/10.3968/j.ccc.1923670020120803.1189.

Olins, W. (2005). *On brand*. Thames & Hudson.

Olukoju, A. (2012). South African business in Nigeria: An emergent global south neo-imperialism? *Global South Magazine, 8*(4), 35–44.

Paster, B. G. (1969). Trademarks – their early history. *Trademark Reporter, 59*, 551–572.

Pennington, J. A. G. (1927). *Advertising automotive products in Africa*. Government Printing Office.

Polkowski, P. L. (2020). Egyptian rock art. In C. Smith (Ed.), *Encyclopedia of global archaeology*. Springer.

Power, M. E. (2014). *Signatures throughout history - Ancient Egypt*. https://www.onespan.com/blog/signatures-throughout-history-ancient-egypt. Accessed January 13, 2020.

Pouwels, R. L. (2005). *The African and Middle Eastern world, 600–1500.* Oxford University Press.

Preston, K. (2009). *History of brands & branding.* Affinity Advertising & Publishing.

Roberts, P. (2006). *Ancient history: Book 2.* Pascal Press.

Rooney, J. A. (1995). Branding: A trend for today and tomorrow. *Journal of Product and Brand Management, 4*(4), 48–55. https://doi.org/10.1108/10610429510097690.

Ruston, G. (1955). On the origin of trademarks. *Trademark Reporter, 45*(2), 128–129.

Sandage, C., & Fryburger, V. (1963). *Advertising theory and practice.* Irwin Publishing.

Settles, J. D. (1996). *The impact of colonialism on African economic development.* https://trace.tennessee.edu/utk_chanhonoproj/182/. Accessed January 15, 2020.

Shank, M. K. (2009). *The meaning of the reliefs at the temple of Abu Simbel.* https://wou.edu/history/files/2015/08/Mary-Kat-Shank1.pdf. Accessed December 28, 2020.

Starčević, S. (2006). Mogućnosti i efekti primene komparativnog oglašavanja. *Ekonomski Anali, 51*(71), 90–102.

Starčević, S. (2007). Evolution of advertising. *Teme, 31*(2), 421–436.

Starčević, S. (2015). The origin and historical development of branding and advertising in the old civilizations of Africa. *Asia and Europe. Maketing, 46*(3), 179–196.

Starčević, S. (2016). *Brand personality: The most difficult difference to copy.* FEFA Faculty, Belgrade.

Stearns, P. N., Adas, M., Schwartz, S. B., & Gilbert, M. J. (2011). *World civilizations: The global experience.* Longman.

Terrel, J. (1990). Storytelling and prehistory. *Archaeological Method and Theory., 2*, 1–29.

Taylor, P. (1997). *The Ancient Greeks.* Heinemann Library, Crystal Lake.

Uckelman, S. L. (2005). *Merchant ship names in the 13th-15th centuries.* http://www.ellipsis.cx/~liana/names/other/ships.html Accessed January 17, 2020.

Unilever. (2020). *Our Unilever South African history.* https://www.unilever.co.za/about/who-we-are/history-of-unilever-south-africa/. Accesses 15 January, 2020.

VerSteeg, R. (2018). Ancient Egyptian roots of trademarks. *The Antitrust Bulletin, 63*(3), 283–304.

Wells, W., Burnett, J., & Moriarty, S. (1989). *Advertising: Principles and practice*. Prentice Hall—A Division of Simon & Schuster, Englewood Cliff.
Wynne-Jones, S., Sulas, F., Out, W., Kristiansen, S. M., Fitton, T., Ali, A. K., & Olsen, J. (2021). Urban chronology at a human scale on the coast of East Africa in the 1st Millennium a.d. *Journal of Field Archaeology, 46*(1), 21–35. https://doi.org/10.1080/00934690.2020.1854549.
Zaghlami, L. (2016). Colonial media and post independence experience in North Africa. *Media & Jornalismo, 16*(29), 159–168.
Zhao, B. (2015). *Chinese-style ceramics in East Africa from the 9th to 16th century. Afriques - Historical debates, methods and fields*. https://journals.openedition.org/afriques/1836?lang=en. Accessed January 18, 2020.

Part I

Practical Perspectives

3

Branding Start-Ups in Africa: A Conversation with Sydney Scott Sam

Sydney Scott Sam and Samuelson Appau

There has been a massive upsurge in start-ups and start-up hubs and incubators in many African countries, and yet we know very little about the brand building strategies of these start-ups and how they market themselves to local and global audiences. This chapter addresses questions about branding start-ups in Africa, and follows a conversational methodology (see for e.g., Figueiredo et al., 2017) based on an interview with Sydney Scott Sam, founder of Workspace Global, a Ghana-based tech-oriented brand communications company and is also a 2019 Forbes 30 under 30 successful entrepreneur in Africa.

S. S. Sam
Workspace Global, Accra, Ghana
e-mail: ceo@theworkspaceglobal.com

S. Appau (✉)
RMIT University, Melbourne, VIC, Australia
e-mail: samuelson.appau@rmit.edu.au

S. Appau (ed.), *Marketing Brands in Africa*, Palgrave Studies of Marketing in Emerging Economies,
https://doi.org/10.1007/978-3-030-77204-8_3

Samuelson Appau [Interviewer]: Let's begin with the extent of start-up growth in Africa. You have a business that focuses on branding start-ups and small businesses and you have travelled around the world to speak to and work with start-ups. When you look at Africa's start-up scene, what is the landscape like? What do you find fascinating about Africa's start-up prospects?

Sydney Sam: We are in era that finally glorifies entrepreneurship. The last 5 to 10 years globally have been quite big on throwing a lot of light on what entrepreneurs are doing. They are the new superpowers over government, over celebrities; start-up entrepreneurs are the new celebrities actually, and that has definitely had its influence on the start-up space in Africa.

Firstly, you know that Africa has one of the highest rates of informal businesses across the world but what we are seeing is that people are now moving a bit more into the formal space where a lot more people are registering businesses. So, we are seeing a significant shift from informal tabletop entrepreneurs towards formalized start-ups and small businesses. There's also been a great awareness about having multiple streams of income. Now the wiser African has more than one stream of income and people who are even in traditional jobs are also starting formal businesses on the side. So, all these things are influencing the rapid rise of start-ups on the African content.

The second thing also is the rise of venture capital opportunities from abroad and also within Africa which are creating more opportunities for access to investment. Obviously, the credit system in many sub-Saharan African countries has not been too great so it's very expensive to get loans and that also created a bit of a barrier to entry for start-ups. But now, there are lot more opportunities; you hear a lot more about pitch competitions and angel investment networks and so on which are influencing these things and that has given a lot of encouragement to new potential entrepreneurs to enter the start-up space.

Lastly the digital boom has also created a lot more access for people who previously will never have anything to do with business to be able to now interact with customers, market themselves and get paid all from their homes or their offices. All these have influenced this recent boom in new start-ups and more entrepreneurs on the continent.

Interviewer: How big is the start-up space in Africa?

Sydney Sam: It is difficult to put a number on how big the start-up space in Africa is. You will notice that even The World Economic Forum and the AfDB all avoid giving a clear number as to how big the start-up space is in Africa. But various organizations have at least been tracking the amount of funding that is entering or is being raised in the African start-up space. For example, it was estimated that about 2 billion dollars of venture capital funding came into Africa in 2019 but with the pandemic, this inflow unsurprisingly dropped in 2020. Still, the Partech Africa report estimated that there were more start-up funding deals done in 2020 in Africa than in 2019 and these included some big deals like Stripe's 200-million-dollar acquisition of Nigeria's payment platform, Paystack. Every projection suggests that this trend will continue on an upward trajectory, so the future is very bright for Africa's start-up scene.

Interviewer: Where are the hotspots in the African start-up space?

Sydney Sam: I would say the hottest spot actually is Nigeria. The thing with Nigeria is just generally the reputation of the country but also in terms of entrance of new businesses and the sheer scaling potential due to the size of the markets. The start-up per capita ratio in Nigeria is huge so in terms of that I think Nigeria is actually the main hotspot for the rise of new start-ups. And there is evidence that this is the case because Nigeria usually gets the highest share of start-up funding on the continent. Kenya is a close second because it is a very stable economy, and they are quite advanced in terms of technology, so Kenya is also really good. South Africa has always been a hotspot for tech start-ups in Africa and has a very vibrant venture capital market. Ghana is also strong and doing very well recently and then there are Rwanda and Uganda. These are the hotspots in sub-Saharan Africa but obviously Northern Africa is also a bustling space for start-ups and in that subregion, Egypt is the major hotspot.

Interviewer: What sectors of the economy is this growth happening across these hotspots?

Sydney Sam: The dominant ones are mainly in fintech and agritech. With agritech there's a lot more innovation in moving from the small traditional farming towards industrialised agribusiness. We are seeing a heavy boom in start-ups focused on agricultural processing because agriculture is a really huge industry in Africa where there is a lot of demand and consumption, so a lot of entrepreneurs are entering that space and bringing tech solutions to capitalise on the opportunities in that space. FinTech is also really big especially in Nigeria and Ghana; that's the most popular sector that also gets a lot of the funding. Retail has also become quite huge due to the pandemic, spanning from retail of cosmetics to food. In Ghana, for example, since COVID-19 hit, there has been a boom in delivery businesses and start-ups because there is this associated boom in retail where people are doing a lot more buying and selling online and on social media and needing to get them delivered. So, that boom in delivery start-ups and businesses is symptomatic of the boom in online retail.

Interviewer: Are there any notable examples of start-ups doing well in these spaces you talked about—agritech, fintech, and retail?

Sydney Sam: Off the top of my head, in terms of fintechs there is Flutterwave, Swipe, and Paystack. In terms of agrictech, I can speak of one of my clients called Crop Doctor; they have developed a technology to help farmers get rid of weeds and also clear their lands for farming. There is also GrowforMe and Agrocenta, which are both in Ghana, iProcure in Kenya and Yellow Beast in South Africa. In terms of retail, there's obviously Jumia, which is probably the most popular. There are some businesses that are following the Jumia model but serve niche markets. For example, there is an e-commerce start-up in Ghana called Kebrea, which focuses on selling home appliances and bathroom supplies like sinks, toilets and so on. So, in the retail space, people are focusing on different niches but that is also booming quite well.

Interviewer: What is driving the growth?

Sydney Sam: There are many possible explanations, some of which I already indicated earlier when I talked about what is driving interest in start-ups in Africa. In addition to that, another main factor driving the growth is financial inclusion and the ease of online transactions. Africa has always been a space with a lot of purchasing power even though that purchasing power is not as well or evenly distributed as you would like. But there has also been a lot of inertia to spend over time especially because of lack of trust; there haven't been the right regulations to support businesses and to protect consumers. So, a lot of our patronage had to do with imports and exports; that is what people going into business focussed on. But now, especially after the COVID scare, and governments taking better control of the e-transaction space and having a lot more secure payments systems like mobile money, it's allowed for payments to be a lot easier and a lot less inertia to transact business with people you haven't seen just using an online platform.

The second thing is, culturally, it is now much cooler to have a business or run your own start-up. Previously, there was a traditional post-colonial African mentality where we put more status on having a profession—being an engineer, being a doctor, being a lawyer, or being an academic. Right now, there is a cultural shift in our understanding where there are other opportunities to make money outside having a traditional job so that cultural shift has also encouraged a lot more people to pursue or take on more risk in terms of the start-up space.

Interviewer: Your business has been to brand Africa's entrepreneurs especially small businesses and start-ups. How important is branding for start-ups in Africa?

Sydney Sam: Being a start-up without branding is almost like walking around as a human being without a name. If you cannot be identified, you cannot be called, and if you cannot be called then people are not very willing to do business with you; people don't trust you. Branding is something that many entrepreneurs and businesses have taken for granted and realise a little too late that branding is something that they need. Literally, right from the inception of your business, as you conceptualise the idea of your business, you need to think about branding. It is one of the most important things you need even as you draw up your business plan; it's really really important.

Interviewer: But do start-ups in Africa take branding seriously?

Sydney Sam: No, and here's why. Let me give you this scenario. You know that often people do not want to pay to get advice from a lawyer before they do something that might require a lawyer; most people take that for granted. But then how much it would cost you to speak to a lawyer to get advice before you take a decision, when you get into trouble after making a bad decision, you end up paying a whole lot more to rectify the situation, assuming that it is not too late. That's just generally the same approach that I'm coming to realise that start-ups in Africa—and perhaps in many other places—have towards branding. Also, because of the slight nuance between branding, marketing, and advertising and because social media has simplified the advertising process, people assume that that ease of advertising automatically translates into how easy branding should be. So, there are a lot of people who either neglect branding altogether or put in very simple measures to create some kind of brand presence or brand awareness. I, therefore, do not think that many start-ups are taking branding as seriously as they should.

However, I find that influencers and online content creators in Africa don't often identify themselves as businesses and are not start-ups, but they consciously or unconsciously work very hard on their brands. Some don't know that what they do is branding but they are very intentional about the kind of impression and image that they create. So, I will say that many start-ups take branding too much for granted but there's also a new flock of content creators and influencers who are unconsciously taking branding very seriously.

Interviewer: That's an interesting contrast that you draw there. Why do you think that this group with more or less human or personal brands unconsciously or even some consciously know and care about their brand, whereas start-ups selling goods and services don't?

Sydney Sam: The thing is, fundamentally at inception, these content creators and influencers understand that the brand is the product; that's just the differences. With influencers, your brand is literally the reason why anyone will pay you money—it's because of your brand image, you have affinity, you have a following, you have a community. It's so clear to them so they have to do that at the beginning. For start-ups and small businesses, especially for those who build good traction early on, money always becomes the distraction because when someone pays them once or twice for their product, they don't immediately associate the fact that their brand is connected to being successful or why they are getting the revenue. They have a delayed period of connecting the two and realising that the bottom line is directly influenced by their brand. They think that if there are people who would interact or who do business with them, then it is not because of their brand and so don't see the need to focus and develop their brand. So, they get carried away and then when competition comes with an equally good product and a well-developed branding strategy, that's when they realise that they need to work on their brand. For example, we know that people care more about values, so you realise that especially in 2020, with all the crazy things happening in the world, we now recognise more that people patronise businesses based on the company's value system and not just based on what the company sells especially in the fashion industry.

Interviewer: So, one might say that this is linked to some misconceptions about branding among start-ups in Africa?

Sydney Sam: Yes, there's some lack of understanding about brands in addition to many other things. Business in Africa is driven by revenue making, by being able to move volumes and not necessarily about the intangible aspect of the business such as branding. So, when you're doing your budgeting, you're thinking about cost of goods, cost of salaries and overheads and then you're thinking about your bottom line; budgeting for building the businesses' brand becomes irrelevant here. Commerce has evolved from the industrial age and now we are in the digital age. In the industrial age, even though there was a great need for brandings it was usually on a direct demand and supply basis and knowing your target market. But in today's age branding has become way more important because what is needed for differentiation is very key to customers choosing to do business with you. That's the lack of understanding or evolution in thinking that is not well rooted yet on the continent, especially for start-ups that you would think will know better.

Another reason is that branding is a little bit expensive; good branding is expensive and also requires a certain level of consistency that most people do not anticipate or want to commit to until it is too late. If you tell a start-up founder that they have to think about their brand every week consistently for the life of the business, they feel it is just too much work. They think, "why don't I just spend time instead working on another part of my business", so there is a low level of priority and a low level of tolerance for the amount of effort it takes to build a brand. But unfortunately, too, the biggest companies they compete with are the biggest brands. So, start-ups know that branding matters, but they just postpone brand building until it is probably too late, not realising that their brand was and should have been an integral part of their business.

Interviewer: Do you have any case studies or examples of some start-up who are taking branding seriously?

Sydney Sam: Absolutely! Let me talk about two of my favourite start-up brands, which are both in Ghana; I have to admit my local bias, but these two brands are doing really well. The first example is HomemedGh, which is an app-based primary healthcare provider that focuses on creating revolutionary, reliable primary healthcare service to its target audience. They provide their customers with tailored healthcare, medical consultations, home nurses, physiotherapy consultations, adult care, medication delivery, and sample collection. The promise HomemedGh makes to their clients is to deliver easy primary healthcare, mobile doctors, and preventative healthcare

One of the major strategies that HomemedGh uses to build brand awareness is through their website which provides extensive knowledge for people who might be interested in the services the company provides. As COVID-19 began to change the way businesses were conducted, the movement of people was largely restricted. Homemedgh was no exception to this, but they took advantage of the situation and carried out campaigns to ensure that people got to know about their brand. The company also used various social media platforms such as Facebook and Instagram to extend the awareness of its brand. Though they don't have a large following on their social media account particularly, their presence on social media gave them the opportunity for their target audience to find them. HomemedGh also did well in incorporating SEO into its branding strategy. Homemedgh also engages in content marketing with the aim of educating their target audience until they are in a position to buy from them. They educate their audience about facts, signs, and symptoms, as well as general information on how they can keep themselves in the best state of health.

Having this branding strategy and executing these tactics have helped HomemedGh carve a particular niche for itself when it comes to how people access primary healthcare in Ghana. Instead of the long queues and the hassle people experience in their quest for medical services, HomedmedGh has consistently sent out the impression that they are the go-to when you want fast and easy access to healthcare all in the comfort of your home. The brand name further entrenches the brand association they have built for themselves. The service experience counts as part of the brand and they have developed perceived brand quality through the use of seasoned and specialized health practitioners in their brand communications. Also, by having several packages that both individuals and groups can subscribe to, this start-up has been able to create an impeccable level of loyalty amongst its growing market.

The second example is a hybrid of a start-up and traditional businesses and is my personal favourite brand—Caveman Watches, a Ghanaian, New York Times endorsed watch business that started just in December 2018. The guy who started the business knew nothing about making and selling watches. What happened was he bought a watch for 200 cedis (Ghana currency) and sold it to someone else for 400 just based on how he was dressed, how he spoke to the person and also that he sold the watch to the person in their home versus the person going out to a shop. So, he then understood that as the differentiating factor, that the difference between his cost price and selling price is literally his brand. So, he went into watch making and selling but built the brand around his watches by creating an authentically African brand called Caveman, drawing inspiration from the early "cave men" who are the ancestors of humanity that is traced to Africa. And he has built a lot of brand associations based on that "class" that he noted early on, so he is very deliberate about who was seen wearing the watch in the beginning. He curated endorsement from high profile celebrities in Africa like Ghanaian rapper Sarkodie, Nigerian actor Desmond Elliot, American singer Akon and so on. He ensured that his watch was represented in the highest and most luxurious settings possible using high level photography, high level videography and great marketing support as well as many other PR tactics. But he sticks to the "authentic Ghanaian" branding story in all of this and keeps that consistency in the brand's positioning. So, these two brands have done a really good job the last few years with their branding in Africa.

Interviewer: What do you think African start-ups can do better with their branding strategy to meet the changing needs of the continent and the world?

Sydney Sam: The first thing I would say is getting professional help because you can't know everything; you need to at least talk to someone you know who understands branding. You don't need to necessarily employ someone to do your branding but talk to someone to at least expand your thinking because branding is very unique to every single business. Even if there are many businesses in the same industry, the context for which you may be operating and then building your brand may be entirely different from that of someone else. So, my advice is to firstly get professional help to at least help you conceptualise where and how branding affects your business.

The second thing is mainly African businesses do not, in my experience, pursue customer centric brand approaches; even for those who take branding seriously they tend to develop the brands based on their perspective of what the brand should be. I believe that it's a balance of both; it should be based om your perspective or what makes you truly you but also what the customer wants to see and what the customer wants to associate with. This also involves a level of testing that people are not spending as much time doing. You test one thing and if it doesn't work you pivot to something else, but most start-ups try to ride through that one approach, even if it's not sticking and then when it fails, they think that branding is a waste of time.

Another thing for African start-ups to consider in their branding is that there is a certain authenticity in branding as an African start-up that businesses should never lose. For example, Mercedes is traditionally German, Toyota is traditionally Asian or Japanese so there's a lot of brand equity from those cultures that makes you want to connect with the brand on that level. So, African brands should not just mimic Western branding strategies because there is a lot of value in being authentically African and investing in that in your story telling and letting your target market know exactly where you came from and share your journey and progress with them. Keep that authenticity; you don't have to pretend to be something you are not because consumers can see through that.

Also, start-ups here need to understand that they cannot separate the business from the brand. The business has to live the brand; your branding should show in your customer service, your payment systems, all of your marketing and even your organisational culture. This sounds like common sense, but it is not common practice, especially in our part of the world where many start-ups think that branding is all about having a business name and a cute logo.

Related to this, it is also very important for your brand if you start the conversation about your business with the purpose of your business; ask yourself, what is your "why". When you are able to answer the question of why my business exists, you are able to understand quite a number of things—what your target market is, what your value proposition is, how your reputation is going to be built. All those things stem from that purpose statement. So fundamentally the first thing all businesses have to do if even if you want to sell candy there needs to be a reasoning behind why this business exists; once that question is answered then you then focus on the what and the how. It helps you decide, for example, why the product is put together the way it is, why the packaging needs to be done a certain way, the way the customer service is designed, and the look and feel of your logo and your website. Once you figure out your business purpose, you can always reference the purpose in making decisions about the different aspects of your business. It becomes the core on which to build your brand into every aspect of your business. If some of these principles can be employed by African start-ups, I believe they have a very good chance of taking on the world.

Interviewer: That is a fine blueprint and a good segue way to my last question. When you started off as a start-up, what did you do in terms of branding, and as you were going along what did you learn, what mistakes did you make and how did you pivot to get to this point. Basically, I want to understand if you walked the walk of the blueprint you have just presented [laughs].

Sydney Sam: [Laughing] I'm not going to lie to you. I think the first two years of my business was "freestyle" so I wouldn't say we did much towards branding our business even though our business was to brand other businesses. The irony is palpable there, and also in the fact that I didn't actually take my own advice until much later when I hit a point where people were suggesting to us that the best way to survive in this country as a creative is to become an advertising agency, which was not what we wanted. You see, if you do not decide your purpose, someone else will decide it for you. So that was really what forced me to take a decision to ask myself what my purpose is: did I come here to advertise peoples' products, or I came here to help people with building and managing their brand identity? This happened about two years after the business started; it was almost like an existential crisis because you know so many different kinds of clients were coming through our door and I wasn't sure who we were. Starting from there, we then took a decision that we wanted to focus mainly on entrepreneurs and then have organisations as a secondary market and that's what really changed the way we did our things.

After that we also realised that agencies in Ghana don't traditionally advertise so we had to find a way to advertise without advertising. That is how we came up with a value giving model where we started to just give free knowledge and assistance and that has been our branding angle for years. In every interaction with an entrepreneur and organisation, we give them something they didn't already know about branding. That then influenced how we did our social media, how our website was designed, why we started events to be able to communicate and create conversations that give value and that's where Openspace, our social engagement initiative, was born. That then started to even change the way we educated our staff and really influence our whole business.

Then we realised that because our business is about supporting so many different brands, we ourselves can't necessarily have a very strong or fixed identity because we are so malleable and agile based on who we need to work with and what the client's needs are. That is when we took on the black and white colour as our brand identity because black and white are base colours, the starting point, it's no colour; it's not red or yellow. That became the baseline identity for us which we started to communicate through all our branding. More recently, by taking my own advice and taking advice from a partner who knows about brands, we have been able to build a positioning on "Ambition", because we came to see that everything that we're doing embodies the pursuit of ambition and supporting others—start-ups, small businesses and entrepreneurs in general—to pursue their ambitions. That is now defining our brand communications.

In terms of mistakes, I think we waited too long to do this, so it created quite a lot of confusion. That has shaped the learning that I have shared with you hopefully to help other emerging start-ups and entrepreneurs avoid making that same mistake. I do appreciate that we have a trial-and-error attitude, so we constantly evolve in our branding strategy even if our overall purpose remains the same, and that's what has helped to build us up to where we are today.

Reference

Figueiredo, B., Gopaldas, A., & Fischer, E. (2017). The construction of qualitative research articles: A conversation with Eileen Fischer. *Consumption Markets & Culture, 20*(4), 297–305.

4

Sustainability Marketing and African University Brands: The Case of the University of Ghana

Ebenezer Asare Effah and Robert E. Hinson

Background and Study Objectives

There is a groundswell of support among academics and industry practitioners alike for the call for corporate organisations to adopt a business approach that strikes a judicious balance between company profitability and overall stakeholder wellbeing. Growing concerns about the impact of contemporary business practices on society and the environment have drawn the sustainability development concept to the front burner for organisations and the larger economies in which they operate (Rudawska, 2018). With contemporary business environments saddled with heightening competition, many are of the view that sustainability development

E. A. Effah (✉)
Central University, Accra, Ghana

R. E. Hinson
University of Ghana, Accra, Ghana
e-mail: rhinson@ug.edu.gh

S. Appau (ed.), *Marketing Brands in Africa*, Palgrave Studies of Marketing in Emerging Economies,
https://doi.org/10.1007/978-3-030-77204-8_4

practices tend to be more responsive to volatile industry circumstance (Wilden & Gudergan, 2015) and can create new sources of competitive advantage (Hampl & Loock, 2013; Hult, 2011; Kolk, 2016; Peloza & Shang, 2011). Indeed, extant literature is replete with studies that draw a positive correlation between corporate sustainability and brand performance (Aguinis & Glavas, 2012; Jiang et al., 2016; Kiron et al., 2015; Kumar & Christodoulopoulou, 2014; Parry, 2012; Saeed et al., 2017; Schaefer et al., 2015; Shirokova et al., 2016), with some scholars arguing that sustainability oriented leadership tends to be more decisive in the integration of resources, processes, and capabilities in various fields of endeavour (Jiang et al., 2016; Katsikeas et al., 2016; Saeed et al., 2017; Shirokova et al., 2016).

A sustainability orientation enjoins organization to demonstrate sensitivity towards their various stakeholders' ideas and interests that enable them to appreciate the environmental, social, and economic issues of interest to them (Brower & Mahajan, 2013; Crittenden et al., 2011), so as to dispense their organizational, physical, financial and human resource capabilities in a manner that reaps favourable outcomes (Kozlenkova et al., 2014). Rudawska (2018) argues that sustainability marketing (SM) be promoted as an inextricable part of marketing with a view to designing business processes that limit the adverse environmental and social effects of marketing (Schaefer et al., 2015), while Kołodko (2013) views SM as an essential corporate requirement whose tenets today's organisation should be compelled to comply with, so as to avoid penalties by the governments (Demirel et al., 2017).

For decades, research on organisational engagements with environmental and social issues has been conducted, with different lines of inquisition (Aguinis & Glavas, 2012; Linnenluecke & Griffiths, 2013; Schaefer et al., 2015; Taneja et al., 2011) including those focusing on sustainability marketing (Anderson, 2012; Crittenden et al., 2011; Kumar & Christodoulopoulou, 2014; Leonidou et al., 2013; Martin & Schouten, 2014; Rudawska, 2018; Trail & McCullough, 2019). Additionally, the role of universities towards a sustainable future is widely recognized and appreciated in the literature (Adams & McNicholas, 2007; Emanuel & Adams, 2011; Fonseca et al., 2011; Fredriksson & Persson, 2011; Lozano, 2011; Palma et al., 2011; Vezzoli & Penin,

2006). The overwhelming part of these academic inquisitions on university sustainability marketing has been undertaken in jurisdictions outside Sub-Saharan Africa whose circumstances are fundamentally different. There is therefore little research on how universities in Africa apply sustainability marketing in their operations.

Universities have become multi-faceted institutions with multiple functions (Laredo, 2007) and multiple missions (Bonaccorsi & Daraio, 2007) (Cañibano & Sánchez, 2009). They are schools of education and research (Whitehead, 1927) typically tasked with the trinity of education, research and service (Krizek et al., 2012), to address societal needs and contribute to national development. They have been largely recognized as nursery of ideas and leaders of thought and practice in achieving socio-economic development; universities have become key stakeholders in achieving a sustainable future (Ferrer-Balas et al., 2008).

The Association of University Leaders for a Sustainable Future [ULSF] (1999) clearly indicates that there are many ways in which universities can be involved in sustainable development (van Weenen, 2000). These approaches vary from aiming to function as environmentally friendly institutions to formulating principles and signing declarations, establishing totally new institutions, or focusing the mission and management of existing university brands on their quest for sustainability. Evidence from the literature suggests that there are promising signs that universities around the world are responding to these opportunities and are beginning to engage in activities that relate to Sustainable development (Ferrer-Balas et al., 2008). These responses are either through campus greening (Ferrer-Balas et al., 2008), development of special courses on sustainability (Ferrer-Balas et al., 2008; Palma et al., 2011) and reporting on sustainability performance (Fonseca et al., 2011; Jiang et al., 2016; Lozano, 2011; Saeed et al., 2017; Shirokova et al., 2016), as well as offering collaborative research opportunities, to mention a few. These differences in approaches to sustainability arise as a result of the concept's multi-disciplinary connotation and implications including its effects on human conditions, and the need for societal perpetuation (Nkamnebe, 2011; citing Barbier, 1989; Ikeme, 2000; Nwankwo et al., 2009; Pearce, 1997).

Despite the remarkable progress towards sustainable development by universities in its various ramifications (Palmer, 2011), one key concern is how these universities themselves are applying the concept of sustainability in their operations to ensure that they continually maintain their relevance to society through the continuous processes of providing teaching, research and extension services to their stakeholders. The question of how universities apply sustainability marketing in their operations has been under-researched even though the higher educational sector globally keeps on expanding. This current study is positioned to explore from University of Ghana's context, the extent to which it is applying sustainability marketing by examining its institutional framework for providing its services to key stakeholders, with a view to making recommendations for possible improvements in that regard.

To achieve the aim of this study therefore, the researchers intend to investigate operational structures in UG that enable its SM implementation; identify possible benefits of SM application in UG's operations; and examine possible constraints that inhibit UG's implementation of its SM programmes.

Literature Review

Sustainability Marketing (SM) Overview

Amid the persistent definitional quagmire that plagues the SM concept, Fonseca et al. (2011) asserts that each study provides an operational conceptualisation for the term that is contingent on its own unique research context as well as peculiarities in its set of objectives (Leonidou et al., 2013). Inspired by this admonition, this paper adopts Nkamnebe's (2011) marketing-oriented conceptualizsations of 'Sustainability' and 'Sustainable Development' as 'Sustainability Marketing' (SM). SM is therefore used interchangeably with sustainability, corporate sustainability, and sustainable development, as there has been no semantic consensus over their differences. The researchers adopt the Brundtland Commission report's (WCED, 1987) and operationally define SM in UG's context as the university's ability to efficiently and consistently perform its core functions—quality and relevant teaching, research and extension services—to meet the needs of its present stakeholders while protecting and upholding the wellbeing of its future stakeholders (Brower & Mahajan, 2013; Crittenden et al., 2011).

The concept of Sustainability Marketing (SM) has enjoyed remarkable ubiquity in the contemporary corporate literature, although there has been lack of consensus in its definition and conceptualization (Anderson, 2012; Martin & Schouten, 2014). As a derivative of sustainable development, several scholars from different backgrounds have written extensively on SM. However, it appears there is no definitional unanimity as far as the term is concerned. SM is a concept with multi-disciplinary connotation and implications (environmental, social, economic, technology, ethical, etc.), including human conditions that point to societal perpetuation (Barbier, 1989; Ikeme, 2000; Nkamnebe, 2011; Nwankwo et al., 2009; Pearce, 1997; Schaefer et al., 2015). In their work titled "Educating Sustainable Societies for the Twenty-first Century", Davis et al. (2003) assert that faculty members and administrators' definitions of SM are in relation to their own disciplines. Nkamnebe (2011) supports this position by arguing that, the enigmatic nature of SM makes a universalistic definition problematic, and its operationalisation difficult (Anderson, 2012; Bhattacharyya, 2010; Crittenden et al., 2011; Kumar & Christodoulopoulou, 2014; Leonidou et al., 2013; Martin & Schouten, 2014; Rudawska, 2018; Stainer & Stainer, 1997; Trail & McCullough, 2019). Smith and Sharicz, (2011) emphasize that a great number of executives are still unclear on precisely what the word sustainability means. The SM concept is thus saddled with definitional nuances that reflect its diversity, both in thought and conceptualization.

From a customer centric perspective, SM could be defined as a management conception which attends to socio-ecological demands and eventually turns them into competitive advantages by delivering customer value and satisfaction. Martin and Schouten (2014) view SM as the process of creating, communicating and delivering value to customers to preserve and enhance both natural and human capital. A generalist perspective could be assumed, and SM has been defined as the collection of activities that involve planning, organizing, implementing and controlling marketing resources and programmes to satisfy consumers' needs and wants while considering social and environmental needs that meet corporate objectives (Schaefer et al., 2015).

From a developmental viewpoint, the Brundtland Commission defines SM as "development that meets the needs of the present without compromising the ability of future generations to meet their own needs" (WCED, 1987, p. 43). Notwithstanding its wide scope, this definition has been largely criticized for leaving room for multiple interpretations; as well as its inherent unrealistic, or at best, over-optimistic assumption of providing "fairness of access to basic resource needs for all populations, both in the present day and in the future" (Ikeme, 2000; Nkamnebe, 2011). Akin to the above generalist definition, Espinosa and Porter (2011) present a fundamentalist view of SM as maintaining the resiliency of the "commons" or common pool resources that are used by all but owned by none; such as clean air, clean water, and the like; while Argyris and Tsaliki (2005) consider SM as a system of affairs that secures continuous and indefinite provision of welfare for society through the implementation of practices which satisfy human needs and, at the same time, take into consideration ethical and environmental issues (Leonidou et al., 2017; Liu et al., 2016; Nkamnebe, 2011). Similarly, Dauncey (2009) describes SM as a condition of existence which enables generations of humans and other species to enjoy social wellbeing, a vibrant economy and a healthy environment (Anderson, 2012; Schaefer et al., 2015) and to experience fulfillment, beauty, and joy without compromising the ability of future generations of humans and other species to enjoy same (Jones et al., 2011).

Such definitions and others with similar generalist orientation have been widely criticized in the extant SM literature for their inherent presumption of quasi-utopian communist perfection.

On the contrary, SM has been conceptualized from a social responsibility perspective as "triple bottom line" (TBL) (Elkington, 1999; Hunt, 2017; Richardson et al., 2015) which emphasizes 'planet, people and profit (triple P) and asserts that organizations consider the environmental, economic and social impacts of their activities (Schaefer et al.,

2015). Additionally, other scholars have conceptualized SM in socio-ecological terms as comprising triple "3Es" connoting economic vitality, environmental quality and equal opportunity (Hult, 2011).

In view of the lack of unanimity in its definition and the accompanying contrasting conceptualizations that are predominantly predicated on industry circumstances, different scholars have used divergent terminology that reflects its scope and purpose. From a management perspective, Asif et al. (2011), for example, conceptualize SM as "corporate sustainability"; while Nkamnebe (2011) terms it "sustainability marketing" from a marketing standpoint. Some researchers however make a flip-side observation arguing that the diversity of opinions on the issue of SM will help enrich and broaden extant literature on the concept (Jones et al., 2011; Robinson, 2003). They however concede that there is an urgent need for scholars to find a generally acceptable terminology to codify the concept, as the absence of precision in meaning renders the concept vague and pointless with the potential to mean virtually anything and therefore, ultimately nothing.

Although the contemporary scholarly literature is replete with works on SM (Asif et al., 2011; Kozlenkova et al., 2014; Kumar & Christodoulopoulou, 2014; Martin & Schouten, 2014; Rudawska, 2018; Rudawska, 2018; Trail & McCullough, 2019), its coverage is limited in the higher education sector, although its practice is abundantly alluded to (Emanuel & Adams, 2011; Engert & Baumgartner, 2016; Grewatsch & Kleindienst 2015; Kumar et al., 2013; Linnenluecke & Griffiths, 2013). Palma et al. (2011) report that the inclusion of new courses that involve sustainability in business administration programmes is irregular and slow among Brazilian federal universities with its scope restricted to universities' contribution to sustainability marketing from a course delivery perspective. Lozano (2011) observes that sustainability reporting in university brands is still at a rudimentary stage as compared to sustainability reporting in corporations. Similarly, Fonseca et al. (2011) used the Global Reporting Initiative (GRI) guidelines and Campus Sustainability Assessment (CSA) tools to analyse the contents of a cross-sectional sample of sustainability reports published by Canada's 25 most populous university brands and concluded that sustainability reporting is an uncommon practice among Canadian universities. Ferrer-Balas et al., (2008) comparative analysis of sustainability transformation of seven universities identified lack of incentive structure for promoting change at the individual level. The main drivers of change identified included "connectors" with society, effective coordination and funding. It was also brought to the fore that, these universities show important strategic efforts and initiatives that drive and nucleate change for sustainability development (Wilden & Gudergan, 2015). These studies focus on universities from developed economies whose circumstances are fundamentally different from those prevalent in emerging markets. We therefore seek to contribute to existing literature by extending knowledge on SM application among university brands in the African context, using UG as a case study.

Benefits and Challenges of SM Application in the University Context

Sustainablility practices, in recent times, have become a subject of strategic importance to corporations, governments, and policymakers (Epstein, 2018). The United Nations' Sustainable Development Goals (SDGs) 2030 call for concerted efforts towards ending poverty, protecting the planet, and ensuring a more sustainable future globally. Consequently, sustainability practices among corporate institutions have gained much attention across the globe (Benn et al., 2014; Kumar & Christodoulopoulou, 2014); encompassing environmental, economic, social, and ethical concerns (Lim, 2016), in order to secure competitive advantage (Porter & Kramer, 2006).

The role of marketing in achieving the SDGs is therefore an ongoing debate (Anwar & El-Bassiouny, 2020), but scholars like Hill (2017), argue that the activities of marketers can help end poverty and improve society, and sustainability marketing could then be seen as building and maintaining sustainable relationships with customers, as well as improving the social and natural environments. We contend in this chapter that given all the ravages of COVID-19, there is a need for marketing to be reviewed to handle overall stakeholder concerns and not just customers'. We believe that the traditional mix of 4Ps or 7Ps should be re-thought to incorporate sustainability practices (Anwar & El-Bassiouny, 2020) and therefore set out in this chapter to investigate sustainability marketing practices in Ghana's oldest University.

The extant SM literature is replete with benefits associated with its effective implementation including reduced costs, increased efficiency, avoidance of or delay in regulatory action as well as enhancing and reinforcing a positive image in the marketplace as a good corporate citizen (Demirel et al., 2017). Other benefits include, encouraging employee productivity through improved corporate culture, employee pride, and gaining overall competitive advantage (Grimstad, 2011) for sustained profitability and growth (Sisaye, 2011; Xie et al., 2016).

Notwithstanding the SM advantages mentioned, certain constraints to its application have also been identified. A cursory review of the literature indicates that, lack of resources—human, financial, material, informational, and infrastructural—can present major impediment in the application of SM among university brands (Asif, 2009). Naeem and Peach (2011) identify lack of human and financial resources and weak inter-sectoral collaboration. Other challenges include lack of dedication and commitment among university management (Asif, 2009); lack of expertise and funds due to reliance on government subvention, and lack of appropriate SM tools within the university system (Naeem & Peach, 2011); as well as different and conflicting stakeholder interests and employee resistance (Asif, 2009). This study intends to ascertain how these challenges, and any others can potentially apply to the UG brand.

Stakeholder Theory

In reviewing existing literature, the researchers find the Stakeholder Theory useful as a basis for UG's effective application of SM in its operations. In the context of this study, this theory advocates that UG should be run in the interests of all of its stakeholders; where the term 'stakeholders' has been defined by Freeman (1984) as individuals or groups that may influence or be influenced by the scope of an organization's objectives (Mainardes et al., 2011). Managing divergent stakeholder interests by integrating and balancing multiple relationships in a consistent manner is necessary for a variety of reasons including sustaining a reliable supply of resources and legitimizing the brand's existence and operations (Asif et al., 2011; DiMaggio & Powell, 1983; Suchman, 1995). Cultivating a stakeholder friendly culture that is responsive to common needs of all stakeholders can be a source of competitive advantage to the firm (Brower & Mahajan, 2013; Kozlenkova et al., 2014).

Following the theoretical foundation of the Stakeholder Theory and review of the literature, this study focuses on how the UG brand can effectively apply SM in its operations by identifying key elements and specification of relationships for diagnostic and prescriptive analysis (Ostrom, 2005). Focal issues in this study include dialogue with key institutional stakeholders, formation of institutional structures for SM operation, perceived SM challenges/constraints, and SM application (Asif et al., 2011; Ferrer-Balas et al., 2008). Thus, UG can execute its SM mandate effectively if it puts in place enabling institutional structures and collaborates with its stakeholders, while minimizing perceived SM challenges expected to serve as a barrier to implementation.

Methodology

Owing to the newness of the phenomenon under investigation and the recognition of the active role that UG staff play in the construction and study of the university's social reality, the study adopts an exploratory research design (Creswell, 2007) and uses the qualitative research approach to address the stated objectives. The adoption of this approach is contingent on the remarkable depth and richness of data collected, as it enables researchers to delve deeper into respondents' thoughts, attitudes, behaviours, impressions, opinions, beliefs, feelings and aspirations (Bryman, 2012; Malhotra, 2010) which are otherwise inaccessible. The study adopts the case study approach that offers the researchers the opportunity to study UG's circumstances (Creswell, 2007) and understand the contextual issues involved (Saunders et al., 2007) in its SM endeavours. The choice of UG in this study is due to its dominance and representativeness of the circumstances of operators in Ghana's university sector (Yin, 2009), whose SM activities need to be investigated in detail to provide rich description and insight into the SM phenomenon.

The purposive sampling technique, specifically expert sampling, was employed in selecting five (5) key administrative Heads of University of Ghana whose qualities, expertise and experiences permit the understanding of the phenomenon in question (Bryman, 2012). This is in line with Creswell (2007) assertion that, for a case study research, four (4) or five (5) interviewees are deemed appropriate in a single case. The five personnel were drawn from the Office for Academics and Students Affairs which has jurisdiction over the Academic Quality Assurance Unit (AQAU); Office of Research, Innovation and Development; and the Human Resource and Organisational Development Directorate of the University. The researchers sought to know the length of time respondents had been on post to be able to determine how familiar and knowledgeable they were a far as UG's internal circumstances were concerned. The Director of Academic Quality Assurance Unit, Assistant Registrar and Researcher Administrator of the Office of Research Innovation and Development (ORID) and the Assistant Registrar had 23, 9 and 8 years working experience with the University, respectively. Similarly, the first Assistant Registrar of Academic Affairs had 18 years working experience while the second Assistant Registrar of Academic Affairs had been working at UG for 16 years.

Data was collected using in-depth, face-face interviews and documented information available at the university. Robson (1993) suggests that interviews offer the researcher the flexibility to modify the line of enquiry, follow up on interesting responses and investigate underlying motives in a manner that unearths deep-seated opinions, feelings, perceptions and impressions of respondents thereby enhancing reliability of data collected. Specifically, the élite type of interviews used involves talking to respondents who are especially knowledgeable about a particular issue and context of inquiry (Yin, 2003). An interview guide containing mainly open-ended questions which resulted from the researchers' operationalisation of the SM concept was used to elicit responses from the respondents. The instrument was pre-tested using a top university executive and modified to ensure reliability. Data collection took place over 2 months.

In all, five hours of long interviews were conducted. Besides the in-depth interviews, secondary data were sourced from university-specific reports; newsletters and other official publications of UG. In analyzing data collected, the interviews were transcribed and subjected to data entry protocols such as editing to find uncompleted questions, coding of open-ended questions and correcting inconsistencies in responses. The interviews were further subjected to inductive data analysis. This technique was deemed appropriate because it offered the researchers the opportunity to group responses thematically by looking at patterns that emerged to make sense and meaning to the researchers (Miles & Huberman, 1994). Responses that were particularly instructive were reported verbatim. The interviews were complemented with content analysis of the documented information obtained from the University.

Presentation and Discussion of Findings

To answer the questions raised in this study, a thematic analysis and clustering of findings from each question was executed in order to achieve a fit with the case study approach. The thematic areas under this section are grouped under four broad sections. The first section focuses on the UG brand's structures of operation. The second section presents the key perceived advantages of SM to the brand, while the third section discusses SM constraints at UG. Lastly, the fourth section presents a discussion of key findings of the study with a view to addressing the study's objectives.

University of Ghana's Structures of Operation that Enable Its SM Implementation

Results from the study indicate that UG is committed to providing teaching, research and extension services that are relevant and address its current and future stakeholder interests. This was confirmed by respondents of the study when asked to briefly describe UG's mission. The Director of Academic Quality Assurance Unit (AQAU) of the University observed:

> We are committed to building on our core strengths of a centre of excellence for high quality teaching, relevant institution and good infrastructure; and our unique competences in the sciences, medicine, humanities, law and business, cultural studies, information technology and other emerging disciplines to ensure and sustain world-class competitive advantages. We are also committed to building deeper awareness of our customers, especially students, the private and public sectors, government and the world community and re-orient our teaching activities and harmonize synergies between disciplines to achieve operational excellence.

The Assistant Registrar of the Human Resource and Organisational Development Directorate (HRODD) had a similar view:

> The University commits itself to providing the manpower needs for both public and private sector development through quality teaching and research using well-trained, technically competent and knowledgeable staff.

The above responses reflect the Basic Laws of the UG (2012, p. 5) which succinctly captures the aims of the University as:

> To provide higher education, undertake research, disseminate knowledge, and foster relationships with outside persons and bodies...... In determining the subjects to be taught therefore, emphasis is placed on courses of special relevance to the needs and aspirations of citizens.

It is instructive to note again that findings from the study indicate that besides the administrative structure of the university where principal office holders such as the Vice-Chancellor, Pro-Vice-Chancellor, Deans, Heads of Departments etc. see to the day-to-day activities of their respective areas of jurisdiction, major decisions made by UG concerning its academic activities are arrived at through a committee System. This committee system of decision-making within the University enhances consultative and participatory decision making and also serves as checks and balances on the operations of the various units within the University. This state of affairs is captured in the following response by the Assistant Registrar of Academic Affairs:

> Departments are responsible for the teaching and research that they carry out. However, proposals made by departments through their Programme/Course Review Committees that are related to their academic programmes (including additions, deletions and changes of courses) in the area of teaching, learning, research and assessment are further sent to their respective College/Faculty/School Board. These Boards then further subject the proposed academic programmes to rigorous scrutiny to ensure that the proposed reviews made by the departments conform to internal guidelines established by the Boards in relation to their academic programmes. The review process ends with the Academic Board which upon liaising with the National Accreditation Board, finally approves all academic programmes that are run by the University.

Although faculty members within departments are given the freedom to develop their own academic programmes, there are internal monitoring mechanisms instituted by the university to regulate the activities of the department. The Assistant Registrar alluded to this in the response below:

> All academic programmes including teaching, learning, research and assessments are regulated by internal guidelines set by the College/Faculty/School Boards and are finally approved by the Academic Board before they are implemented.

Stakeholder dialogue is a key component of this study in applying SM in UG's operations. It was observed from the findings that UG dialogues with clearly identified key stakeholders at all levels of decision making, including all those who have forward and backward linkages with the university. This was confirmed by the following response by the First Assistant Registrar of Academic Affairs:

> Yes, the University Council consisting of several stakeholders of the University determines the strategic direction of the University including mission, vision, long-term academic plans and key performance indicators. These stakeholders include representatives from government, alumni, National Council for Tertiary Education (NCTE), staff, students both undergraduate and postgraduate, convocation, and other members or professionals from accomplished careers whose expertise are of relevance to the University brand".

In tandem with the above position, the Assistant Registrar of Academic Affairs corroborated a section of the Basic Laws of UG (2012) by indicating that:

> the College Councils of the Colleges within the University dialogue with relevant partners in overseeing the development and progress of the College as well as keeping the Colleges' academic activities under constant review......There are also Student-Staff Consultative Committees in every department with representations at all levels that meet at least once a semester to evaluate teaching and courses at the departments.

Additionally, findings from the study indicate that the university has a periodic review mechanism manned by the Academic Quality Assurance Unit (AQAU) that evaluates its academic activities with a view to addressing emerging stakeholder needs. This review system is underpinned by key principles including rigorous and comprehensive coverage in evaluations, internal and external peer review, stakeholder involvement, rapid and effective feedback, and evidence-based assessment.

This was confirmed by the Director of AQAU when he indicated that:

> We advise the Academic Curriculum, Quality and Staff Development Committee on the determination and maintenance of acceptable levels of academic standards with respect to teaching, learning and research....We additionally disseminate on a regular basis, matters that are related to quality enhancement to the wider community and beyond; organize annual exit surveys of graduating classes, and periodically undertake tracer and employer surveys. We also undertake a host of reviews to ensure rigorous and comprehensive coverage in our evaluations.

In answering a question on the nature of internal stakeholder involvement and feedback systems prevalent within the University, the Assistant Registrar of Academic Affairs intimated:

> Academic staff feedbacks are obtained through departmental meetings, committees, working groups, evaluations of staff development sessions, validation and review of events and consultation exercises about specific projects.

When asked about how review mechanisms used by the university work in practice, the Assistant Registrar of Academic Affairs gave the following response:

> All Departments seek feedback from students on individual courses as well as lecturers within programmes of study at the end of each semester or academic year, through paper and electronic questionnaires. The findings are then communicated to students by the department indicating any actions to be taken to address key concerns raised, or reasons for not taking action. This regular assessment of courses and lecturers help the departments to know whether the purposes for which the courses were mounted have been achieved so as to address problems that arise during courses.

The foregoing analyses of responses amply indicate that UG has operational structures in place for its SM implementation. These structures and mechanisms ensure that the university brand continuously attracts, develops, motivates, monitors and retains the highest calibre of academic staff in meeting the varying needs of both internal and external stakeholder constituents in a sustainable manner. There is also evidence that UG collaborates and dialogues with its stakeholders on a regular basis in executing its mandate—a fertile condition for SM implementation.

Advantages Associated with SM Application at UG

A major objective of the study was to investigate the advantages of SM application in UG's operations. In tandem with observations in the extant SM literature, findings from the study indicate that the UG brand stands to gain numerous advantages from efficient implementation of its SM initiatives. In affirming the above stance, the Assistant Registrar and Research Administrator made the following observation:

> SM is very advantageous.....enhancement of research profile, increasing visibility, increasing research income, attracting competent graduate students and production of researchers that will lead discussions in public discourse will be the main advantages to our brand.

The view of the Assistant Registrar of Academic Affairs was not different:

> SM enhances stakeholder satisfaction, attracts highly qualified, experienced and competent academic staff and highly qualified students; and promotes and increases innovation.

A similar view was expressed by the Director of AQAU who opined:

> The University will gain social acceptance and support from its key stakeholders when it continuously provides services that are relevant to its stakeholders.

Analyses of responses thus far corroborate findings in the literature by indicating that the UG brand stands to gain numerous advantages from efficient and effective implementation of its SM programmes and activities.

Challenges that Confront University of Ghana in the Implementation of Its SM Operations

The study reveals a number of challenges with the potential to impede effective SM application in the university. One of such constraints identified by the researchers is lack of academic freedom. Although faculty members are given the freedom to develop their own academic programmes, the running of those programmes is ultimately determined by a higher authority. In making this observation, the Director of AQAU opined:

> All proposals made by the Programmes/Course Review Committee concerning academic programmes are sent to the College/Faculty/School Boards for further review to ensure adequacy of the academic unit's review; and that the proposal is consistent with the broader goals and programmes of the College/Faculty/School, as well as with the mission of the university. The final authority which approves all academic programmes run by the university is the Academic Board.

Another key constraint identified is lack of structures to incentivise the institution's staff as the University was unable to offer attractive remuneration packages to its academic staff. As the Assistant Registrar of HRODD put it:

> All academic staff are on government payroll; there is no other special incentive given to faculty members.

Among factors that influence the inadequate incentive structure of UG is the university's over-dependence on government subvention for salaries; absence of innovation in fundraising; ineffective strategy for marketing the brand; inability to charge realistic fees for cost recovery; and poor programme-industry fit to respond to volatile industry circumstances. In addition, unavailability of resources and low commitment by management to effective application of SM were found to hamper its operations in that regard, as amply indicated in the response below by the Director of AQAU:

> For me, I see lack of resources and management commitment. This unit did not have any administrative head for two years and therefore was not in operation within those years until I assumed office. Again, the AQAU does not have permanent staff who can assist me in carrying out the operations of the unit.

Responses gathered from the study therefore unveil a number of challenges that the UG brand needs to address to see its way clear in implementing its SM programmes and activities.

Discussion and Conclusion

With the wind of SM blowing across industries all the world over, visionary leadership that is sufficiently responsive to changing societal needs is a prerequisite for its successful application by universities brands (Jiang et al., 2016; Saeed et al., 2017; Shirokova et al., 2016). UG is equipped with relevant structures that effectively assign responsibility and offer rewards, albeit inadequate, in the execution of its triple mandate of teaching, research and extension services that address divergent current and future stakeholder interests (Kotler, 2015). This observation conforms to an earlier assertion by Krizek et al. (2012) that institutions of higher education are typically tasked with the trinity of education, research and service. UG's disposition towards SM is exhibited in its consultative governance structure that ensures effective dialogue between the university and its key stakeholders at all levels of decision making. The governance structure of UG enhances information inflow and has inherent checks and balances which provide fertile grounds for balancing stakeholder interests with organizational fortunes.

Perhaps, UG's level of interaction with its key stakeholders is borne out of its recognition that different stakeholder groups provide various resources that are more or less critical to the University's long-term success (Brower & Mahajan, 2013; Freeman, 1984; Maignan et al., 2005). According to Kolk (2016), cultivating a stakeholder-friendly culture that is responsive to varying, sometimes contrasting interests is a source of competitive advantage for the university brand (Leap & Loughry, 2004).

The UG brand's commitment to SM is evident in its administrators' involvement. Key personnel such as the Chairperson of the University Council, Vice-Chancellor, Pro Vice-Chancellors, and Deans were found to be involved in providing its core services. Findings of the study however suggest that in practice, management commitment to the endeavor is rather minimal as indicated by the Director of AQAU.

Findings of the study further suggest that several advantages can accrue to the University brand from its effective application of SM. These include attracting highly qualified, experienced and competent academic staff; improved reputation; and maintaining the brand's relevance in national development. Other benefits include increased innovation; brand visibility; access to funding; and overall stakeholder satisfaction. This confirms early observations that the most significant opportunities for actively pursuing more sustainable approaches to business include improved operational efficiency (Asif et al., 2010, 2011); preservation of operating license (Nejati et al., 2010); enhanced brand value and reputation (Aguinis & Glavas, 2012; Kiron et al., 2013, 2015; Kumar & Christodoulopoulou, 2014); improved access to capital and innovation, staff and customer attraction and retention, identification of new opportunities (Nejati et al., 2010); and overall competitive advantage (Grimstad, 2011; Hampl & Loock, 2013; Kolk, 2016; Nejati et al., 2010).

Notwithstanding the numerous benefits the UG brand derives from its effective application of SM, certain constraints/challenges are associated with the adoption and implementation of same. These include over-centralisation and bureaucratic decision-making systems, poor incentive structures, lack of management commitment, lack of resources and absence of academic freedom. In ascertaining success factors for SM application, Asif (2009) identified as instrumental, dedicated efforts on the part of management and employees (Engert & Baumgartner, 2016; Katsikeas et al., 2016), as well as efficient allocation of resources in addressing stakeholder needs, as expounded by the Stakeholder Theory. SM is a strategic management tool aimed at providing quality and relevant teaching, research and extension services that continuously address current and emerging stakeholder requirements of the university brand. Its effective application is precipitated by efficiency in internal institutional structures and consistent stakeholder dialogue. SM operations can be saddled with challenges, so it is incumbent on university management to consciously institute appropriate structures and commit sufficient resources that will aid its effective implementation, as the benefits associated with sustainability practices far outweigh accompanying costs.

Study Implications and Limitations

Extant sustainability literature and findings of this study portray SM as a formidable precipitant of institutional profitability and overall university brand reputational wellbeing. SM adoption by university brand managers will promote a symbiotic relationship in which Africa's universities will work to promote the interests of their numerous stakeholders on whom their brands' survival and growth depend (Xie et al., 2016; Zhang et al., 2016; Zhao et al., 2011). At the institutional level, offices responsible for marketing and institutional advancements must make deliberate and sustained efforts to develop clear-cut, actionable SM marketing plans that would be reviewed periodically to reflect changing circumstances of their stakeholders. In view of its demonstrable benefits to the numerous publics of the university brand, a ministerial level policy framework should be developed to regulate SM practices of universities on which mandatory annual sustainability reports should be submitted for possible governmental action. The study provides a worth of tactical implementation details that stand to guide university brands in their adoption and execution of SM programmes. Theoretically, the working definition proffered, and the blend of dimensions adapted for the study, provide a sound basis for further research in the current blurry university SM terrain.

This study is limited in scope with its focus on UG. A future study involving a good number of African university brands with diverse geographical and socio-economic circumstance would enhance findings generalisability. Again, the key structures, constraints and benefits of SM identified were based on responses as they relate to the university sector.

SM pertaining to varied industry sectors could be considered in a future study. Notwithstanding these limitations, findings of this study provide useful insights into key issues of concern to university brands that policy makers need to consider in their attempts to implement SM not only in Ghana but across Africa and beyond.

References

Adams, C. A., & McNicholas, P. (2007). Making a difference: Sustainability reporting, accountability and organisational change. *Accounting, Auditing & Accountability Journal, 20*(3), 382–402. https://doi.org/10.1108/09513570710748553

Aguinis, H., & Glavas, A. (2012). What we know and don't know about corporate social responsibility: A review and research agenda. *Journal of Management, 38*(4), 932–968.

Anderson, J. (2012). Reflective journals as a tool for auto-ethnographic learning: A case study of student experiences with individualized sustainability. *Journal of Geography in Higher Education, 36*(4), 613–623.

Anwar, Y., & El-Bassiouny, N. (2020). Marketing and the Sustainable Development Goals (SDGs): A review and research agenda. In *The future of the UN Sustainable Development Goals* (pp. 187–207). Springer.

Argyris, A., & Tsaliki, P. V. (2005, June). Is sustainable development feasible?. In *Contribution of marketing to peace and prosperity, proceedings of the 9th International Conference on Marketing and Development (ICMD)* (pp. 8–11). Aristotle University of Thessoloniki.

Asif, M. (2009). Sustainable energy options for Pakistan. *Renewable and Sustainable Energy Reviews, 13*(4), 903–909.

Asif, M., Fisscher, O. A., de Bruijn, E. J., & Pagell, M. (2010). Integration of management systems: A methodology for operational excellence and strategic flexibility. *Operations Management Research, 3*(3–4), 146–160.

Asif, M., Searcy, C., Garvare, R., & Ahmad, N. (2011). Including sustainability in business excellence models. *Total Quality Management & Business Excellence, 22*(7), 773–786.

Barbier, E. B. (1989). Cash crops, food crops, and sustainability: The case of Indonesia. *World Development, 17*(6), 879–895.

Benn, S., Edwards, M., & Williams, T. (2014). *Organisational change for corporate sustainability*. Routledge.

Bhattacharyya, S. S. (2010). Exploring the concept of strategic corporate social responsibility for an integrated perspective. *European Business Review, 22*(1), 82–101.

Bonaccorsi, A., & Daraio, C. (Eds.). (2007). *Universities and strategic knowledge creation: Specialization and performance in Europe*. Edward Elgar Publishing.

Brower, J., & Mahajan, V. (2013). Driven to be good: A stakeholder theory perspective on the drivers of corporate social performance. *Journal of Business Ethics, 117*(2), 313–331.

Bryman, A. (2012). Sampling in qualitative research. *Social Research Methods, 4*, 415–429.

Cañibano, L., & Sánchez, M. P. (2009). Intangibles in universities: Current challenges for measuring and reporting. *Journal of Human Resource Costing & Accounting, 13*(2), 93–104.

Creswell, J. W. (2007). Five qualitative approaches to inquiry. *Qualitative Inquiry and Research Design: Choosing among Five Approaches, 2*, 53–80.

Crittenden, V. L., Crittenden, W. F., Ferrell, L. K., Ferrell, O. C., & Pinney, C. C. (2011). Market-oriented sustainability: A conceptual framework and propositions. *Journal of the Academy of Marketing Science, 39*(1), 71–85.

Dauncey, G. (2009). Towards sustainability. Available at www.towards-sustainability.co.uk/infodir/susquote.html. Accessed on 10 May 2014.

Davis, S. A., Edmister, J. H., Sullivan, K., & West, C. K. (2003). Educating sustainable societies for the twenty-first century. *International Journal of Sustainability in Higher Education, 4*(2), 169–179.

Demirel, B., Erdem, C., & Eroglu, I. (2017). The crowding out effect from European debt crisis perspective: Eurozone experience. *International Journal of Sustainable Economy, 9*(1), 1–18.

DiMaggio, P. J., & Powell, W. W. (1983). The iron cage revisited: Institutional isomorphism and collective rationality in organizational fields. *American Sociological Review, 48*(2), 147–160.

Elkington, J. (1999). Triple bottom line revolution: Reporting for the third millennium. *Australian CPA, 69*(11), 75–76.

Emanuel, R., & Adams, J. N. (2011). College students' perceptions of campus sustainability. *International Journal of Sustainability in Higher Education, 12*(1), 79–92.

Epstein, M. J. (2018). *Making sustainability work: Best practices in managing and measuring corporate social, environmental and economic impacts*. Routledge.

Engert, S., & Baumgartner, R. J. (2016). Corporate sustainability strategy–bridging the gap between formulation and implementation. *Journal of Cleaner Production, 113*, 822–834.

Espinosa, A., & Porter, T. (2011). Sustainability, complexity and learning: insights from complex systems approaches. *The Learning Organization, 18*(1), 54–72. https://doi.org/10.1108/09696471111096000

Ferrer-Balas, D., Adachi, J., Banas, S., Davidson, C. I., Hoshikoshi, A., Mishra, A., Motodoa, Y., Onga, M., & Ostwald, M. (2008). An international comparative analysis of sustainability transformation across seven universities. *International Journal of Sustainability in Higher Education, 9*(3), 295–316.

Fonseca, A., Macdonald, A., Dandy, E., & Valenti, P. (2011). The state of sustainability reporting at Canadian universities. *International Journal of Sustainability in Higher Education, 12*(1), 22–40.

Fredriksson, P., & Persson, M. (2011). Integrating sustainable development into operations management courses. *International Journal of Sustainability in Higher Education, 12*(3), 236–249.

Freeman, R. E. (1984). Strategic management: A stakeholder approach. *Journal of Human Resource and Sustainability Studies, 2*(2). https://doi.org/10.2139/ssrn.263511

Grewatsch, S., & Kleindienst, I. R. (2015). Exploring the link between corporate sustainability and the development of capabilities. *Academy of Management Proceedings* 1, 16893. Briarcliff Manor, NY 10510: Academy of Management.

Grimstad, S. (2011). Developing a framework for examining business-driven sustainability initiatives with relevance to wine tourism clusters. *International Journal of Wine Business Research, 23*(1), 62–82. https://doi.org/10.1108/17511061111121416

Hampl, N., & Loock, M. (2013). Sustainable development in retailing: What is the impact on store choice? *Business Strategy and the Environment, 22*(3), 202–216.

Hill, R.P. (2017). Poverty and deprivation: What's a marketer to do? Available at https://www.ama.org/2017/09/13/poverty-and-deprivation-whats-a-marketer-to-do/. Accessed on 13 January 2020.

Hult, G. T. M. (2011). Market-focused sustainability: Market orientation plus! *Journal of the Academy of Marketing Science, 39*, 1–6.

Hunt, S. D. (2017). Strategic marketing, sustainability, the triple bottom line, and resource-advantage (RA) theory: Securing the foundations of strategic marketing theory and research. *AMS Review, 7*(1), 52–66.

Ikeme, J. (2000). *Sustainable development, globalisation and Africa: plugging the holes*. www.afbis.com/analysis/Jekwu.html. Accessed 12 August 2009.

Jiang, P., Xu, B., Geng, Y., Dong, W., Chen, Y., & Xue, B. (2016). Assessing the environmental sustainability with a co-benefits approach: A study of industrial sector in Baoshan District in Shanghai. *Journal of Cleaner Production, 114*, 114–123.

Jones, P., Comfort, D., & Hillier, D. (2011). Sustainability in the global shop window. *International Journal of Retail & Distribution Management*, *39*(4), 256–271. https://doi.org/10.1108/09590551111117536

Katsikeas, C. S., Leonidou, C. N., & Zeriti, A. (2016). Eco-friendly product development strategy: Antecedents, outcomes, and contingent effects. *Journal of the Academy of Marketing Science, 44*(6), 660–684.

Kiron, D., Kruschwitz, N., Haanaes, K., & Reeves, M. (2015). Joining forces: Collaboration and leadership for sustainability. *MIT Sloan Management Review, 56*(3).

Kiron, D., Kruschwitz, N., Haanaes, K., Reeves, M., & Goh, E. (2013). The innovation bottom line. *MIT Sloan Management Review, 54*(3), 1.

Kolk, A. (2016). The social responsibility of international business: From ethics and the environment to CSR and sustainable development. *Journal of World Business, 51*(1), 23–34.

Kolodko, G. W. (2013). *Where the world is going: The political economy of the future*. Prószyński i S-ka.

Kozlenkova, I. V., Samaha, S. A., & Palmatier, R. W. (2014). Resource-based theory in marketing. *Journal of the Academy of Marketing Science, 42*(1), 1–21.

Krizek, K. J., Newport, D., White, J., & Townsend, A. R. (2012). Higher education's sustainability imperative: How to practically respond? *International Journal of Sustainability in Higher Education, 13*(1), 19–33. https://doi.org/10.1108/14676371211190281

Kumar, V., & Christodoulopoulou, A. (2014). Sustainability and branding: An integrated perspective. *Industrial Marketing Management, 43*(1), 6–15.

Kumar, V., Rahman, Z., & Kazmi, A. A. (2013). Sustainability marketing strategy: An analysis of recent literature. *Global Business Review, 14*(4), 601–625.

Laredo, P. (2007). Revisiting the third mission of universities: Toward a renewed categorization of university activities? *Higher Education Policy, 20*(4), 441–456.

Leap, T., & Loughry, M. L. (2004). The stakeholder-friendly firm. *Business Horizons, 47*(2), 27–32.

Leonidou, L. C., Christodoulides, P., Kyrgidou, L. P., & Palihawadana, D. (2017). Internal drivers and performance consequences of small firm green business strategy: The moderating role of external forces. *Journal of Business Ethics, 140*(3), 585–606.

Leonidou, L. C., Leonidou, C. N., Fotiadis, T. A., & Zeriti, A. (2013). Resources and capabilities as drivers of hotel environmental marketing strategy: Implications for competitive advantage and performance. *Tourism Management, 35*, 94–110.

Lim, W. M. (2016). A blueprint for sustainability marketing: Defining its conceptual boundaries for progress. *Marketing Theory, 16*(2), 232–249.

Linnenluecke, M. K., & Griffiths, A. (2013). Firms and sustainability: Mapping the intellectual origins and structure of the corporate sustainability field. *Global Environmental Change, 23*(1), 382–391.

Liu, W., Oosterveer, P., & Spaargaren, G. (2016). Promoting sustainable consumption in China: A conceptual framework and research review. *Journal of Cleaner Production, 134*, 13–21.

Lozano, R. (2011). The state of sustainability reporting in universities. *International Journal of Sustainability in Higher Education, 12*(1), 67–78. https://doi.org/10.1016/j.jclepro.2007.01.002.R

Lozano, R., Lukman, R., Lozano, F. J., Huisingh, D., & Lambrechts, W. (2013). Declarations for sustainability in higher education: Becoming better leaders, through addressing the university system. *Journal of Cleaner Production, 48*, 10–19.

Maignan, I., Ferrell, O. C., & Ferrell, L. (2005). A stakeholder model for implementing social responsibility in marketing. *European Journal of Marketing, 39*(9–10), 956–977.

Mainardes, E. W., Alves, H., & Raposo, M. (2011). Stake-holder theory: Issues to resolve. *Management Decision, 49*, 226–252.

Malhotra, N. K. (2010). Introduction: Analyzing accumulated knowledge and influencing Future research. In *Review of marketing research* (pp. xiii–xxviii). Emerald Group Publishing Limited.

Martin, D. M., & Schouten, J. W. (2014). The answer is sustainable marketing, when the question is: What can we do? *Recherche Et Applications En Marketing (english Edition), 29*(3), 107–109.

Miles, M. B., & Huberman, A. M. (1994). *Qualitative data analysis: An expanded source book* (2nd ed.). Sage.

Naeem, M. A., & Peach, N. W. (2011). Promotion of sustainability in postgraduate education in the Asia Pacific region. *International Journal of Sustainability in Higher Education., 12*, 280–290.

Nejati, M., Bin, A. S., & Amran, A. B. (2010). Sustainable development: A competitive advantage or a threat? *Business Strategy Series, 11*(2), 84–89.

Nkamnebe, A. D. (2011). Sustainability marketing in the emerging markets: Imperatives, challenges, and agenda setting. *International Journal of Emerging Markets, 6*, 217–232.

Nwankwo, S., Chaharbaghi, K., & Boyd, D. (2009). Retrieved 12 August 2009. http://homepages.uel.ac.uk/D.A.C.Boyd/IJTMSD%20Multidisciplinary%20paper.pdf

Ostrom, E. (2005). Doing institutional analysis digging deeper than markets and hierarchies. *Handbook of new institutional economics* (pp. 819–848). Springer.

Palma, L. C., de Oliveira, L. M., & Viacava, K. R. (2011). Sustainability in Brazilian federal universities. *International Journal of Sustainability in Higher Education, 12*(3), 250–258.

Palmer, C. (2011). Place-historical narratives: Road—or roadblock—to sustainability? *Ethics, Policy & Environment, 14*(3), 345–359.

Parry, S. N. (2012). Environmental responsibility in micro-enterprises: Exploring the relationship between disclosure and practice. In *Social and sustainable enterprise: Changing the nature of business* (pp. 97–117). Emerald Group Publishing Limited.

Pearce, D. (1997). Substitution and sustainability: Some reflections on Georgescu-Roegen. *Ecological Economics, 22*(3), 295–297.

Peloza, J., & Shang, J. (2011). How can corporate social responsibility activities create value for stakeholders? A systematic review. *Journal of the Academy of Marketing Science, 39*(1), 117–135.

Porter, M. E., & Kramer, M. R. (2006). The link between competitive advantage and corporate social responsibility. *Harvard Business Review, 84*(12), 78–92.

Richardson, J., Grose, J., O'Connor, A., Bradbury, M., Kelsey, J., & Doman, M. (2015). Nursing students' attitudes towards sustainability and health care. *Nursing Standard (2014+), 29*(42), 36.

Robinson, R. R. (2003). Consumers' perspectives on purchasing sustainably produced foods and dietitians' perspectives on integrating issues of sustainability into professional practice.

Robson, C. (1993). *Real world research*. Blackwell Publishers, Oxford.

Rudawska, E. (2018). From sustainable market orientation to sustainability marketing. In E. Rudawska (Ed.), *The sustainable marketing concept in European SMEs: Insights from the food & drink industry* (pp. 53–79). Emerald Publishing Limited.

Saeed, M. A., Waseek, I., & Kersten, W. (2017). Literature review of drivers of sustainable supply chain management. In *Digitalization in maritime and sustainable logistics: City logistics, port logistics and sustainable supply chain management in the digital age. Proceedings of the Hamburg International Conference of Logistics (HICL)* (Vol. 24, pp. 159–184). epubli GmbH.

Saunders, M., Lewis, P. H. I. L. I. P., & Thornhill, A. D. R. I. A. N. (2007). Research methods (Business Students 4th ed.). Pearson Education Limited.

Schaefer, M., Goldman, E., Bartuska, A. M., Sutton-Grier, A., & Lubchenco, J. (2015). Nature as capital: Advancing and incorporating ecosystem services in United States federal policies and programs. *Proceedings of the National Academy of Sciences, 112*(24), 7383–7389.

Shirokova, G., Osiyevskyy, O., & Bogatyreva, K. (2016). Exploring the intention–behavior link in student entrepreneurship: Moderating effects of individual and environmental characteristics. *European Management Journal, 34*(4), 386–399.

Sisaye, S. (2011). Ecological systems approaches to sustainability and organizational development. *Leadership & Organization Development Journal., 32*(4), 379–398.

Smith, P. A., & Sharicz, C. (2011). The shift needed for sustainability. *The Learning Organization, 18*(1), 73–86.

Stainer, A., & Stainer, L. (1997). Ethical dimensions of environmental management. *European Business Review., 97*, 224–231.

Suchman, M. C. (1995). Managing legitimacy: Strategic and institutional approaches. *Academy of Management Review, 20*(3), 571–610.

Taneja, S. S., Taneja, P. K., & Gupta, R. K. (2011). Researches in corporate social responsibility: A review of shifting focus, paradigms, and methodologies. *Journal of Business Ethics, 101*(3), 343–364.

Trail, G. T., & McCullough, B. P. (2019). Marketing sustainability through sport: Testing the sport participant sustainability behaviour model. *European Sport Management Quarterly*, 1–35.

University Leaders for a Sustainable Future. (1999). *Sustainability assessment questionnaire*. ULSF.

University of Ghana. (2012). Basic Laws of the University of Ghana. https://www.ug.edu.gh/paddocs/Basic_Laws.pdf

Van Weenen, H. (2000). Towards a vision of a sustainable university. *International Journal of Sustainability in Higher Education, 1*(1), 20–34.

Vezzoli, C., & Penin, L. (2006). Campus: "lab" and "window" for sustainable design research and education. *International Journal of Sustainability in Higher Education, 7*(1), 69–80.

WCED, S. W. S. (1987). World commission on environment and development. *Our Common Future, 17*(1), 1–91.

Whitehead, A. N. (1927). Universities and their function, address to the American Association of the Collegiate Schools of Business, Harvard University.

Wilden, R., & Gudergan, S. P. (2015). The impact of dynamic capabilities on operational marketing and technological capabilities: Investigating the role of environmental turbulence. *Journal of the Academy of Marketing Science, 43*(2), 181–199.

Xie, H., Wang, W., Yang, Z., & Choi, Y. (2016). Measuring the sustainable performance of industrial land utilization in major industrial zones of China. *Technological Forecasting and Social Change, 112*, 207–219.

Yin, R. K. (2003). Designing case studies. *Qualitative Research Methods*, 359–386.

Yin, R. K. (2009). How to do better case studies. *The SAGE Handbook of Applied Social Research Methods, 2*, 254–282.

Zhao, Y., Li, Y., Lee, S. H., & Bo Chen, L. (2011). Entrepreneurial orientation, organizational learning, and performance: Evidence from China. *Entrepreneurship Theory and Practice, 35*(2), 293–317.

Zhang, C., Bengio, S., Hardt, M., Recht, B., & Vinyals, O. (2016). *Understanding deep learning requires rethinking generalization.* arXiv preprint arXiv: 1611.03530.

5

Marketing Oil and Gas Brands in Africa

Riverson Oppong

The Oil and Gas Industry in Africa

Africa is regarded as one of the continents with considerable oil and gas resources that can accelerate the growth of its economy when it is strategically used. Even though new resources are discovered progressively, the resources are not distributed evenly or equally. For instance, thirty-eight (38) African countries are net oil importers currently. Globally, the oil and gas (energy) industry serve as one of the leading sectors towards the advancement of the economies of oil-rich nations, and Africa has one of the largest oil and gas reserves, and the industry serves as one of the leading sectors towards the development of the continent. The

R. Oppong (✉)
Ghana National Gas Company, Accra, Ghana
e-mail: riverson.oppong@ghanagas.com.gh

Accra Campus, Ghana Technology University College and Coventry University, Accra, Ghana

S. Appau (ed.), *Marketing Brands in Africa*, Palgrave Studies of Marketing in Emerging Economies,
https://doi.org/10.1007/978-3-030-77204-8_5

energy sector constitutes 80% of African's economy, and it provides over 98% of the primary energy supply needed (Mehdi-Zadeh, 2012; Seyyed-Javadeyn et al., 2010; Thompson & Gamble, 2013; Vallaster & Adam, 2011).

Depending on the production, oil and gas serve as the primary source of energy supplies, but it acts as capital, liquidity, and wealth to the African economy. This is attributed to the fact that the economies of oil-rich states obtain massive foreign exchange from it compared to other sectors like agriculture that require investment and the needed funds and budgets. When there is any challenge to the industry's validity, it is regarded as a huge challenge that faces those economies in providing basic needs. A decline in foreign exchange that comes from the exportation of crude oil results in the deterioration in the oil-rich countries' economic situations and leads to reductions in the imports of intermediate goods. And the decline in production can also lead to a decline in imports of capital goods and a decline in investment. A decline in oil revenues leads to a decrease in public funding and disturbs the budget balance and increases inflation (Onojaefe, 2001).

To suggest that the oil and gas sector is enormous is an understatement. In reality, the oil and gas sector is vast and has its own unique ecosystem of industries. From independent small companies (like Springfield Petroleum) to field service providers (like Baker Hughes) to super major oil corporations (like Royal Dutch Shell and ExxonMobil), the oil and gas industry comes in many different sizes and shapes. These corporations use different marketing strategies to get the word out about their brands. However, when you look at them on the whole, the business purpose appears to fall into one of three groups. Firstly, corporations aim to strengthen investor relations to establish mutually beneficial relations and finance their drilling projects. Secondly, they strive to address recruitment processes and beef up brand perception within the sector. Thirdly, corporations aim to enhance public relations and community engagement to engender positive brand perception outside the sector (Jones, 2005; Kumar et al., 2013; Miller & Merrilees, 2013).

Yet, even with the massive amount of money the oil and gas industry invest in accomplishing these goals, they remain probably the most maligned business sector on the planet. There are numerous explanations for this. One of the primary reasons is the sector's impact on the natural environment through oil drilling and the contributions of their consumption on global warming. Another reason is that many of those in the sector hesitate to "meet people where they are at" and show the real (and nearly miraculous) benefit oil and gas bring to the globe (Minton & Rose, 1997; Peattie, 2001; Porter & van der Linde, 1995). Today, oil and gas serve as one of the most significant commodities, and at the same time, the most political commodity globally. For this reason, policies about this natural resource in the oil-rich countries constitute the central part of the national policies of these economies. In these countries, any policy is influenced by the oil policies, with potential for conflict and even civil wars (Hosseini & Abolfazli, 2009; Qayyumi et al., 2011).

Underpinned by environmental and sustainability agendas, regulatory and technological changes in the oil and gas (energy) industry have compelled these organisations to reconsider their existing business models that contributes to a speculated "utility death spiral' (Hartmann & Apaolaza-Ibáñez, 2012; Larsen, 2017). In recent literature, the word 'sustainable' has emerged as a common notion. It addresses the underlying principle that while fulfilling customers' needs and wants, corporations have a duty to preserve nature. Recent environmental issues necessitate management to formulate strategies for reducing pollution and the conservation of natural resources. This is still a challenge, and it is difficult for many oil and gas managers to incorporate sustainability into their corporations. However, the green economy is a competitive segment comprising green goods, organic farming, clean technology, renewable energy and natural resources that marketers consider an opportunity for competitive advantage (Saxena & Khandelwal, 2010). Therefore, many corporations these days follow a green corporate strategy to guarantee sustainable growth by embracing their business operations' green attributes. Although these initiatives are voluntary, more and more corporations have taken up this initiative, becoming the primary plan and critical strategic consideration among corporations. There are some indications that after transitioning to a green manufacturing process, different types of corporations that turn to green strategies—such as conventional manufacturing companies—become more profitable (Ashley & Leonard, 2009; Hasan & Ali, 2015; Taylor et al., 2013).

The call to give consumers access to modern (environmentally friendly) energy services and expand the usage of renewable energy sources has transformed the oil and gas (energy) sector—formerly full of monopolistic practices—on its head (Yadghar & Tadayyon-Tahmasebi, 2006). These variables have prompted a paradigm shift in the mentality that energy is a desirable 'commodity' that is assumed to be a 'constant.' How can energy companies reinvent themselves to succeed in a dynamic, consumer-driven marketplace from traditional methods and ways of thinking?

Considering the challenges in the oil and gas environment, marketing managers need to develop a strong relationship with all stakeholders that will be able to tailor the right products and services based on the needs of customers. A decline in the price of oil affects oil production, which causes a drop in revenue related to oil supply or production. Exploring novel marketing strategies is needed to remain competitive and profitable in any given sector, especially the oil and gas industry (Appiah-Adu & Amoako, 2016). This chapter explores the African oil and gas (energy) industry and the branding strategies employed to build and market energy brands in Africa.

The Concept of Branding in the Oil and Gas (Energy) Sector

The American Marketing Association described a brand as a name, term, design, symbol, or any other feature that identifies one seller's good or service as distinct from those of other sellers. Although the concept of branding is not a recent phenomenon, there has been little examination of branding strategies in the oil and gas (energy) industry. Energy branding can be defined as a corporate ideology that determines an oil and gas (energy) company's entire strategic practice, which is expressed both externally and internally in its operations" (Larsen, 2017). It is about a two-way customer communication; it is about understanding who the customer is and how to connect in ways that the customer understands. It is all about being willing to use the energy company's resources as part of the brand's storytelling for businesses outside of the energy sector. Some super-brands in the energy sector have raised the benchmark in their communication with customers. For instance, in the case of BP, the petroleum company uses content marketing for its lead generation. BP uses its active social channels and blogs to promote their services and offers. This type of content drive and active social media visibility and engagement are invaluable in boosting the number of leads generated through its website.

Evermore companies and businesses have found and are improving the drawbacks of the oil and gas (energy) through their branding efforts (Larsen, 2017). A strong brand can contribute to marketing success and branding also stimulates consumer-brand interaction. The exponential growth of distributed generation and renewables may be one of the most important industry developments impacting the conventional oil and gas (energy) model. For a sector that has so far been marked by an over-reliance on 'dirty power,' the shift away from fossil fuel-generated energy to renewable energy is a significant step forward. This will continue to constitute part of the main messages of the rebranding strategies of many energy companies as a multitude of marketing campaigns are being pursued with sustainable connotations. Energy companies, therefore, emphasise 'clean and sustainable' and ensure that they create value in other areas that matter to consumers, e.g., product extension, customer service and pricing (Glowik & Smyczek, 2012).

Additionally, many energy companies are now conscious of a good brand's value in the more competitive markets and are taking measures to shift more towards careful branding strategies (Larsen, 2017). The drawback is that energy companies are large ships, and changing the system requires time for them. For branding to be effectively introduced, literally the entire company requires to be on deck. And training an engineer to respond in a fresh perspective can be challenging when his whole professional life has centred on something completely different. Often, numerous individuals want the company to go deeper into branding, but management is often much more oriented on the company's engineering portion and does not recognise the value of a good brand (Larsen, 2017).

Energy companies ought to be extremely visible via advertisements that attempt to improve the negative perceptions of energy companies and their environmental consequences through explaining unique support programs to save biodiversity and protecting water bodies, as well as focusing on a sector-wide rebranding strategy (Keller, 2012). The exponential implementation of smart grids and renewables is perhaps one of the very important industry dynamics impacting the traditional energy model. This will continue to be part of a major messaging of the rebranding energy approaches (Kotler & Keller, 2005).

Due to the dependence on oil reserves, continuity of gas supplies and geopolitical situations, there is the need to enhance energy management effectiveness (Yadghar & Tadayyon-Tahmasebi, 2006). To achieve each of these broad and long-term goals, there is the need for strategic management in every sector of the oil and gas industry to support a balanced development and growth (Qayyumi et al., 2011). The industrial marketing environment is changing rapidly, and any industry that is not adapting to these rapid changes is inevitably excluded from competition.

The recent revolution in the global economy, especially the continuity of economic crises, has resulted in a fiercely competitive and uncertain environment. For this reason, industrial enterprises are challenged with the need to differentiate their products and services within the global market. In such a situation, companies try to distinguish themselves by enhancing their brand to achieve a competitive advantage in the market (Kotler & Pfoertsch, 2006).

The primary identity of a company's brand can be determined based on its stated goals and objectives. Therefore, with any change in its perspective and interaction with and reaction to people and customers, the identity can be changed over time. For example, the approach to developing an integrated strategy and selecting the slogan "Beyond Petroleum", where the new brand of BP was introduced in July 2000, was based on four central values of performance, innovations, protection of the environment, and assertiveness. From 2001 to 2005, this was so when several of the oil and gas companies had lost their customer satisfaction. However, with this approach, BP could enhance its strength, as it increased market share to about 27%, and the company's intangible assets value increased to over $7 million (Keller, 2012). The approach to creating a global brand to compete in the international arena needs a global and international identity in every aspect. Next, I discuss the main branding strategies that have been used to develop and market oil and gas brands in Africa.

Branding Strategies Used in the African Oil and Gas Industry

The energy industry in Africa has witnessed some tough times for the past half-decade—expected paradigm shift in the global energy mix, implementation of the Sustainable Development Goals, and COVID-19 related issues. There are some global upstream oil and gas companies who are trying to redefine their operational activities in a new marketing era. But many do not reserve respectable portions of their budget for their marketing, even though the marketing landscape has changed drastically. Because many of these companies are B2B, they do not invest a lot in branding efforts unlike those who also do or are midstream or downstream and therefore are customer-facing. Below, I discuss of some of the more common branding strategies that oil and gas businesses that operate in Africa have adopted to deliberately or unconsciously influence positive brand perceptions about their business.

Brand Social Responsibility

Unsurprisingly, the most common branding strategy used by many oil and gas businesses in Africa is through brand social responsibility to the communities, regions and countries where they operate. A good example is Springfield, an oil and gas company whose business model operates as a fully integrated entity across the entire value chain of the oil and gas industry, with the intention to become the very first Ghanaian indigenous company to develop and operate an offshore oil and gas field. Even before Springfield announced its discovery of oil and gas in December 2019, the company has focused on building its branding models around community engagement and social investments. Springfield's social investment policy is predicated on the belief that natural resources are for the collective benefit of the citizenry and that the communities in which they operate must enjoy positive impacts from their operations. Springfield's approach is to integrate elements of the United Nations' Sustainable Development Goals (SDGs) into its operations with the explicit aim of ensuring better living standards for all people. In this regard, Springfield focuses on the following SDGs: affordable and clean energy, ending poverty, good health and wellbeing, quality education, gender equality, decent work and economic growth; and building partnerships to achieve the goals. These social investments include buying health supplies for local hospital emergency units, paying for the surgeries of infants and children, building schools and supporting medical training. The company suggests that the goal of these social investments is to compensate the cost of their operations in the communities they operate.

This is similar to the brand social responsibility approach and objective of Angola's Sonangol, which overseas oil and gas production in the country. Songangol, in addition to being the biggest donor to the state budget, is responsible for carrying out various social initiatives in an endeavour called "Together with the Community." Sonangol is deeply involved in improving the welfare of the community and helps rebuilding and building schools, kindergartens and hospitals across the country. Over $6 million was allocated to areas such as public health, education, culture, sports and agriculture in 2003 alone. And this support comes with massive branding along the streets of Angola. The corporation also sponsors many sporting events, including national sports competitions and the national sports teams, among others. It was also the title sponsor for the motorsport event entitled 'Superleague Formula by Sonangol' which happened between 2009 and 2010.

Nigeria is Africa's largest oil producer and the Nigerian National Petroleum Corporation (NNPC) which regulates and operates petroleum production in the country also has a similar brand social responsibility approach with strategic investments in health, education and economic empowerment, sport, art and culture, and charitable/professional donations. The NNPC's stated aims are to improve the general health and well-being of their stakeholders and residents of the host community through sustainable policies and activities throughout the community. They also participate in brand social responsibility initiatives to enable local economies to thrive in all geographical operational areas. Similarly, as part of its brand social responsibilities, the Nigerian Agip Oil Company (NAOC) also declared it aided farmers' cooperative societies, youths and women groups in its areas of operation with micro credit facilities between (Vanguard, 2009).

Brand social responsibility is not limited to indigenous African oil and gas companies. Foreign or international brands operating in Africa also adopt a similar branding approach and initiatives. For example, the international oil companies in Nigeria have spent various sums in this regard. In 2010, Shell Petroleum Development Company (SPDC) spent a total of US$65 million in funding development projects in 244 communities in Nigeria (Shell in Nigeria, 2011). Another company, Chevron, spent a total of US$56.7 million on 425 communities in six years to fund various developmental and social welfare programmes (Chevron: 2011 Nigeria Corporate Responsibility Report). Exxonmobil affiliate companies in Nigeria invested about US$280 million between 2000 and 2009 on strategic and sustainable community 9 investments in healthcare, education and capacity building initiatives (Vanguard, 2010). Thus, many oil and gas brands operating in Africa adopt this brand corporate social responsibility approach with the aim of gaining local acceptance and also to offset any negative brand perceptions that may arise from the brand's activities, especially in places most affected by the oil and gas brands' operations.

Customer-Brand Relationship

Another branding strategy—adopted often by downstream companies—towards developing a stronger brand is building better relationships with customers through improved services, processes and customer engagement. For example, Ghana Oil Company Limited (GOIL), Ghana's foremost local Oil Marketing Company (OMC), have introduced an upgraded electronic prepaid card to assist customers in reducing the volume of physical cash business transactions. The purpose of the upgraded GOIL Advantage Cards (G-Cards) also seeks to help existing and prospective customers manage fuel consumption and reduce waste. According to GOIL's Chief Operating Officer, the upgraded GOIL Advantage Card has special security features to protect the customers, as well as make it easy for customers to load cash onto the card at any GOIL fuel station.

Another customer-brand relationship approach is incentivizing customer referral. A good example of an oil and gas brand that uses this approach is Stream Energy, which was named the "Most Innovative Marketer of 2016", at the Energy Marketing Conference for Retailers. The company found an innovative way to reach customers: selling energy by word of mouth. Stream Energy encourages current customers to refer new customers in exchange for discounted—even free—energy. This approach taps into customer-created content to reach a broader audience of potential customers. Plus, the company consistently publishes content to educate its audience on how to cut costs and make more decisions that benefit the environment. All of these efforts build Stream Energy's credibility and enable the company to keep its customers informed and excited about what the company is doing.

A few of these brands also rely on social media to build more engagement with their customers. Springfield, for example, have a very active social media following especially on LinkedIn. The brand shares frequent stories about the businesses' journey, activities and brand social responsibility. They also share social content like working from home advice, supporting women in the workplace, engaging in topical local news and celebrating their indigenous Ghanaian identity. These social media posts often engender a lot of engagement with their followers and build a better brand-customer relationship.

Another energy company that has taken a similar approach in its branding efforts in Africa is Georgia Power, an international brand with operations in Africa. The energy company have a social media centre located at the company y's head office. It is meant to facilitate accurate, timely social media communication with customers during inclement weather. Even when the weather is not severe, the firm engages with its customers more than 6000 times a month on social media, answering service questions, helping with payment options, offering up energy efficiency advice, and more. This focus on sharing content with customers on social media allows the company to help its customers become more informed about energy consumption and gain confidence in the brand as a trusted voice in the energy sector.

Brand Identity Building

A third strategy that oil and gas brands use in Africa is brand identity building. While all oil and gas businesses invest in minimal brand elements like a name and logo, not many really commit to building a distinctive brand identity. Oil and gas companies which have retail operations tend to do this better, often (re)positioning or refreshing different aspects of their brand to project their differentiated brand offering. For example, GOIL recently unveiled a new brand logo and launched its new rebranding as one of its marketing strategies. According to GOIL, the rebranding is a reflection of their commitment to grow their business by being better positioned in the minds of all stakeholders including employees, consumers, regulators, investors and even its competitors (GOIL Annual Report, 2019).

Some other brands build their positioning on addressing environmental concerns, which is an issue that has universally and consistently generated negative perceptions about the oil and gas industry. A good example is the case of Eni, a multinational oil company with vast operations in Africa, which is building brand positioning rooted in protecting and preserving the environment by means of creating programs and technologies that will be able to reduce the emission of greenhouse gas. This caused the company to launch the "Eniday", which is an online magazine that discusses innovations in the energy industry, as well as the people who do the hard work of transforming natural resources into energy. This online content is made up of a mix of written content and visual programs that educate and inspire its audience about the brand's positioning on "energy as a good".

Similarly, in keeping with its five-year (2018–2022) strategic objectives, Angola's Sonangol has committed to designing its activities in order to ensure the least impact on the balance between the environment and communities that rely on it, with the focus on solid sustainability principles. With regard to Sonangol's operations, such as petroleum exploration and development that have a greater environmental impact, the business relies on the application of sustainable practices and on the viability of an unforeseen evaluation of available resources.

Springfield, however, is a good example of a non-retail (upstream) oil and gas company that also invests in building a unique brand identity around its brand social responsibility and African heritage but perhaps more notably also on the personal brand of its CEO, Kevin Okyere. Okyere enjoys a celebrity status in Ghana, has a large social media following, especially on LinkedIn, engages in very publicised philanthropy, receives extensive media coverage by local and international news media and has close relations with local and international celebrities like American comedian and TV host, Steve Harvey. Okyere's well managed personal brand and its effect on the Springfield brand is akin to the effect of Elon Musk on the Tesla brand, reflecting a new generation of CEOs whose personal brand is shaped by and influences the brand identities of their corporate brands. In this case, Okyere's personal brand and Springfield have a shared identity of an authentic home-grown African success story that gives back to the community that birthed and nurtured its success.

Conclusion

Branding should be about much more than how your company is graphically represented. It's about adopting a new philosophy of doing business and expressing that strategically through your brand. A great brand represents a company's current activity and—to some extent—its aspirations, informing both its internal and external environments or worlds. In the case of oil and gas, Ryan O'Keefe, Director of Communications at Enel rightly notes that "the world of energy (oil and gas) needs to face this reality and prepare to give people more power, to work more closely with consumers, inviting them into the energy conservation and transforming them into actors of a world that before belonged just to utilities. Brands are essential in writing the terms of this new relationship, and they have to articulate this strategic approach in a new company positioning. All good brand work is done at the molecular level – it's the core that defines how a company approaches everything else." When an organisation invests in a brand, it paves the way for the business to achieve long-term success. This shift towards a brand orientation will help transform energy (oil and gas) companies from production-oriented, conservative and self-referential businesses into a business model that engages consumers, partners, and stakeholders in an open, people-centric and transparent way.

References

Appiah-Adu, K., & Amoako, G. K. (2016). The execution of marketing strategies in a developing economy: A case study of selected market leaders. *African Journal of Economic and Management Studies, 17*(1), 9–29.

Ashley, C., & Leonard, H. A. (2009). Betrayed by the buzz? Covert content and consumer brand relationship. *Journal of Public Policy and Marketing, 28*, 212–280.

British Petroleum (BP) plc. (2016). *BP energy outlook of 2035*. http://www.bp.com/en/global/corporate/energy-economics/energy-outlook-2035.html.

Glowik, M., & Smyczek, S. (2012). *International marketing management*. De Gruyter.

Goil Annual Report. (2019). https://goil.com.gh/investor-relation/annual-reports/.

Hartmann, P., & Apaolaza-Ibáñez, V. (2012). Consumer attitude and purchase intention towards green energy brands: The role of psychological benefits and environmental concern. *Journal of Business Research, 65*(9), 1254–1263.

Hasan, Z., & Ali, N. A. (2015). The impact of green marketing strategy on the firm's performance in Malaysia. *Procedia—Social and Behavioral Sciences, 172*, 463–470. Retrieved on 11 November 2020, from: https://doi.org/10.1016/j.sbspro.2015.01.382.

Hosseini, S. M., & Abolfazli, S. A. (2009). The study of the influence of brand equity on consumer response. *Commercial Management Outlook, 32*.

Jones, R. (2005). Finding sources of brand value: Developing a stakeholder model of brand equity. *Journal of Brand Management, 13*(1), 10–32.
Keller, K. L. (2012). *Strategic brand management* (A. Bathayi, Trans.). Siteh.
Kotler, P., & Keller, K. L. (2005). *Marketing management* (Vol. 12). Prentice-Hall Edition.
Kotler, P., & Pfoertsch, W. (2006). *B2B brand management*. Springer.
Kumar, V., Sharma, A., Shah, R., & Rajan, B. (2013). Establishing profitable customer loyalty for multinational companies in emerging economies: A conceptual framework. *Journal of International Marketing, 21*(1), 57–80.
Larsen, F. (2017). Green energy branding. In F. Larsen (Ed.), *Energy branding* (pp. 111–145). Palgrave Macmillan.
Mehdi -Zadeh, M. R. (2012). Identity, brand and organization logo: Reviewing the development of the brand of Iran's oil industry in comparison with two oil companies. *Management and Human Resources of the Oil Industry, 3*(11).
Miller, D., & Merrilees, B. (2013). Linking retailer corporate brand and environmental sustainability practices. *Journal of Product & Brand Management, 22*(7), 437–443. Retrieved on 8 November 2020, from: https://doi.org/10.1108/JPBM-10-2013-0417.
Minton, A. P., & Rose, R. L. (1997). The effects of environmental concern on environmentally friendly consumer behaviour: An exploratory study. *Journal of Business Research, 40*, 37–48.
Onojaefe, D. P. (2001). *Branding essentials in the South African petroleum industry* (Unpublished Masters Dissertation). Cape Technikon, IN.
Porter, M. E., & van der Linde, C. (1995). Green and competitive: Ending the stalemate. *Harvard Business Review, 73*(5), 120–134.
Peattie, K. (2001). Towards sustainability: The third age of green marketing. *The Marketing Review, 2*(2), 129–146. Retrieved on 5 November 2020, from: https://doi.org/10.1362/1469347012569869.
Qayyumi, Z., Mobini-Dehkordi, A., & Shrifian, M. A. (2011). The role of the senior managers in the implementation of Iran's Oil Industry Perspective. *Iranian Journal of Energy, 14*(2).
Saxena, R., & Khandelwal, P. K. (2010). Can green marketing be used as a tool for sustainable growth? A study performed on consumers in india—An emerging economy. *The International Journal of Environmental, Cultural, Economic & Social Sustainability, 6*(2), 277–291.
Seyyed-Javadeyn, S. R., Amini, A., & Amini, Z. (2010). The assessment of the effect of a brand on industrial customer's loyalty. *Commercial Management Outlook, 36*, 57–73.

Taylor, P., Chuang, S., & Yang, C. (2013). Key success factors when implementing a green-manufacturing system. *Production Planning & Control, 25*, 923–937.

Thompson, A. A., & Gamble, J. A. (2013). *Strategic management, principles and practices* (2nd ed., M. A. and H. Nikumaram, Trans.). Moballeghan.

Vallaster, C., & Adam, L. (2011). Formation: Brand actors and the Corporate brand strategy situational context for a business-to-business. *Brand Industrial Marketing Management, 40*, 1133–2114.

Yadghar, A., & Tadayyon-Tahmasebi, M. (2006). *Strategic marketing management in oil, gas and petrochemical industry (a case study): Strategic planning marketing model in Iranian GC enterprises.* International Conference on marketing management.

6

Branding and Marketing Nigerian Churches on Social Media

Oluwadamilola Blessing Ayeni

This chapter builds on Einstein (2007)'s argument that religion is a brand. The fact that "religion is personal and religion is packaged and sold the same way as other marketed goods and services" (Einstein, 2007, p. 78) is very pertinent in understanding how religious organisations promote and market themselves within their immediate and external communities. While a variety of positions exist on religious branding, this chapter will use Einstein (2007)'s central argument as a background in exploring churches, marketing perspectives and promotional tools. In particular, the use of social media platforms amongst other media tools will be considered as they play a very important role in the promotional strategies employed by churches (Niemandt, 2013). Often, research has shown that churches may adopt social media platforms as a marketing

O. B. Ayeni (✉)
Department of Media and Communication, Swinburne University of Technology, Hawthorn, VIC, Australia
e-mail: oayeni@swin.edu.au

S. Appau (ed.), *Marketing Brands in Africa*, Palgrave Studies of Marketing in Emerging Economies,
https://doi.org/10.1007/978-3-030-77204-8_6

tool for promotion and visibility in the market (Muchuki, 2017). How this is achieved will also be explored in this chapter.

More specifically, this chapter explores the religious scene in Nigeria which is catching up in significant ways to the changing media landscape. Religious organisations and bodies in Nigeria consist of several individuals and groups who hold religious beliefs. Examples are Islam, Christianity and other Traditional forms of beliefs or individual spirituality. While this chapter will focus on the religious environment, the focus is on the Christian faith and churches in Nigeria because, in the last decade, there has been a rapid increase in marketing activities by churches and spiritual leaders in Nigeria. Nigerian religious leaders are constantly seeking to influence and grow their communities as large as they can (Dowd, 2016). This chapter will also address why there is an increasing need for churches to brand and promote themselves to members and external communities. In this regard, this chapter reviews research on the branding and promotion strategies by churches in Nigeria focusing on how and why these religious organisations position their brand on the social media platforms available to them. As rightly argued by Einstein (2007), churches are a source of product and messages, hence it is important to explore how and why these churches create and maintain brand visibility to their audience and market and endorse these religious products.

In this regard, this chapter explores two questions: how do churches adopt secular branding approaches in promoting their brand and the message, and in particular, how does the use of social media in brand promotion apply to churches in Nigeria? To answer these questions, I will introduce the concepts of religions as brands and how religions can adopt branding approaches such as promotions in communicating with their target market. This chapter concludes that there are very valuable perspectives on social media branding by churches in Nigeria that need to be illuminated. These approaches may not apply to all churches at large, however, its exploration is vital in understanding how social media promotions are applicable in religious environments.

Religion and Religious Organisations

Religion is defined by scholars in different ways. Stolz and Usunier (2019) define religion as a cultural symbolic system that responds to the problem of meaning and is linked to a divine reality. Religion to some is based on God-centeredness (Knauss, 2016). It could also be viewed based on self-individuality and spirituality (Stolz & Usunier, 2019). Many religious organisations and religious bodies just like any other not-for-profit organisations have a brand name, which draws from their faith—Christianity, Islam, Judaism. The brand also has differentiated symbols such as the cross for Christianity, Yin-Yang sign for Taoism, Crescent and star for Islam. Places of worship in most cases reflect these signs and names (Stolz & Usunier, 2019). For example, during the development of the Presbyterian church in the United States of America, a new corporate seal was created to represent the symbolic and theological positions of the Presbyterian church (Mulder, 1991). Likewise, the Methodist Church adopted the official denomination logo—Cross and Flame Sign and the Disciples of Christ Church—the Chalice (Shirley, 2012). The unique differentiation through the specific religion, the logos, symbols, seals distinguishes the brand as a whole in the minds of the target audience (Mottner, 2007). Aside from the symbolic representations, such as logos, seals, and names, churches also promote their core values and doctrinal message to differentiate themselves from other churches (Abreu, 2006). Most of the symbolic visual representations are maintained over time. For example, till today, the Presbyterian churches in the USA still embrace the seal of the church for most of their branding (Shirley, 2012).

Why Market or Brand Religion?

There is now a consensus among scholars that religion is a brand or a product that is marketed like commercial products and services (Stolz & Usunier, 2019). Two important perspectives explain this trend—the changing needs of consumers of religious service and the actions of the religious organisation. First, as Stolz and Usunier (2019) suggest, consumers are seeking solutions to their needs and religious bodies have always positioned themselves as capable of meeting these needs. While it is important to explore the marketization of religious organisations, brands, and their products, it is important to understand the growing unmet needs of the religious consumer that religious organizations are failing to address. Consumers are a part of the religious consumer society and what this means is that if an individual's expectations are changing, the religious organisations should also change how they meet those expectations (Stolz & Usunier, 2019). Consumers expect that products and services must be tailored to their needs and these expectations are also directed to religious organisations. Religious organisations will in turn have to fulfil these needs and expectations as much as they also need to fulfil their marketing needs.

As Einstein (2007) asserts, more and more religious bodies are now seeking to understand consumers' needs and ensure these are met through advertising and branding. Some of these are evident in marketing Christianity. Churches face so many challenges, one of which is that they are competing with other churches with similar or different doctrinal values. Membership problems such as low numbers are continuing, and the questions remain if churches are adopting a more efficient or a combination of effective marketing approaches (Angheluta et al., 2010). Thus, for churches, the main challenges motivating their need to market or promote their brands are stagnant or declining membership or followers (Joseph & Webb, 2000; Webb, 2012), and differentiating from other churches with competing ideologies, church doctrines and structures (Webb, 2012). This oftentimes leads churches to adopt rigorous approaches to improve the image of the church, increase attendance and loyalty (Angheluta et al., 2010) through marketing and promotional strategies. For example, in Romania, the Orthodox church utilised marketing tactics to enhance its position in the Romanian society and also to increase and retain its members (Coman, 2019). The need to address the challenge of declining membership requires creative marketing approaches and strategies. Just like secular brands, the need to attract more members and followers shows an interesting link and similarity to the growing need for brands to attract more customers and meet their needs.

How Do Churches Promote Their Brands?

The preceding section highlighted the reasons why some religious organisations such as churches market and promote their brands. Churches adopt many marketing strategies to be visible, promote the brands thereby maintaining and sustaining church membership. These strategies can best be categorized into two approaches—the traditional approach and the contemporary or new approach. For a better understanding, the traditional methods will be discussed first in this section and a more detailed section about new approaches will be discussed under the social media section.

Church leaders have been using several traditional marketing strategies ever since the early 1970s. Traditional methods of marketing involve the use of advertising on radio and newspapers (Stolz & Usunier, 2019), promotional materials such as referrals, bulletins, direct mails, and yellow page advertisements (Webb, 2012). In a study conducted among Southern Christians in the US, 44–53% of respondents attested using to word of mouth as a tool for church promotion (Coleman, 2002). Door to door marketing techniques was argued to be effective in some cases (Gazda et al., 1984). The Romanian Orthodox church through the use of the TV station shared news, interviews, documentaries and church music to their global audience (Coman, 2019). The Romanian Orthodox church also promoted itself through organising religious activities such as tourism and pilgrimages (Coman, 2019). Most of these approaches and strategies were integrated to meet marketing needs. There does not seem to be a clear cut approach or a promotional tool that is most successful in this case (Stolz & Usunier, 2019). Integrating more than one marketing promotional tool is efficient in meeting a brand's growing need.

Despite all of these attempts at promoting churches, church organisations continue to face several criticisms and prejudice about church advertising (Angheluta et al., 2010). Some popular opinions are that marketing by religious organisations desacralizes religion (Abreu, 2006). Some also argue that when religious messages are advertised, the sacred message is lost (Stolz & Usunier, 2019). While this may be challenging, separating religion and secularity especially in branding may pose some marketing challenges for religious organisations. One way to negotiate this challenge is to ensure that the marketing and branding techniques and practices are clear and the communication is clear (Stolz & Usunier, 2019). Also, if marketing is properly applied, it should not diminish the values of religious organisations (Angheluta et al., 2010). More specifically, marketing does not have to change the message or the goal of religion. As Abreu (2006) asserts, the use of several programmes and strategies are just a technique that should not be replaced by the organisation's mission.

Contemporary Approaches—Social Media

Social media is a broad term that encompasses different services and ways of interacting with various users. Social media rests on what is popularly called Web 2.0 (Ogunsola & Raji, 2019). Each service has its strengths, develops a particular user community and has a distinct style for interaction (Hogan & Quan-Haase, 2010). Social media users can share and control their messaging and content (Ellison & boyd, 2013; Kaplan & Haenlein, 2010; Postman, 2009) in a very timely manner without interruption at a very low cost, and can be adopted by both individuals and organisations (Kaplan & Haenlein, 2010). Each media service is used for different types of communication and each type of content such as videos and pictures have direct value to the platform. For example, social networking sites such as YouTube are interactive and encourage users to create and disseminate contents to their audience (Kaplan & Haenlein, 2010). Some social media platforms that exist are Facebook, Twitter, Instagram, and TikTok (Ogunsola & Raji, 2019).

Social media platforms are unique in such a way that businesses can reach both internal and external audience on different platforms (Schlagwein & Hu, 2017). According to Nah and Saxton (2013), businesses can also own multiple social media accounts across platforms to communicate with their external audience. This also allows them to build relationships with this audience through messages that create engagements (Nah & Saxton, 2013).

Even if the traditional forms of communication appear to be effective, it is not the single and only important one to be considered

(Keller, 2009). Marketing needs to be supported with all other forms of communication methods such as social media. For a brand to build communication effectively, they should consider spaces where consumers reside which is on-line (Keller, 2009).

Social media according to Mangold and Faulds (2009) is a "hybrid" element of the promotion mix. This is because it encourages a two-way type of communication. Brands can communicate directly to consumers and consumers can engage directly with brands and other consumers (Mangold & Faulds, 2009). This is one factor that differentiates from the traditional promotional mix whereby the brand can control to an extent the message as well as the timings. Mangold and Faulds (2009) also argue that in adopting this promotional mix, brands must produce unified messages, and achieve organisational objectives. The focus should also be on building brand communities (Balakrishnan et al., 2014). This is because if community members are loyal to the brand, it leads to attachment and ultimately to repurchase and positive word of mouth. Religious organisations will in no doubt miss out if they do not incorporate social media platforms into their traditional forms of communication.

Social Media and Religion

The idea that religious organisations are now approaching engagement with new media is a topic that requires utmost attention (Campbell, 2010). This idea is very pertinent in this discussion and very crucial in understanding why church leaders and churches brand and promote on social media. Online churches use the internet to offer religious products such as worship, discussions, and friendships (Hutchings, 2011). The most obvious one is a modified form of televangelism and a focus on the leader who in this case is the preacher (Hutchings, 2011). Due to the ubiquitous nature of social media and the diverse benefits it affords, many churches have been increasingly moving to that area (Hutchings, 2011; Sircar & Rowley, 2020). For example, churches such as the Church of England and Hillsong, UK adopt several social media platforms such as Facebook, Twitter, Instagram and YouTube to strengthen church member relationships through sharing of contents and live streaming videos to members (Sircar & Rowley, 2020).

Social media is also a very useful tool in connecting church members, building an online community, and also reaching and attracting new members (Ogunsola & Raji, 2019). For some churches who approach social media platforms as a tool, it may also be due to the limitations that exist in the conventional traditional church space, especially in cases where members are unable to access the physical space and location. However, with social media platforms and the internet bridging these gaps, accessibility is not an issue (Badmos, 2014). Social media creates a space for online worship, thereby resulting in the emergence of an "internet church" which is available to individuals who want to worship online or belong to the church online (Chiluwa, 2012). Also, messages can be transmitted and shared for free online and the church can also utilise social media platforms for publicity, church sermons and upcoming programmes (Badmos, 2014).

Nigeria as a Religious Country

Nigeria has the largest Christian population in Africa (Ojo, 1995) and the sixth-largest in the world. According to Ojo (1995), there have been several developments that have occurred in the Christian faith since the twentieth century to the date. This gave rise to several denominations and faith which has since paved the way for the current Christian denominations in the country. According to the Pew report in 2015, Christians were only 43% of the population, but that is equivalent to over 86 million Christians in Nigeria, constituting the largest number of Christians in African. It is projected that there will be 174 million Christians in Nigeria by 2060 (Diamant, 2019).

In the context of Nigeria, traditional forms of marketing are a more common tool to reach members and prospects in the community. The use of outdoor advertising (billboards, posters), outdoor crusades and house to house visitations are effective means for advertising and promoting the message and very effective to attract new members to the church (Anyasor, 2018). Similarly, findings from a study conducted reveals that in five Nigerian cities, respondent reported 76% listen to Christian music, 56.7% read Christian books, 86% listen to Christian programs on television or radio and 80% read or view outdoor advertisements in the form of bills and posters (Ukah, 2008). Also, the projection of churches and church leaders in Nigeria as a form of celebrities aids in visibility and church promotion (Ihejirika & Okon, 2014).

Social Media and Churches in Nigeria

Before discussing social media use by churches in Nigeria, it is important to highlight that Facebook, Twitter, Instagram and LinkedIn are the major social networking site used by most Nigerian businesses (Lawore, 2016). A more recent data conducted by Statista reveals that as of the third quarter of 2019, about 94% of internet users in Nigeria use WhatsApp. This is followed by Facebook with 87% and YouTube has 76%. In total, in Nigeria, social media users reached approximately 25 million people in 2019; this is expected to almost double by 2021 (Varrella, 2020).

As discussed previously, as Nigeria has the largest Christian population in Africa, the dissemination of the Christian religious message and branding of the church are now becoming more flexible due to the presence of the internet. Churches in Nigeria are now adopting the use of social media to transmit messages to both local and global audiences (Chiluwa, 2012). Christians on the other hand in Nigeria, individually use social media to share information about their faith (Ogunsola & Raji, 2019). Among the networking sites available, some popular ones used in Nigeria for church outreach according to Amanze and Wogu (2015) are Facebook and Twitter. Facebook in particular is used to share church activities and to connect with members (Amanze & Wogu, 2015). YouTube, Facebook, Twitter and Instagram are employed to regularly update members of activities and programmes and also recruiting prospective members to their church (Eke & Enweani, 2019). Some churches in Nigeria use Facebook to promote activities such as advertise programmes, devotionals, and promote upcoming activities (Eke & Enweani, 2019). YouTube is utilised to share religious messages, past sermons, or live sermons. Lastly, Eke and Enweani (2019) finds that churches also use Instagram to share images of church flyers.

Consistent with the previous discussion, this section now highlights important communication and media techniques applied in specific churches. Some of the techniques and practices were leveraged by churches by applying some of the social media benefits and functionalities highlighted in the previous section. These practices include creating content, using several communication narratives, images, video sharing, live streaming, and brand engagements. As evidenced, these techniques and practices need to be selected carefully and work in synergy with church mission and communication objectives.

Method

This chapter is situated upon analysis of the available literature on social media use in Nigerian by Nigerian churches for promotion and engagement. Due to the scarcity of research in this area, I adopted a descriptive content analysis of their social media pages. Content analysis according to Krippendorff (2018) is useful when describing and understanding contents and messages in the context they are used. Also, to support the content analysis, I incorporated a review of the literature on social media platforms and the church in Nigeria

I adopted a media studies approach to Nigerian churches branding and promotion, focusing on a hybrid of brand promotion which is the use of social media. The two main sources of literature for this chapter were specific to social media as well as marketing: promotions. The identified churches were selected as one of the five best digital churches in Nigeria (Olaniyan, 2021). The purpose of this section is to provide real-life examples of how some Nigerian churches use social media platforms to promote the church, engage and meet the spiritual needs of their members. Churches in Nigeria have not only adopted social media for church promotion and sharing their message, but they have also found ways to ensure that their presence is felt across more platforms. Hence platforms like Facebook, YouTube, Instagram, Twitter, LinkedIn, mobile apps are all incorporated in their communication channels.

Social Media Channels Used for Church Brand Engagement in Nigeria

YouTube

Certainly, churches in Nigeria do have a strategy to communicate and engage and they consider the visual aspect of a platform to be an important part of achieving their goal. Even though religious organisations have been promoting the message and the word through traditional channels, churches in Nigeria promote their messages through any available platforms that meet that goal. For example, YouTube is used by some churches to broadcast live sermons, share recorded events, and worship sessions. In a practical example, churches like Daystar Christian Centre, The Commonwealth of Zion Assembly Ministry (COZA) named (COZATV, 2021) have a YouTube Channel and a bustling community of subscribers. They are dedicated to sharing worship and praise musicals from the different church ministries to meet the spiritual needs of members and promote church activities. Aside from promoting church programs and message through video uploads, during the online live streaming, the church encourages viewers to engage in the chatbox with the host. Engagement occurs in the live chat section on the YouTube Channels, viewers use words like "Amen" to respond to the prayers and sermons delivered (Daystar Christian Centre, 2021).

An important point to consider here is motivations for using YouTube in brand promotion. In a study conducted by Oh and Syn (2015), motivations for using YouTube could be linked to its ability for users to share videos, photos, and audio form. Hence, these churches may turn to YouTube due to its functionality of enabling video sharing, promoting community building and engagement. Lastly, due to the permanence of the uploaded contents, members can refer to old videos when needed. Hence, members and audience are more likely to engage with themselves and the church through these online platforms that are made available to them.

Mobile Apps

The use of mobile apps is increasingly becoming popular in church settings in Nigeria, especially among the digitally focussed churches. Churches develop mobile apps for members to stay connected and access most of the church programs, broadcast schedule and events. For example, Daystar Christian Centre has a mobile app called *Daystar Mobile* where most of the members can get connected on the go. On the app, the church promotes programs, announce events and provide external links to other social media pages of the church. Members are also encouraged to use the mobile app to stay connected to online communities through the different features available (Daystar Mobile, 2021). The House on the Rock, another church located in Lagos, Nigeria also has its app available to both Android and Apple users. The purpose of their app is to stream live services, provide information so members can learn about upcoming events, connect with friends and families and locate any of the physical branches for church attendance (House on the Rock, 2021). Another church, The Redeem Christian Church of God—City of David through the username COD uses a radio app called *Mixlr* to broadcast live audio of sermons to church members. Members also participate during the live sermon by responding intermittently through the chat box during the scheduled programming (COD Radio, 2021). The ability to share audio from *Mixlr* to other social media platforms is one of benefits as the churches can promote these sermons on other platforms.

WhatsApp

WhatsApp is a mobile app that aids in communication through text, voice, videos and photos using an internet connection. It is one attractive app because of its ability to share messages and make free calls compared to the use of SMS text function on mobile phones (Montag et al., 2015). WhatsApp is a preferred social media application in Nigeria for its ability to initiate voice calls, build intimate connections and privacy. In a study conducted by Ogunsola and Raji (2019), the voice call option of WhatsApp allows church leaders to call members directly when needed regardless of location, both locally and abroad (Ogunsola & Raji, 2019). Asides from direct calls and messaging, community and church groups are created to keep in contact with members and provide public announcements to members promptly (Ogunsola & Raji, 2019).

Instagram

Instagram is popular for its image sharing functionality (Moreau, 2017). It has several appealing inherent features such as the ability to create short stories, customise reels, which inherently improves engagement. More specifically, on Instagram, users can share short fun casual stories which last for 24 hours and this can be viewed by their followers (Instagram, 2020). Reels, another feature allows users to create short multi-videos of up to 30 seconds which are combined into a video using filters available (Instagram, 2020). The IGTV is another feature that exists on Instagram for its users. IGTV is a long-form video compared to stories and reels, and it allows users to create and share longer videos with friends and followers (Instagram, 2020).

Churches are seen to actively utilise some of these features of Instagram to promote their church messages and activities. On Instagram for example, Daystar Christian Centre, with a high following utilises Instagram stories to share church activities. The *Highlights* feature of Instagram is also used to promote messages and to highlight stories that were once posted. Daystar showcases testimonies, conferences and even programs on their *highlights*. This is the same for the City of David church as they showcase worship days and Expos on their highlights. The permanence of Instagram Highlights makes it an alluring feature for churches as members can continually access this information and contents on their page. Other new features like stories, Reels, IGTV was also used alongside posts to share short videos during worship sessions, church activities and events. The City of David Church used IGTV and reels extensively to promote church programs and activities. Some churches also promote their church leaders and lead pastors on their Instagram pages. For example, the COZA church showcases motivational posts from the church leader on Instagram to their followers. House on the Rock Instagram page also highlights images of church leaders.

Twitter

Twitter is a social networking site that allows its users to communicate in short messages (Gil, 2020). The use of concise and constricted characters limit on posts allows users to adopt creative ways of communicating contents across (Gil, 2020). Although this platform initially focused on allowing users to share personal updates, it is now used as a channel for sharing information containing links, images and video (O'Reilly & Milstein, 2011).

Churches like Daystar Christian Centre on Twitter uses quite several hashtags related to their posts. Their Twitter is majorly used to share both images of church programs as well as quotes from the lead pastor of the church. Images during church programmes are shared on Twitter with a text following the sermon of the day and the bible verse.

The engagement of the City of David church on Twitter is quite different, as the church focuses on sharing short snippet videos form church programs. This is an attempt at showing their followers what they may experience if they attend. Also, here, hashtags are generously used to accompany the videos and texts posted. Another type of content shared on Twitter is prayers from a church leader. The Elevation Church Nigeria- another church located in Lagos, Nigeria uses Twitter to share prayers as tweets accompanied with hashtags to increase its reach and visibility within and outside its community.

Facebook

Facebook is a social media platform that gives people voices, helps users build connections and community in a safe environment (Facebook, 2021). Asides from the ability to connect with friends, families and co-workers, Facebook users can create profiles, personalise them by including photos, information about themselves, their interests, activities and locations (Ayu & Abrizah, 2011) The reason for churches sharing

Facebook may not be clear, however, Oh and Syn (2015) suggest that Facebook users are motivated to share information on their page that helps their friends or anyone who comes across their post.

The Facebook pages of most of the churches viewed were majorly used to share images and videos of church services. Hashtags were incorporated as well as links to other social media pages. For example, a close look at the RCCG City of David Facebook shows a substantial engagement from the church in terms of post frequencies and responses. Also, features like the ability to create events were utilised by the church on these platforms. COZA church and Elevation Church use the platform in promoting and announcing church activities, and events such as Expos. The use of posters and images of the church leaders was also evident on the Facebook page of the House on the Rock official page; this also included the live streaming of sermons and worship.

In summary, these churches presented above embrace most if not all the social media platforms popular in Nigeria to communicate key religious messages and promote their brand. The messages are consistent across these platforms; however, they are modified to fit within the structures and affordances of each of the platforms utilised. Churches, if equipped with the right resources can successfully market and promote their brand on social media.

COVID-19 and Church Attendance

The use of social media platforms and the concept of the online church has also changed in recent times due to the impact of COVID-19 on church attendance. The COVID-19 pandemic struck the whole world including Nigeria and impeded normal church activities. The first confirmed case of the virus in Nigeria was recorded in Lagos, Nigeria on 27 February 2020 (Nigerian Centre for Disease Control [NCDC], 2020). The virus quickly spread to other states in the country. To stop the spread of the virus, churches were forced to cancel services their activities that required congregations gathering (Tama & Jacob, 2021). One of the strategies utilised by churches was the inclusion of online church services. This forced change brought a certain flexibility to the way churches provide services to members and attract prospects. Members who cannot attend physical church spaces can still participate and be involved in the church by attending online churches (Ogunsola & Raji, 2019). This also normalized and helped churches in Nigeria to use social media to transmit messages to both local and global audiences (Chiluwa, 2012). This use of social media not only aid in the spread of the church's brand message, but it also served as a tool for evangelism, promotes church growth, church networking and communication (Ogunsola & Raji, 2019). While the effects of the COVID-19 lockdown on churches in Nigeria is not the main focus of this chapter, it is important to touch on it especially as some of the strategies used by churches during this time helped solidify and project social media presence. What the pandemic has brought to religious organisations and churches, in particular, is to be resilient, diversify media tools and extend promotional tactics beyond the traditional forms (Tama & Jacob, 2021).

Conclusion

This chapter is conscious of the fact that the definition of a social media platform is diverse. It also draws in on the reality of the scanty resources on social media use by churches and church leaders in Nigeria. From the review of previous literature, several points are linked. The reason for branding remains the same notwithstanding the platform used. The channels differ but the challenges that these churches face, and messages shared remains constant. As an exploratory investigation, this chapter also presents very important areas that can be applied in brand promotion and communication on social media. In the context of Nigeria, this chapter draws upon the social media branding and promotion of several digitally driven churches in Nigeria. These churches were selected based on their active engagement and their ability to fully incorporate social media in their church promotions.

That said, it is evident from the literature that the church and its leaders, on one hand, are constantly seeking new ways to promote their brands and their message. It is also clear that the traditional medium is not ignored but rather adopted and incorporated in branding, marketing, and church promotion in Nigeria. After examining the available literature, this chapter makes some recommendations for future research and practice.

More research needs to be conducted in this area especially as social media is ubiquitous and evolving. It should also be examined in depth with a diverse case study group. Secondly, church leaders and churches in Nigeria need to adopt several strategies that best suit their brands, financially and doctrinally in spreading their message. Churches should look at ways through which they can promote and engage with their audience on social media. Social media use by Nigerian churches will only increase especially as it is projected that 70% of churches in Nigeria will have an online presence (Chiluwa, 2012). Finally, the main point of discussion is that religion and more specifically, the church is a brand, and therefore needs to work like one to ensure it meets the changing needs of the market.

References

Abreu, M. (2006). The brand positioning and image of a religious organisation: An empirical analysis. *International Journal of Nonprofit and Voluntary Sector Marketing, 11*(2), 139–146.

Amanze, P. O., & Wogu, C. N. (2015). Internet evangelism: An effective method for soul-winning in the Seventh-Day Adventist Church in Nigeria. *Asia-Africa Journal of Mission and Ministry (AAMM), 11*, 149–170.

Angheluta, A. V., Strambu-Dima, A., & Zaharia, R. (2010). Church marketing-concept and utility. *Journal for the Study of Religions and Ideologies, 8*(22), 171–197.

Anyasor, O. M. (2018). *Advertising motivations of church advertising in Nigeria.*

Ayu, A. R., & Abrizah, A. (2011). Do you Facebook? Usage and applications of Facebook page among academic libraries in Malaysia. *The International Information & Library Review, 43*(4), 239–249.

Badmos, K. (2014). *Effect of social media on the church.* Paper presented at the 2014 Annual Conference of theological friends and fellows.

Balakrishnan, B. K., Dahnil, M. I., & Yi, W. J. (2014). The impact of social media marketing medium toward purchase intention and brand loyalty among generation Y. *Procedia-Social and Behavioral Sciences, 148*, 177–185.
Campbell, H. (2010). *When religion meets new media*. Routledge.
Chiluwa, I. (2012). Online religion in Nigeria: The internet church and cyber miracles. *Journal of Asian and African Studies, 47*(6), 734–749.
COD Radio [C. Radio]. (2021). *City of David*. Available at: https://mixlr.com/cod-radio. Accessed February 22, 2021.
Coleman, B. C. (2002). Appealing to the unchurched: What attracts new members? *Journal of Nonprofit & Public Sector Marketing, 10*(1), 77–91.
Coman, D. (2019). Branding elements in the Romanian Orthodox Church. *Romanian Journal of Journalism & Communication/Revista Romana de Jurnalism si Comunicare-RRJC, 14*(1).
COZATV [@COZATV]. (2021). *COZA Sunday celebration service* [YouTube]. Retrieved February 22, 2021.
Daystar Christian Centre [D. C. Centre]. (2021). *Daystar online service* [YouTube]. Retrieved February 22, 2021.
Daystar Mobile [D. C. Centre]. (2021). [*Google Play*]. Retrieved February 22, 2021.
Diamant, J. (2019). *The countries with the 10 largest Christian populations and the 10 largest Muslim populations*. https://www.pewresearch.org/fact-tank/2019/04/01/the-countries-with-the-10-largest-christian-populations-and-the-10-largest-muslim-populations/.
Dowd, R. A. (2016). Religious diversity and religious tolerance: Lessons from Nigeria. *Journal of Conflict Resolution, 60*(4), 617–644.
Einstein, M. (2007). *Brands of faith: Marketing religion in a commercial age*. Routledge.
Eke, U. V., & Enweani, C. C. (2019). *Use of social media by religious organizations in Nigeria: Lessons for libraries and information centres*.
Ellison, N. B., & boyd, D. M. (2013). Sociality through social network sites. In *The Oxford handbook of internet studies*. Oxford University Press.
Facebook. (2021). *About Facebook*. https://about.fb.com/.
Gazda, G. M., Anderson, C. I., & Sciglimpaglia, D. (1984). *Marketing and religion: An assessment of the clergy*. Paper presented at the Proceedings of the southern Marketing Association.
Gil, P. (2020). *What is Twitter & How does it work?* https://www.lifewire.com/what-exactly-is-twitter-2483331#:~:text=Twitter%20is%20an%20online%20news,to%20someone%20in%20your%20audience.

Hogan, B., & Quan-Haase, A. (2010). Persistence and change in social media. *Bulletin of Science, Technology & Society, 30*(5), 309–315.

House on the Rock. (2021). [*Subsplash Inc*]. Retrieved February 22, 2021.

Hutchings, T. (2011). Contemporary religious community and the online church. *Information, Communication & Society, 14*(8), 1118–1135.

Ihejirika, W. C., & Okon, G. B. (2014). Mega Churches and megaphones: Nigerian Church leaders and their media ministries. *A Moving Faith: Mega Churches Go South, 62.*

Instagram. (2020). *Instagram features | Discover new features on stories, shopping & more*. https://about.instagram.com/features.

Joseph, W. B., & Webb, M. S. (2000). Marketing your church with advertising and promotion strategies that work. *Journal of Ministry Marketing & Management, 6*(1), 19–34.

Kaplan, A. M., & Haenlein, M. (2010). Users of the world, unite! The challenges and opportunities of social media. *Business Horizons, 53*(1), 59–68.

Keller, K. L. (2009). Building strong brands in a modern marketing communications environment. *Journal of Marketing Communications, 15*(2–3), 139–155.

Knauss, S. (2016). "Get to know the unknown": Understanding religion and advertising. *Journal of Media and Religion, 15*(2), 100–112.

Krippendorff, K. (2018). *Content analysis: An introduction to its methodology*. Sage.

Lawore, O. (2016, May 31). 4 top social media platforms for Nigerian businesses. https://pacemediasite.wordpress.com/2016/05/31/4-top-social-media-platforms-for-nigerian-businesses/.

Mangold, W. G., & Faulds, D. J. (2009). Social media: The new hybrid element of the promotion mix. *Business Horizons, 52*(4), 357–365.

Montag, C., Błaszkiewicz, K., Sariyska, R., Lachmann, B., Andone, I., Trendafilov, B., ... Markowetz, A. (2015). Smartphone usage in the 21st century: Who is active on WhatsApp? *BMC Research Notes, 8*(1), 1–6.

Moreau, E. (2017). What is Instagram, anyway? Here's what Instagram is all about and how people are using it. *Lifewire*.

Mottner, S. (2007). Marketing and religion. In *The Routledge companion to nonprofit marketing* (pp. 92–107). Routledge.

Muchuki, P. G. (2017). *The effects of social media marketing on churches: A case study of PCEA Evergreen Church*. United States International University-Africa.

Mulder, J. M. (1991). *Sealed in Christ: The symbolism of the seal of the Presbyterian Church (USA).*
Nah, S., & Saxton, G. D. (2013). Modeling the adoption and use of social media by nonprofit organizations. *New Media & Society, 15*(2), 294–313.
NCDC. (2020). *First case of Corona virus disease confirmed in Nigeria.* https://ncdc.gov.ng/news/227/first-case-of-corona-virus-disease-confirmedin-nigeria.
Niemandt, C. (2013). A network society, social media, migration and mission. *Missionalia, 41*, 22–39. https://doi.org/10.7832/41-1-19
O'Reilly, T., & Milstein, S. (2011). *The Twitter book.* O'Reilly Media.
Ogunsola, K., & Raji, D. A. (2019). Qualitative study of the use of social media by church personnel for religious activities in Ibadan, Nigeria. *African Journal for the Psychological Studies of Social Issues, 22*(3), 189–204.
Oh, S., & Syn, S. Y. (2015). Motivations for sharing information and social support in social media: A comparative analysis of Facebook, Twitter, Delicious, YouTube, and Flickr. *Journal of the Association for Information Science and Technology, 66*(10), 2045–2060.
Ojo, M. A. (1995). The charismatic movement in Nigeria today. *International Bulletin of Missionary Research, 19*(3), 114–118.
Olaniyan, O. (2021). *Five best digital churches in Nigeria.* https://rccgmps.org/five-best-digital-churches-in-nigeria/.
Postman, J. (2009). *SocialCorp: Social media goes corporate.* Peachpit Press.
Schlagwein, D., & Hu, M. (2017). How and why organisations use social media: Five use types and their relation to absorptive capacity. *Journal of Information Technology, 32*(2), 194–209.
Shirley, T. (2012). *Branding church: The role of corporate branding imagery in mainline denominations.*
Sircar, A., & Rowley, J. (2020). How are UK churches using social media to engage with their congregations? *Journal of Public Affairs, 20*(1), e2029.
Stolz, J., & Usunier, J.-C. (2019). Religions as brands? Religion and spirituality in consumer society. *Journal of Management, Spirituality & Religion, 16*(1), 6–31.
Tama, S. S., & Jacob, D. K. (2021). Impact of the 2019–20 Coronavirus (COVID-19) pandemic on the church in Nigeria. *COOU Journal of Arts and Humanities (CJAH) Formerly Ansu Journal of Arts and Humanities (AJAAH), 5*(3).
Ukah, A.F.-K. (2008). Roadside Pentecostalism: Religious advertising in Nigeria and the marketing of charisma. *Critical Interventions, 2*(1–2), 125–141.

Varrella, S. (2020). *Leading social media platforms in Nigeria 2019*. https://www.statista.com/statistics/1176101/leading-social-media-platforms-nigeria/.

Webb, M. S. (2012). Church marketing: Building and sustaining membership. *Services Marketing Quarterly, 33*(1), 68–84.

7

Political Party Brand Management in Ghana

Kobby Mensah

Introduction

Ghana's political brands are maturing and transitioning from their early days since the country was returned to a democratic path (Mensah, 2011, 2016). Just as most countries of similar electoral rules, Ghana has experienced a duopolistic dominance with the major players being the National Democratic Congress and the New Patriotic Party. These two parties have alternated power between them and seem to pursue similar programmes. They however differ significantly in their behavioural forms, including style of leadership, communication, organisation and mobilisation. These factors influence voters' perceptions about them and underpin their political brand image. This chapter will look at how these factors shaped the political brand image of one of the two dominant

K. Mensah (✉)
Department of Marketing and Entrepreneurship,
University of Ghana Business School, Legon, Accra, Ghana
e-mail: kobbymensah@ug.edu.gh

S. Appau (ed.), *Marketing Brands in Africa*, Palgrave Studies of Marketing in Emerging Economies,
https://doi.org/10.1007/978-3-030-77204-8_7

political parties in Ghana, the New Patriotic Party (NPP). It will track the intra and inter party behaviours that facilitated the brand image change.

Branding in marketing enables customers to make product and service choices (de Chernatony & McDonald, 1998, p. 28) through the use of both tangible and intangible attributes that differentiate and identify products or services. According to the political branding literature (Needham, 2006; White & de Chernatony, 2002), the brand's notion of creating *difference* and *identity* is well transposed into politics. The literature on political branding observes that political parties, just as commercial entities, differentiate themselves from each other using functional (cognitive) and emotional (affective) attributes associated with the *party*, the *candidate* and the *policy* (Needham, 2006; White & de Chernatony, 2002). In the literature on political brands, there are diverse approaches to political brand building.

Traditionally, political brand identity reflects the left—right ideological continuum. Ideology is defined 'as a way of looking at things.' This means ideology is central to a party's policy initiatives; shapes the leadership style of the party; and identifies the likely supporters. This traditional approach to branding—recognizing only party ideology as a means to creating difference and identity—is considered obsolete and ineffective in political marketing literature (Lees-Marshment, 2001; Needham, 2006; Reeves et al., 2006; Scammell, 1999; Worcester & Baines, 2006) given that social and political trends are increasingly changing. This approach to party identification and differentiation is akin to product orientation in marketing where companies only organize their commercial activities based on production capabilities internal to the organisation without regard to customer interest (Lees-Marshment, 2001). Hence, the argument in the literature that political brands based on ideological leanings is unsustainable and susceptible to failure as it misses the fundamental ingredient of voter needs (Needham, 2006; Reeves et al., 2006) (Fig. 7.1).

Other studies have focused on policy and candidates' attributes as means to developing a political brand (Mensah, 2016; Needham, 2006; Reeves et al., 2006; Scammell, 1999; Worcester & Baines, 2006). The

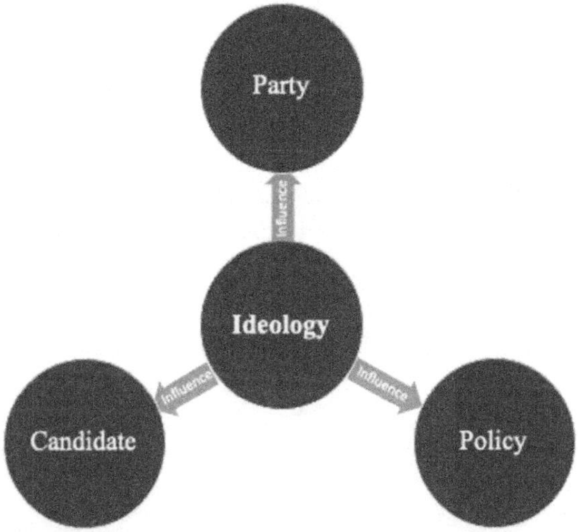

Fig. 7.1 The product oriented (traditional model) political brand management (Adapted from Mensah, 2011)

focus of this breed of literature is the need to build market oriented political brands where voter need is central. This need, expressed in many forms including economic, health and security issues, as well as aspirations, for example, could be achieved by having policy development and party candidate's selection tailored to voters' views. Thus, political brand theories in extant literature, such as Needham's (2006) and Reeves et al (2006), focus on attributes associated with candidates and policies as sources of creating political brand identity. These political brand theories have led to increasing use of voter databases to inform policy making and candidate selection (Hay, 1999; Needham, 2006; Norris & Gavin, 1997; Reeves et al., 2006). Though appropriate, the policy and candidate branding approaches to building voter centric political brands misconstrue the market orientation concept by not recognizing internal party attributes as part of the ingredients in brand building. This approach has the potential of increasing the instances of political convergence where parties look alike to voters and make it difficult for them to choose amongst them (Hay, 1999). The approach also harbours the tendency to limit electoral opportunities by alienating segments of voters

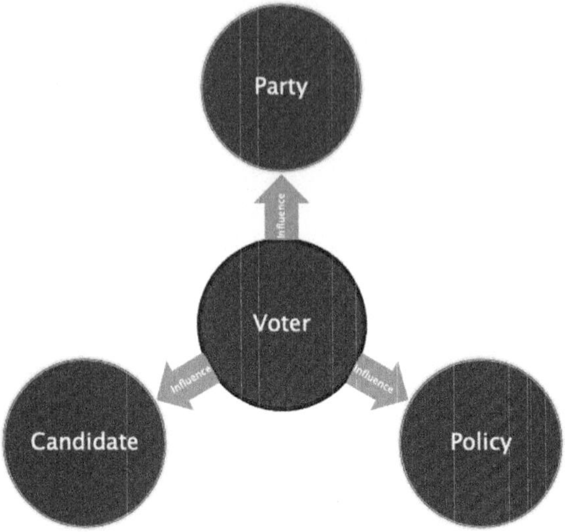

Fig. 7.2 The voter-oriented approach to political brand management (Adapted from Mensah, 2011)

who are connected to the party based on the relegated attributes. This may result in electoral resentment and protest voting eventually. Therefore, this chapter demonstrates how attributes such as party leadership behaviour and communication could still be applied in rebranding an existing political party brand that has suffered an image problem going into a crucial election. It draws on the case of the New Patriotic Party (NPP) in Ghana as an example. First, however, I review the literature on the marketing of political parties as brands (Fig. 7.2).

Approaches to Political Party Marketing

Some researchers have argued that the marketing concept of customer-orientation and its notion of exchange is applicable to non-commercial activities and entities such as politics (Kavanagh, 1995; Kelley, 1956; Kotler, 1999; Lees-Marshment, 2001; Newman, 1994; Scammell, 1995, 1999; Wring, 1999, 2002). A number of political marketing research have conceptualized party organization and management in the same manner that we understand the commercial firm. Lees-Marshment (2001) has analysed the phenomenon using the behavioural perspectives of political parties. The Comprehensive Political Marketing model (CPM) by Lees-Marshment (2001) argues that modern political party behaviour has moved from the politics of conviction to one influenced by voter needs. It categorizes party behaviour into three: a product-oriented party (POP), a sales-oriented party (SOP), and a market-oriented party (MOP). The argument here is that a POP, illustrated in Fig. 7.1, is an ideological dogma organisation. This is an inward-looking party that focuses on what the party thinks is good for the people and develops policies alongside this belief with the hope that when presented before the electorate, they will rally behind it and eventually vote for it. Just like the product-orientation theory in marketing, policy formulation, development and communication reflect the ideological positions of the party. For example, a party that perceives and advances state control of the forces of production as the best means to manage the economy becomes a POP if that position is contrary to the beliefs of the majority of the people. In a POP, party political communication activities and messages are designed to advance ideological positions with the view that voters will be convinced to shift their positions to the party's position and eventually vote for it.

The SOP is similar to the POP in policy behaviour but differs in its communication approach. Just like a sales-oriented company, they believe in persuading the target audience with a superior communication ability regardless of the relationship between the product or service offering and the needs of the audience. This means even if they do not have the right product or service that respond to the need, they should be able to sell through a compelling communication effort. The SOP applies marketing techniques such as opinion survey to determine voters' position on the issues in order to design party communications to respond to that position. In this direction, campaign messages and themes are carefully developed along polling and opinion survey findings. The SOP uses communication mechanisms to direct political debate in an attempt to influence voter opinion. It employs modern persuasive selling techniques

(Smith & Hirst, 2001) like sound bites, advertising, direct mail, and telemarketing alongside traditional communications channels to convince voters.

The MOP, which is the third and final stage of the CPM model, according to Lees-Marshment, designs its entire behaviour, policy, organisational and communication, in a manner that could respond effectively to voter needs and offer satisfaction. As illustrated in Fig. 7.2, it has the voter at the centre of its activities, applying market intelligence to identify voter demands and design its product (policy and candidate brands) to suit them (Lees-Marshment, 2001). It proclaims the long-term application of the marketing concept in party management; in government or in opposition (Coxall et al., 2003; Lees-Marshment, 2001; Newman, 1994; Nimmo, 1999; Smith & Hirst, 2001). The MOP makes a comprehensive, integrated, and continuous use of market research, segmentation, branding, integrated communication, the marketing mix instruments amongst others in party organization and management (Lees-Marshment, 2001; Lilleker, 2005; Newman & Sheth, 1985; Scammell, 1999; Smith & Hirst, 2001). In structure, the MOP is characterized by the establishment of a permanent department staffed with marketing and communication professionals with a mandate to coordinate day-to-day political management activities, using marketing concepts and instruments mentioned above. In character, the CPM model argues that the MOP is interactive. Policy development involves a continuous marketing research and intelligence gathering, analysing speculative feedbacks in the media and from voters, and inculcating these findings into policy development and implementation (Sparrow & Turner, 2001). A number of case studies (Lees-Marshment, 2001; Lilleker, 2005; Smith & Hirst, 2001; Wring, 1999) in political marketing literature have demonstrated this behaviour of the MOP.

However, there are situations when party values become the crucial dividing lines based on which competing parties define themselves and offer choice. There are other instances when these party values become the 'political equity' (value or devalue) based on which to offer (or not to offer) trust, confidence and credence to the political brand being presented to the electorates. As a result, the decision to build a political brand should take into consideration the changing political market contexts. The brand building decision should recognize the electoral situations, including voter and competitor environments, party position within the political market and internal party situation in considering the political brand strategy. The argument is that political branding process should be conceptualised in the context of "brand architecture management" exercise that seeks to assess and organise multiple brands portfolio to reflect the brands' roles to the political goals and to create structures for marketing success. In this case, a political brand framework that considers varied attributes to political brand development and management is appropriate. This multi-attribute political brand management programme considers all political elements of electoral relevance and their relative strengths and weaknesses with the target markets in building political brands. Based on this information, the role of the political elements is predetermined at the start of the process and their relationship with the target voters identified.

From the above discussion it is noted here that in framing a political brand identity, political parties need to consider and identify any political element that has positive equity—market value—to serve as an endorser to the party in achieving its goals. The strengths and roles of the political element have to be identified, organized and managed within a brand system that aims to develop a cohesive political brand identity capable of relating to their target electorates. This approach is informed by the commercial brand notion where a brand is most valuable when seen as a point of connection to sell products to customers, aid communication and to guide multiple stakeholder impressions and actions towards the corporation's goal. According to the literature on corporate branding (Brown et al., 2006; Dacin & Brown, 2006; Handelman, 2006), the function and management of commercial brands are understood in the context of their entire set of stakeholders and their importance in building brands. In the event where only one of the many stakeholder groups is identified, there is the tendency for the organization to inadvertently cut off others in its brand building strategy. On the other hand, problems could equally occur when all stakeholders are considered however without being managed according to their level of relevance to party's brand strategy. Hence, it is necessary that the right balance is ensured.

Akin to commerce, party political elements in the form of the candidate, the party and the policy are the connecting points that link various stakeholder groups to a party's electoral agenda. These political elements of the party system become the defining points through which active and prospective voters make voting decisions; other political actors make participation decisions; sponsors make funding decisions etc. Against this background, it is thus right to assume that a political party stands to gain if it is able to identify and manage as many political elements that could potentially serve as connecting points to the party. These political elements should be considered, with their strength and weaknesses identified and roles predetermined, as part of a strategy in developing and managing the political brand. In this way, a party is likely to gain a maximum level of access to potential stakeholders as a number of political elements of electoral relevance are given a fair chance and proportional level of resources to contribute to the party's electoral goals.

Based on the above discussions, with the use of a case study of a political party in Ghana, the chapter attempts to offer an alternative view of political brand marketing strategy where all major political elements of electoral relevance are considered in building and managing the political brand, as illustrated in Fig. 7.3. It conceptualises political brand building and management in the form of "architecture," known as the 'Political Brand Architecture' (PBA) (Mensah, 2011, 2016). The PBA concept aids the process of identifying, organizing and managing political elements necessary to build a political brand. The PBA concept is derived from the commercial marketing literature, the brand architecture theory, to describe how a political party organises its political brand portfolio and their relationships within them and with their target markets (Aaker & Joachimsthaler, 2000). It shows how the management of such relationships will offer *clarity* to the party's campaign in order to minimize voter confusion by specifying brand roles and how they relate to voters; *synergy* in ensuring that brands are working together to maximize electoral fortunes but not competing against one another for voters' attention; and *leverage* to effectively target all key segments within the marketplace.

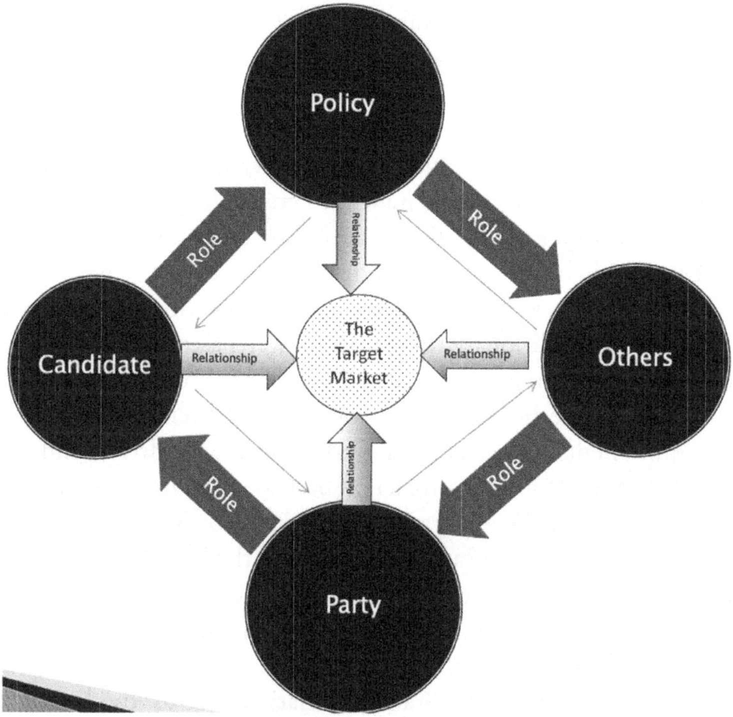

Fig. 7.3 The multi-factor approach to political brand management (Adapted from Mensah, 2011)

The Two Dominant Architecture Forms in Branding.

In the branding literature there are three forms of branding. The first, corporate-dominant brand architecture, is the process of managing products based on a common corporate identity or value, where the visibility and recognition of the corporate brand identity exerts the strongest influence on consumer decision-making (Uggla, 2005). The second, product-dominant brand architecture, entails identifying and developing an individual identity and value for each product to influence their own customers. The third, a hybrid, entails the development of products with some degree of association to the corporation, while allowing them to exercise their own values. These three architecture patterns are further classified into two main approaches, namely branded house (which includes the first pattern) and the house of brands (involving the second and third patterns). Analogous to the commercial environment is the situation found in politics. Political parties have to manage political elements (party, candidate, policy) to ensure they achieve a common goal. Parties no longer deal with 'captive voters' who pledge allegiance solely because their ancestors did, nor with a set of voters with homogenous needs. Parties are largely influenced by various internal and external interests, where coalitions with diffuse power bases operate to a much greater extent than in commercial organisations (Lock & Harris, 1996).

In managing the branded house or house of brands, there are three main requirements: (1) establishing portfolio roles—driver, endorser or descriptor (Aaker & Joachimsthaler, 2000)—so as to understand the relationship between different brands within the portfolio; (2) identifying the brand's relationship to target markets, and the brand/market relationship (Kapferer, 2004); and (3) establishing the 'brand association base' (Uggla, 2005)—a semiotic reference point or imagery used to crystallise the brand's identity/personality in the minds of target customers. Uggla (ibid., 789–790) defines the brand association base as 'the link a brand establishes with its stakeholders through, for example, people, places, institutions that add to (or subtract from) customers' knowledge of the brand'. The implication of such a system is the management of different political products capable of satisfying the interests of different 'political stakeholders' in the market. Thus, the 'one-political-product-satisfies-all' (Lees-Marshment, 2001) approach cannot manage the situation—rather, a multi-product is needed for multiple segments of the political market, where each segment has wide-ranging aspirations and interests to satisfy. This means the party, candidate and policy are equally relevant to the campaign, and must be managed in a way that will target a specific audience (Table 7.1).

Table 7.1 Attributes for political brand management

Themes	Attributes
Party brand	ideology, tradition, history, track record, dominant tribe of leadership, dominant religion of leadership, class of leadership, attitude and behaviour of leadership, organisational structure and capacity to function
Candidate brand	Personality (temperament and build), competence, ideology, track record, tribe, religion, class, behaviour
Policy brand	Ideology based issue position, ideology-based policy development, social benefits, internally driven (party oriented), externally driven (voter oriented), competitor response

Note The themes and attributes in this table were generated from the analysis of 85 sampled news report (nr), advertisement (ad) and advertorial (adv) items and transcripts of interviews and FGDs

Managing the Political Party Brand

Managing a party brand includes repositioning the image of an existing party. For example, a party of centre right ideological leanings is usually associated with elitism. Left leaning critics maintain that right leaning political parties are usually of and for the rich in society and are mostly out of touch. They claim such parties are the mouthpiece of the affluent in society and their leadership and membership are dominated by private businessmen and women, professionals such as lawyers, medical officers and academics, hence their policy positions are pro-affluent. Critics of left leaning parties argue that they are wasteful, big government, and promote unproductive society as they become welfare dominant.

Prior to the 2000 elections in Ghana, the NPP had that kind of identity problem of a centre right party. The damage to the image of the NPP party as elitist and tribal, and the need to amend it before going into Elections 2000 preoccupied the leadership and their approach to the campaign. The leadership was under no illusion that the party's image was important, and resolving it needed a strategic way of mobilizing political resources, including those external to it. This led to the adaptation of the party's ideological positions to issues, and the prioritization of social justice policy positions such as transportation, health and education. The party also enhanced its engagement on democracy and good governance, issues seen as less ideological, and deliberately reduced its voice on hard core neoliberal economic policies. The party's attitude and behaviour towards policy choices and communication leading to the campaign led to a perceived shift towards the centre of the Ghanaian political market. In an interview, a party official claimed that:

> The NPP is a broad-based ideological party, including people who are very far to the left and those far to the right. Somehow, we managed some sort of existence within centrist platform. At one stage one of our leaders led an NPP delegation to an international liberals' forum, at the same time another leader had taken us to the right-wing conservative association. Then there was a small debate as to why are we being associated with liberals when we are right of centre; and also, we have been painted right of centre. (Interview, PR-3, March 2008)

From the quotation above, it is clear that the NPP party relaxed its posture on ideological leanings, relegating any inkling to ideological dogma and preferring to 'focus on the things that bring voters of any ideological position together. The party officials argued that focusing on reconciliation and the commitment to democracy and the rule of law embraces everyone. People do not have to be of the left or right, so long as they recognised that the best form of government is democracy, and the party is offering that, they will join hands in realising it (Interview, PR-3, March 2008). Based on this thinking on the part of the party hierarchy, the party's campaign message focused on two areas. The first was to shape the party's image around its traditional democratic credentials. Thus, issues of good governance, the rule of law, leadership and corruption were to take a centre stage. Secondly, the party relied on its historic past and current personalities to promote reconciliation and a unity government, as explained in the sections that follow.

The Use of Party Tradition and Democratic Credentials

It is observed that one of the areas in which the party was to shape its image was the use of its traditionally perceived democratic credentials to demonstrate its tolerance with other political views, according to PR-3

(Interview, March 2008). As a result, the party proposed an all-inclusive administration with ministers from all the political parties in opposition and a broader policy agenda in line with both sides of the political divide as illustrated in the following text below.

Text NR.1	Myjoynews item (18/12/2000)	'NPP will form a broad-based government'

The above Text NR.1, a news item from the website of one of the leading news organisations Joy FM reported that the then NPP candidate J. A. Kufuor reiterated at a rally organised in Accra that the party will form a broad-based government if it wins power in the December elections. The rally, organised to thank the people of Accra for their support, was also to give the platform for the rest of the opposition parties to openly endorse their support for the NPP flagbearer, Mr. Kufour. The news report noted the opposition parties present at the rally, including the Convention Peoples Party (CPP), the United Ghana Movement (UGM), the People's National Convention (PNC) and the National Reform Party (NRP). Of the four (4) parties present, three—namely the CPP, the PNC and the NRP—are to the left of the NPP ideologically. Only the UGM ideologically aligned to the NPP having come out of the party as a break away in the run up to the elections. Amongst the parties in show of solidarity with the NPP, of significance was the CPP, the foremost of the left-wing parties and the NPPs long standing competitor. According to the report, the Flagbearer of the CPP, Prof. George Hagan, pledged his party's co-operation with the NPP to dislodge the NDC rule.

This show of force involving the leaders of these two traditionally opposed parties, and most importantly the attitudinal and behavioural change to ideological leanings, were significant to voters and quite remarkable in the political history of Ghana, as noted by political analysts. The adaptation of policy positions that followed was seen as the NPP party's preparedness to adapt its '…traditional policy position of a Westminster capitalist party where they believe that individuals other than government manage the economy and all that government does is to ensure the enabling atmosphere' (Gyimah-Boadi, 2001; Interview: MR-1, March 2008). In this direction, in terms of the key issues that the party promoted, the NPP party managed to focus a lot of media attention on specific programmes such as mass transportation, national health insurance, low-cost housing and school feeding programme. These perceived social policies became the flagship policies of a party that is centre right, and they occupied the centre stage of its media interactions. These policies, according to party officials and other experts interviewed, were key to transforming the party's image as socially responsive to the majority of the people in Ghana.

However, from a political history standpoint, the NPPs attempt to adapt its ideological position on the issues that concerned majority of Ghanaians in order to reflect their wishes was not new. In the early 1990s, the People's National Defence Council (PNDC), a military regime that governed as a centre-left administration, and later became the National Democratic Party (NDC) when constitutional rule was installed in 1992, had begun a liberalization programme that was aimed at expanding the economic base of the country (Carbone, 2003). In the PNDC's liberalization programme, majority of state-owned institutions and industries, including the state media, were deregulated. The liberalization and deregulation programme by a PNDC administration, which is to the left of the NPP, according to Carbone (2003, p. 10), was strategic to convince the growing middle class who are usually attached to the NPP, of its preparedness to modernize the economy of the country. To Carbone, Rawlings and his PNDC's (and later NDC) decision to locate themselves in-between social justice ideals and neo-liberal economic philosophy was strategic to capture a cross section of the Danquah-Busia network (the NPPs base) that proclaimed economic privatization. This approach, according to Carbon was central to Rawlings and the NDCs two successive electoral gains in 1992 and 1996.

What differentiated the NPPs approach in 2000 from the NDCs in 1992, however, was the 'broad-based government' concept that the NPP promoted. This is because not only did they talk about adapting the party's traditional neo-liberal policy standpoint but also the inclusion of politicians from across the ideological aisle who could be useful to the national interest. The 'all-inclusive government' concept was also perceived as a strategy to convince the electorates, who under the face of immense political tension in the country were anticipating a uniting front, that the NPP party was prepared to work with even its opponents as the party sought to calm tensions in the country leading to the elections. It was, in other words, 'a physical evidence' to the party's newly found identity of being 'tolerant' and 'inclusive' aimed at separating the current party image from its perceived dogmatic past.

Though the NPP managed to focus media attention on its perceived adaptation of leftist policy positions such as mass transportation, national health insurance, school feeding programme and affordable housing, moving away from its traditional neoliberal economic stance (Gyimah-Boadi, 2001, p. 114), it is also important to note that there were other major policies that remained right leaning, but were less focused on in public discourse. For example, according to a party official, the NPP leadership had insisted that any long-term economic programme should be 'wealth creation' as against 'poverty alleviation' which was favoured by the left leaning smaller parties, which they sought support from (Interview: PR-3, March 2008). The disagreement amongst the party leadership obviously indicates an unsettling environment in the party's attempt to adopt a 'multi-layered' view of itself.

In communicating its new attitudinal and behavioural form of being a believer in collectivism—ideologically all embracing, the party was conscious and deliberate in the kinds of language it employed in public discourse. According to van Dijk (1996, 2001) and (Schöpflin, 2001) the ordering of words and word choices in discourse serves a crucial function to collectivists in the conveyance of ideas. Its social function is to co-opt support, maintain dominance and to enlarge membership as the collectivist succeeds in persuading other groups with this text structure. The same could be said of the NPP in managing its newly found party image. The NPP managed to keep in its political vocabulary, and in the media spotlight, certain phrases to demonstrate its image as a true national party concerned about the interests of the nation. An example is the text below.

Text AD.1	*The Daily Graphic* (23/11/2000)	'A *new* Ghana, A *new* kind of leadership, An *All-inclusive* government'
Text ADV.1	*The Daily Graphic* (24/11/2000)	'Your country needs you... *come together* if *we* want *our* democracy to work and give hope to young people'

The above texts, which are paid advertisement and advertorial placed in the *Daily Graphic*, a state-owned national newspaper, use collectivist and amplification rhetorical devices to emphasize the newness of the party's agenda for Ghana. According to Harris (2017) in the 'handbook of rhetorical devices,' amplification involves repeating a word or expression while adding more detail to it in order to emphasize what might otherwise be passed over. In other words, amplification allows you to call attention to emphasis and expand a word or idea to make sure the reader realizes its importance or centrality in the discussion. In the case of Text AD.1, the NPP campaign tries to draw readers' attention on the significance of the word 'new,' implying that Ghana is set to become a new place with the kind of 'new' leadership the party proposes to offer, which is embodied in their concept of 'an all-inclusive government.'

Text ADV.1 uses an advertising technique called appeal to loyalty. This technique suggests that humans as social beings possess strong emotive attachment to groups and advertisers seek many ways to appeal to this kind of emotions. One of such ways is the general appeal to loyalty, which operates on the notion that one should act in concert with (what is claimed to be) the group's best interests regardless of the merits of the particular case being argued. The other is the Bandwagon effect, which creates the impression that everybody is doing it and so should you. In the instance of the first, appeal to loyalty, text ADV.1 is an example where the party takes a nationalist—collectivist—stand projecting itself in what could be described as a 'concerned citizen' interested in the wellbeing of the nation instead of its own and encourages the citizenry to follow suit. The party, in this case, hides its own interests and brings into prominence instead, the interest of the nation in the phrases 'if you want our democracy to work…'.

Having demonstrated the commitment to the democratic principles through its political activities, the party is able to entrench its perceived 'identity' as the most democratic through this kind of advertising discourse. Since the 1991 referendum that ushered in the constitutional rule for the fourth republic, any party that seems to exhibit democratic principles is perceived as the 'best' party to belong to. And with this understanding, the NPP laid a claim to such position by virtue of its historic tradition as well as its organisational behaviour.

On another front, a segment of the electoral audience is targeted with the party's democratic credentials through the phrase '…and give hope to young people' in anticipation of their likely break away from their older folks and from the status quo. From political history perspectives, the younger Ghanaian generation, especially those between 18 and 30 years by the 2000 elections had only lived and experienced only one type of government, which is the Rawlings' administration from the PNDC regime to the NDC. Altogether, the two regimes had ruled Ghana for about 20 years by the 2000 elections. Therefore, the understanding about this bloc of electorates was that of a group 'tired' of being under 'one party' rule in their adult life. Hence, the propensity that the majority of this electoral bloc was going to vote NPP, especially those that are 'non—aligned' to any party and those aligned but to less viable parties, was high and worth targeting.

The party's continued engagement on discourses such as the commitment to democracy, human rights, free speech and other democratic principles enhanced opinions on its democratic 'identity.' The party's behaviour towards the media, for example, enhanced its traditionally held view as the most democratic and a pursuer of good governance. Its proposed policies such as the abolition of the criminal libel and sedition laws (*The Independent* newspaper, 2 November 2000) geared towards ensuring press freedom and entrenchment of free speech was enormously welcomed, especially within the media fraternity, the civil society and the international community. Typically, one would expect the atmosphere of free speech to be part of a democratic state like Ghana. However, the story was different prior to the 2000 elections. The ability to speak freely was not for the faint hearted. Not even the hard-core defenders of the fourth estate, the media could withstand the wrath of the criminal libel law in place at the time. Therefore, the NPPs announcement of the repeal of this law that stifled press freedom and curtailed many other freedoms even within the academia went a long way to demonstrate their commitment to democratic principles that they have always guaranteed the people. The eventual effect was that members of the media became an 'apparent part' of the opposition machinery.

The Use of Party Leadership and Historic Ties

The social backgrounds of certain personalities of the party hierarchy, including the candidate, the wife of the candidate and the vice-presidential candidate as examples, became crucial to the campaign. Also observed was the evocation of the party's historic past in campaign discourse in an attempt to demonstrate how prospective audience may relate to the party, evidenced in the examples below.

Text NR.2	Joy FM (20/11/2000)	'Opposition leader on reconciliation for Ghana.' The party's position on uniting the country
Text NR.3	*The Statesman* (17/09/2000)	'NDCs world bank is under threat... the NPPs links with the region dates back to the Second Republic, when the Progress Party, under the leadership of Dr. K.A Busia laid most of the infrastructure that the region has today'

In Text NR.2 above, the presidential candidate is reported to have said that the government of NPP, if voted into power, will seek as priority a reconciled nation devoid of any type of discrimination. The presidential candidate supported this position by saying that his choice of running mate, Alhaji Aliu Mahama, who is a Muslim and from the northern part of the country, is a manifestation of the party's commitment to reconciliation, which is necessary for socio-economic and political development (news report, Joy FM, 20 November 2000). He continued to say that he is a Christian and comes from the southern part of the country while

Alhaji Aliu Mahama is a Muslim from the north. Thus, the two have come together in harmony as leaders of the opposition party to promote reconciliation which the country needs to heal the wounds within the rank and file of the populace (ibid.). From socio-political perspectives the candidate creates an impression of a divided country based on religion and tribe, hence their candidacy, as a Christian from the south and a Muslim vice candidate from the north, is symbolic in bridging that divide. The assertion, however, was not the case in respect to the country but rather was limited to how people perceived their party as a result of the party's past record. It is on record that since the country's independence in 1957, varied religious, tribal and other social groups have cohabited until the 'Aliens Compliance Order (ACO),' a policy passed in the 1970s by the Progress Party (PP), which the NPP descended from, demanded migrants to leave the country (Interview, PR-2 and PR-3, March 2008).

The passage of the ACO by the PP forced migrants, especially Nigerians out of Ghana. The policy had become a symbol of intolerance on the image of the party, especially to settler communities in Ghana usually referred to as the 'Zongos,' which is widespread in southern Ghana. Although the NPP does not habour similar policy positions, as the party maintains, critics of the party always attempt to link the two in political discourse. Thus, the need for the NPPs leadership to address the issue before the election 2000. In the same instance, critics of the party, in the past and leading to the 2000 elections, had always labelled the party tribal as a result of certain utterances by its past leadership which to many, tend to divide the country. For example, a *Daily Graphic* report dated 17th May 2000 quoted a leading member of the Democratic People's party (DPP), Mr. Dan Markin as saying:

> Ghanaians have not forgotten about Mr. Victor Owusu's s remarks that the people of Volta region are "inward looking." This remark inflicted deep cuts on the mental faculties and created festered sores in the minds of the people of the Volta Region which have not healed up till now. (news report in the *Daily Graphic* newspaper, 17 May 2000)

The supposed remark by Victor Owusu, a prominent figure and once the leader of the NPP, is regarded in Ghanaian politics as one of the most damaging to the already sour relations between the NPP and the Ewe tribe. This background, amongst others such as its elitist accusations partly explains the challenges the NPP faced going into elections 2000 and their campaign strategies thereon.

In a news report featured in the centre right *Statesman* newspaper, Text NR.3 above, the NPP party sought to remind people that it was actually under the government of its predecessor party in the Second Republic, the Progress Party (PP), when most of the infrastructure the Volta region has today were developed. The story goes on to suggest that the dominance of the NDC in the Volta region was under threat given the resurgence of the NPP nationwide, hence the NDC and their allies' desperate attempts to smear the party. This kind of attack on the NPPs image as tribal led to a number of activities, including community outreach programmes and media advertisements and advertorials in their attempt to counter the attack. See the text below.

Text NR.4	Joy FM (01/05/2000)	"NPP launches Operation Reach the Communities in their Hamlets"

In Text NR.4, an example of the NPPs community outreach programme code-named "Operation Reach the Communities in their Hamlets" is reported in a Joy Fm online news. The programme is said to have been initiated by the NPP to target people in communities where the party's negative image is perceived. In the report, Mr. Jake Obetsebi-Lamptey, the NPP National Campaign Manager called on the people of such communities to debunk the anti-alien and anti-Ewe smear campaign by opponents against the NPP. He told the campaign team to try hard to build the party's confidence in the people and let them know that the NPP does not hate any tribe or ethnic group but accepts all people who share in its aims and principles. He further stated that the programme:

> ...is to enable the party to interact with, educate and sensitise six Ewe and Dangme communities in the Greater Accra constituency area on the

political and economic situation prevailing in the country. (news report, Joy FM, 1 May 2000)

The attempt to counter the attack on the party's image was replicated in the media, using advertisement and advertorials, as noted above. The advertorials, usually a quarter, half and sometimes full page long, presented a detailed background of the NPP party's historic links with such communities that they are accused of being 'anti' to. These advertorials were usually placed in the state-owned and nationally circulated *Daily Graphic* Newspaper with notification that it is being paid for by a group known as 'the Citizens Committee for Democratic Change' (CDDC). As is always the case, general elections in Ghana always attract para-political groups who speak in favour of a particular party under certain guises. In this direction, where the message is placed in the *Daily Graphic*, not the centre right newspaper, the *Statesman* known to be the NPPs mouthpiece, and is paid by a group known as 'the Citizens Committee for Democratic Change,' the attempt is made to remove the partisan source out of the message. As observed by Deighton, a claim must possess grounds that are not in dispute and part of achieving this includes having a source that could be considered credible and verifiable (Deighton, 1985, p. 433) although the credibility and verifiability of this organisation could be a matter of challenge. On the other hand, placing such advertorials in the nationally circulated *Daily Graphic* is an attempt to reach the majority of the people as ethnic groups in Ghana are not necessarily geographically bound. As a result of seeking economic gains, different ethnic groups are found in settler communities all over the country. An example of the advertorials sponsored by the CDDC is found in the text below.

Text ADV.2	*Daily Graphic* Newspaper (23 & 27/12/2000)	"Roots of the NPP are deep in the north. NDC falsifies history to deceive the north"
Text ADV.3		"Can you imagine the level the NDC will go to deceive the people?"

In Text ADV.2, the party sought to highlight its historic ties with the targeted communities where it had image issues. The CDDC sponsored a number of advertorials 'intended to educate and encourage Ghanaians to vote for change,' the group claims (CDDC in the *Daily Graphic*, 23 December 2000). One of such advertorials targeting those communities reads:

> The propagandist of the NDC will tell you the NPP is historically an Akan party. The first NPP in Ghana was the Northern people's party (NPP) led by Tolon Na. it was the principal partner of the Togoland Congress and the Anlo youth of the Volta region and the NLM of Ashanti who together formed the United Party. The second person to lead the UP after K.A Busia had gone into exile was Chief S.D Dombo who was the leader of opposition until Ghana became a one party state. Victor Owusu, Joe Appiah, R.R Amponsah all served under the leadership of Chief Dombo. The UP was thus the first national party to be led by a Northerner.
>
> Indeed, the NPP today is a historical tribute to the tremendous contribution made by the Northern people's party to the evolution of democracy in Ghana through the illustrious leaders like Tolon Na, Jatoe Kaleo, Chief Kaboe and Chief J. A Brimah (these chiefs of significant influence during Ghana's independent struggle who hail from the North of the country). Put an end to the NDC falsehood. The rest of the country has seen through their deceit and the mood for change is now irresistible. The northern and upper regions should be a central part of the process of change. If you miss the message of change on December 7, you can make amends on December 28. Be true to the heritage of Chief Dombo; join the national mood for change. (CDDC advertorial in the *Daily Graphic* newspaper, 23 December 2000)

Conclusion

In conclusion, this chapter has demonstrated how the New Patriotic Party (NPP) in Ghana applied the brand personality and endorsement concepts in marketing to craft an identity as democratic and national in character 'congruent' to the ideal audiences they sought to persuade.

The party had done so through the communication of its tradition and ties to the communities it targeted; the personalities within its rank and file and the perceived democratic credentials it beholds besides ideology. The chapter argues that attributes inherent in a political party, including its leadership behaviour, communication behaviour, organisational and managerial abilities, historic ties, membership characteristics, are effective inputs in developing a compelling political brand, as demonstrated by the NPP.

The chapter however notes that the application of the model evidenced in the NPP case should be emulated with caution. Although the techniques articulated here offered the case party the opportunity to create a multi-layered image consistent with, and appealing to, individual groups of people it targeted, as commercial brands do, there is a side effect, however, as tensions arose during discussions on the party's economic policies. There is a possibility of the approach being criticised as "propaganda" peddled only to persuade voters. To the ideological purists, a party that attempts to respond to the demands of the people in contention with its ideological base is not a principled entity, and not truthful to its soul. A situation of disgruntled membership could arise if there is a significant voice of ideological purists in the party. This limitation for example, brings into focus the discourse about the total 'fit' of commercial marketing techniques and strategies in politics raised in political marketing literature.

Finally, the chapter has also illustrated how the party brand is managed as part of the comprehensive Political Brand Architecture (PBA) model (Mensah, 2016). It supports the idea that the political party as an entity builds and maintains at least three political brands in their portfolio, namely the party brand, the candidate brand, and the policy brand, with which to target different segments of the voter market. In this view is the assumption that each of these political brands—the party, the candidate, and the policy, appeals to different categories of the voter population, hence abandoning one could result in the alienation of a potential support base. Therefore, a party as an entity stands to connect with multiple voter targets with its portfolio of three political brands.

References

Aaker, D. A., & Joachimsthaler, E. (2000). *Brand leadership*. Free Press.

Brown, T. J., Dacin, P. A., Pratt, M. G., & Whetten, D. A. (2006). Identity, intended image, construed image, and reputation: An interdisciplinary framework and suggested terminology. *Journal of the Academy of Marketing Science, 34*(2), 99–106.

Carbone, M. G. (2003). *Developing multi-party politics: Stability and change in Ghana and Mozambique* (Working Paper No. 36).

Coxall, B., Robins L., & Leach R. (2003). *Contemporary British politics*. Palgrave.

Dacin, P. A., & Brown, T. J. (2006). Corporate branding, identity, and consumer response. *Journal of the Academy of Marketing Science, 34*(2), 95–98.

De Chernatony, L., & McDonald, M. (1998). *Creating powerful brands in consumer, services and industrial markets*. Butterworth-Heinemann.

Deighton, J. (1985). Rhetorical strategies in advertising. In H. Morris, H. Elizabeth, & A. Ann (Eds.), *Advances in consumer research* (Vol. 12, pp. 432–436). MI: Association for Consumer Research.

Gyimah-Boadi, E. (2001). A peaceful turnover in Ghana. *Journal of Democracy, 12*(2), 103–117.

Handelman, J. M. (2006). Corporate identity and the societal constituent. *Journal of the Academy of Marketing Science., 34*(2), 107–114.

Harris, R. A. (2017). *Handbook of rhetorical devices*. Taylor and Francis.

Hay, C. (1999). *The political economy of New Labour: Labouring under false pretenses?* Manchester University Press.

Kapferer, J. N. (2004). *The new strategic brand management: Creating and sustaining brand equity long term*. Kogan Page.

Kavanagh, D. (1995). *Election campaign: The new marketing of politics*. Blackwell.

Kelley, S., Jr. (1956). *Professional public relations and political power*. Johns Hopkins Press.

Kotler, P., & Kotler, N. (1999). Political marketing: Creating effective candidates' campaigns and causes. In B. I. Newman (Ed.), *Handbook of political marketing*. Sage.

Lees-Marshment, J. (2001). *Political marketing and British political parties*. Manchester University Press.

Lilleker, D. G. (2005). Political marketing: The cause of a democratic deficit? *Journal of Non-Profit & Public Sector Marketing, 14*(1/2), 5–26.

Lock, A., & Harris, P. (1996). Political marketing—Vive la différence! *European Journal of Marketing, 30*(10/11), 14–24.

Mensah, K. (2016). Political brand architecture: Towards a new conceptualisation of political branding in an emerging democracy. *African Journalism Studies, 37*(3), 61–84.

Mensah, A. K. (2011). *Political brand management: Forms and strategies in modern party politics* (PhD thesis). The University of Sheffield.

Needham, C. (2006). Brands and political loyalty. *Journal of Brand Management, 13*(3), 178–187.

Newman, B., & Sheth, J. A. (1985, September). Model of primary voter behaviour. *Journal of Consumer Research, 12*(2), 178

Newman, B. I. (1994). *The marketing of the president*. Sage.

Nimmo, D. (1999). The permanent campaign, marketing as a governing tool. In B. I. Newman (Ed), *Handbook of political marketing* (pp. 73–86). Sage.

Norris, P., & Gavin, N. T. (1997). *Britain votes, 1997*. Oxford University Press.

Reeves, P., de Chernatony, L., & Carrigan, M. (2006). Building a political brand: Ideology or voter driven strategy. *Journal of Brand Management, 13*(6), 418–428.

Scammell, M. (1995). *Designer politics*. Macmillan.

Scammell, M. (1999). Political marketing: Lessons for political science. *Political Studies, 47*, 718–739.

Schöpflin, G. (2001). *The construction of identity*. Österreichischer Wissenschaftstag.

Smith, G., & Hirst, A. (2001). A new approach for a new era of political marketing. *European Journal of Marketing, 35*(9/10), 1058–1073.

Sparrow, N., & Turner, J. (2001). The permanent campaign—The integration of market research techniques in developing strategies in a more uncertain political climate. *European Journal of Marketing, 35*(9/10), 984–1002.

Uggla, H. (2005). The corporate brand association base a conceptual model for the creation of inclusive brand architecture. *European Journal of Marketing, 40*(7/8), 785–802.

Van Dijk, T. A. (1996). Discourse, power and access. In C. R. Caldas-Coulthard & M. Coulthard (Eds.), *Texts and practices: Readings in critical discourse analysis* (pp. 84–104). Routledge.

Van Dijk, T. A. (2001). Critical discourse analysis. In D. Schiffrin, D. Tannen, & H. E. Hamilton (Eds.), *The handbook of discourse analysis* (pp. 352–371). Blackwell.

White, J., & De Chernatony, L. (2002). New Labour: A study of the creation, development and demise of a political brand. *Journal of Political Marketing, 1*(2/3), 45–52.

Worcester, R. M., & Baines, P. R. (2006). Voter research and market positioning: Triangulation and its implications for policy development. In P. J. Davies & B. I. Newman (Eds.), *Winning the election with political marketing* (pp. 11–28). Haworth Press.

Wring, D. (1999). The marketing colonisation of political campaigning. In B. I. Newman (Ed.), *Handbook of political marketing* (pp. 159–173). Sage.

Wring, D. (2002). Images of labour: The progression and politics of party campaigning in Britain. *Journal of Political Marketing, 1*(1), 23–37.

Part II

Critical Perspectives

8

A Brand Named 'Shatta': Self-Branding in Global Enterprise Culture

Samuel K. Bonsu

Introduction

Contemporary capitalism has facilitated the emergence of an enterprise culture, particularly in Western societies, characterized by the blurring of boundaries between culture and economy. Individuals are "encouraged to view their lives and identities as a type of enterprise, understood in relation to the self based ultimately on a notion of incontestable economic interest" (McNay, 2009, p. 56). The business press seems to offer a mobilizing discourse for the enactment of this culture (Vallas & Cummins, 2015), supported by the increasing use of electronic venues such as YouTube, Facebook, Twitter and Instagram. Some have gained fame and riches through self-branding (e.g., The Kardashians), encouraging others to pursue similar strategies to material success. This

S. K. Bonsu (✉)
GIMPA School of Business, Ghana Institute of Management and Public Administration (GIMPA), Achimota, Accra, Ghana
e-mail: sbonsu@gimpa.edu.gh

S. Appau (ed.), *Marketing Brands in Africa*, Palgrave Studies of Marketing in Emerging Economies,
https://doi.org/10.1007/978-3-030-77204-8_8

Self-as-Enterprise culture has become a common feature of Western society, with self-branding as its close corollary. As Hearn (2008, p. 198) observed:

> Self-branding involves the self-conscious construction of a meta-narrative and meta-image of self through the use of cultural meanings and images drawn from the narrative and visual codes of the mainstream culture industries. The function of the branded self is purely rhetorical; its goal is to produce cultural value and, potentially, material profit.

Material profits call for attracting enough eyeballs—that is, building a large following who will watch the antics of the self on public display, and valorized through advertising and other means (Bonsu et al., 2010). People, therefore, post information about themselves and their activities, sometimes contrived, for competitive attention. Spectacularizing occurs when traditional boundaries (e.g., self/social, reality/representation, production/consumption, private/public, substance/appearance, fact/fiction, economy/culture) are blurred to render the "self" as a "spectacle"—a highly dramatized representation of reality that is enacted through branding and public relations (Debord, 1977).

Reduced to their ideological function, spectacularized selves, as commodities, become economic objects of consumption. It is not surprising then that contemporary celebrities measure their success by the number of followers they have on Twitter or the number of "views" of their postings on social media. The self-branding associated with the spectacularizing of the self cuts across media platforms and leaves very little, if any, meaningful distinction between the self as a commodity and other commodified spectacles.

Debord identified spectacles and spectacularization as features of late capitalism, implying its presumed absence in non-Western pre-modern societies. Indeed, Capitalism and its logics rest on Western ideologies, leading to the logical expectation that spectacularization and the enterprise culture that funds it will be confined to the West. However, as capitalism and its processes have taken an aggressive global turn, its logics have extended into all corners of the world, even into places where conditions for capitalism are not quite rife. Attempts to standardize meaning and value across contexts (e.g., Levitt, 1983) have failed as brands and branding can mean and be valued differently by different people in different places (Pike, 2013, p. 325).

Establishing enterprise culture smoothly across the globe calls for reconstitution of non-Western actors as capable entrepreneurs and active consumers in the neoliberal sense, with the assumed ability to take charge of their own lives (Bonsu & Polsa, 2011). It is partly through this complex globalization apparatus that the developing world is rendered amenable to foreign cultural intervention and control. Such is the situation in Ghana where the meaning and value of brands may be unique and local, even though they are informed significantly by the global.

It is within the arena of global capitalist ideologies that I explore the commodification of the self-branded spectacle called *Shatta Wale*. Shatta Wale is the pseudonym of a popular Ghanaian entertainer who has successfully transformed himself into a musical commodity that is produced, exchanged and consumed. He is the self-proclaimed King of African Dancehall Music. Shatta has used the media deftly to craft a particularly marketable image of himself that has granted him significant economic returns. In what follows, I draw on publicly available dimensions of Shatta's life as a musician—from his failed act as Bandana (another pseudonym) and his transformation to the current—to define his efforts as an entrepreneur of the self.

Shatta Wale is no doubt a spectacle, employing cultural emblems from around the globe to create a particular image of himself that translates into economic value. Following Hearn (2008), I present Shatta Wale as a reflexively constituted brand subject to transaction and exchange, employing practices and discourses of post-Fordist modes of capitalist production, albeit in a non-Western location. In so doing, I explore answers to the following core question: how does the self-branding Shatta Wale address multiple and, at times, conflicting demands of target audiences, maintaining a coherent brand identity across diverse markets? In other words, how has the Shatta self-brand been spectacularized and commercialized for financial benefit? Through this pursuit, I identify the contrived Shatta Wale as a manifestation of spectacle, subjecting the brand to materialist analysis. The case will help unearth some of the complex developmental processes of spectacle as a universal ideological system.

The Spectacle of Self-Branding in Enterprise Culture

> Regardless of age, regardless of position, regardless of the position we happen to be in, all of us need to understand the importance of branding. We are CEOs of our own companies: Me, Inc. To be in this business today, our most important job is to be head marketer for the brand called You. Start right now: As of this moment you're going to think of yourself differently! You're not an "employee" of General Motors, you're not a staffer at General Mills… Forget the Generals! You don't "belong to" any company for life, and your chief affiliation isn't to any particular "function". You're not defined by your job title and you're not confined by your job description. Starting today you are a brand. (Peters, 1997, p. 83)

Integrated spectacle, according to Debord (2011), references representations of reality that have been separated from its underlying reality, and produce a false consciousness that masks reality. The spectacularization process transforms social relations into a series of commodity exchanges whereby reality is (re)constructed to conform with one's imagined perspectives. McNay's (2009) review of the business press indicates the depth of integrated spectacle in Western society, that allows consumers to be put to work (cf. Zwick et al., 2008) as part of the process. The media and related cultures that fund the spectacular encourage the use of corporate branding tools as a means to shaping individual imaginations, dispositions and skills. Branding, therefore, has become a core relational tool for spectacularization as they facilitate building of connections among producers, consumers and society at large (Newman & Giardina, 2011).

The above epigraph is quintessential advice on spectacular self-branding, in an era where citizens are constituted as individuals whose identities are tied to market logics, within a power structure that creates self-producing subjects—individuals who work on themselves towards enhancing their socio-economic value (Foucault, 2010). Such advice invites individuals to reconceive themselves as capitalist firms in their own right, establishing their own personal brands as a means to creating and managing demand for themselves as market offerings. Spectacular self-branding is a chief outcome of the process.

There is no better example of the phenomenon than non-traditional events that that followed the November 2020 American Presidential elections. All factual evidence proved that Joe Biden won the elections but Donald Trump and his acolytes used social media and other rhetorical devices to create an "alternative reality" that suggested that Trump had won by a landslide. This false representation of the election results seems to be the reality for many who besieged the US Capitol on January 6 to "stop the Steal". Indeed, during the siege on the US Capitol where rioters knew they were committing crimes bordering on treason, many still found time to support "Me Inc" through their unique attire and photos transmitted to followers or posted on social media. Several rioters were identified through such posts that they had placed to highlight their own roles in the riots—in a sense to hype their self-brands.

This Foucauldian power structure that undergirds the constitution of individuals as self-producing subjects supports the construction of the individual as an entrepreneur of his own life (Bonsu & Polsa, 2011), relating to others mainly as competitors. Here, as Vallas and Cummins (2015) notes,

> the marketing of one's own assets... is conjured as an essential source of human agency and empowerment... Here one finds the mantra that success in one's personal career can best be pursued by emulating the branding tactics for which large corporations are so well known ...individuals ought to take stock of their assets, regard the self as a profit-seeking entity, and establish the personal brand with which they can actively produce demand for their services (p. 303)

Ultimately, the individual is made responsible for the life project of fulfilling seemingly self-determined goals that suggest an empowered, meaningful, and prosperous life. That is what makes the brand—the brand of the self.

The Branded Self

Emerging merely as markers of quality and origin, brands have become financial assets as well as symbols of identity and status (Aaker, 1991; Moor, 2003) that owe their value to consumer meaning creation processes (Arvidsson, 2005). Not too long ago, a product needed only to be of good quality and supported by strong promotion to be successful. Over time, all products came to meet a minimum level of quality and there were so many competing options that products had to differentiate themselves creatively. This market condition was marked by excess capacities of similar products vying for the same consumers. Under these circumstances, merely satisfying consumers with functional value was not enough to prevent customer defection (Haughton, 2005). Branding stabilized in this competitive environment as marketers sought to create unique identities for their products and to solicit emotional attachments from consumers (Akgun et al., 2013; Yoo & MacInnis, 2005). The brand now references an entire 'virtual context' for consumption that 'stands for a specific way of using the object, a propertied form of life to be realized in consumption' (Arvidsson, 2005, p. 244). The brand is in constant flux in terms of meaning and value, producing aestheticizied modes of justification for life under capital (Goldman & Papson, 2006). Applying these processes to the self is not extraordinary in contemporary society.

Although there are many historical references to the self as a commodity amenable to processes akin to branding, it was not until the 1990s that it received wide appeal (Hearn, 2008). Popularized by business consultants such as Peters (1994, 1997, 1999), self-branding has gained even more favour in the age of precarity (Standing, 2011). While some have questioned how accurately the notion of increasing precarity captures the reality of employment as a recent and global phenomenon (Choonara, 2020), there is no question that the heightened sense of job insecurity by reason of flexible contemporary employment contributes to increased development of the self as a commodity and self-branding to facilitate sale of the offering. The ability to do this has been buoyed significantly by the proliferation of information technologies (The Internet in particular) that has democratized access to some markets. The resulting

> branded self is a commodity sign; it is an entity that works and, at the same time, points to itself working, striving to embody the values of its working environment. Here we see the self as a commodity for sale in the labour market, which must generate its own rhetorically persuasive packaging, its own promotional skin, within the confines of the dominant corporate imaginary. As such the branded self must be understood as a distinct kind of labour; involving an outer-directed process of highly stylized self-construction, directly tied to the promotional mechanisms of the post-Fordist market. Within promotional culture, the branded self may be seen as the 'significative supplement'...of the commodity-self, transforming what it doubles and extends, producing a version of self that blurs distinctions between outside and inside, surface and depth. This 'persona produced for public consumption' reflects a 'self, which continually produces itself for competitive circulation' ......and positions itself as a site for the extraction of value. (Hearn, 2008, p. 201)

In this culture, the value of a dollar is not its pedigree but its destination. That such a culture marked by the ubiquity of spectacular promotional discourse is a truly postmodern one (Debord, 1977), raises the question of whether a society which was never truly modern can leapfrog to employ postmodern techniques of self-branding. It is to this spectacular promotionalism that we turn now to explore how it is deployed in the Ghanaian context.

Methodology

My methodological approach was aimed at exploring the Shatta Wale brand and its location in the global world of self-entrepreneurship. This suggested the need to explore the evolution of the brand over time and the processes that have gone into its creation. To this end, I examined a wide variety of data sources especially those on the internet. I began by typing "Shatta Wale" in the google search engine. After filtering explicit results using SafeSearch, this exercise yielded over 10.5 million results, 2.6 million of which was video. This was supplemented by sampling newspaper stories on Shatta Wale. Some of these stories were also published on related websites. Such items were counted only once to avoid duplication. Filtering by date and relevance to my purpose led to a focus on 50 videos and 100 media articles, including documentaries, news reports of events involving Shatta Wale, self-sponsored articles, interviews with celebrity hosts and, of course, music videos. Much of the data was in English (pidgin sometimes), blended with local languages.

Research data was explored through the use of cultural analysis to yield a set of life-history case studies on Shatta Wale. This approach is based on the view that stories express themes by which socio-psychological conceptions are represented in life experiences (Thompson, 1997, p. 442). Like Martin et al. (1983), the data was read carefully to identify themes that express the essence of self-branding. This analysis began with watching/reading all the sampled data as a whole, which served as a starting point for understanding the transformational history of the Shatta Brand. I surmise that I adopted a socio-cultural reading (Goldman, 1992) of media representations of Shatta Wale to suggest the presumed embeddedness of spectacular self-branding in his life and music in a world where socio-economic conditions invite individuals to be architects of their destinies. I discuss my observations in this and in other regards in the following interpretation of the data.

Findings

From Charles to Shatta[1]

Shatta Wale, legally christened Charles Nii Armah Mensah Jr. at birth, was born at the Police Hospital in Accra, Ghana on October 17, 1982. He attended Seven Great Princes Academy at Dansoman, a suburb of Accra. His parents were separated very early in his life and so he was under the care of his father, supported by other family members. His father introduced him to reggae music at home and brought him gifts of music CDs from his trips. Charles attended Winneba Secondary

[1] This biography was distilled from information from Wikipedia, media reports and interviews granted by Shatta Wale to many people including Abeiku "Santana" Aggrey, Deloris Frimpong-Manso (Delay) and Rev Erskine.

School but was kicked out, moving to complete his secondary education at Anfoega. After a misunderstanding regarding education and career choices, Charles left home and lived on the streets. He is quoted as saying that

> There were many times I slept without food. I have been through all the hustle in life, I mean hell. I have lived with the people and became one of their own. No wonder my music easily resonates with the people. I am thankful to God for making me see the daylight.

He devoted his time to music while on the streets. It was during this time that he took the stage name Bandana. Bandana had a hit, "Moko Ho" that garnered him a nomination at the 2004 Ghana Music Awards. He had a couple of other hits including "Obaa Yaa" and "Anastasia", but he wanted bigger and better things. He disappreared from the music scene, apparently retreating to hone his dancehall craft. He returned to the industry as Shatta Wale in 2013, after a 9-year public absence. Shatta Wale and his crew struggled for gigs, accepting to play even at unpaid events just for the publicity. He was invited to perform at the "Rapperholic" Festival in 2014—an annual musical event held by Sarkodie, arguably Ghana's biggest rap artiste. In his biographicsl documentary, Shatta Wale credits this performance as the primary break into this current status:

> One day, we got the opportunity to perform on Rapperholic [Sarkodie's show]. I told the crew this was our chance; we had been performining too much on sapele stages and wawa stages..[so] we need to make our mark. I believe we went there and really made that mark…that was where we endorsed the name Shatta Wale to the whole public.

The Shatta Wale brand was born and invigorated that evening, and Shatta Wale knew it. He started receiving heavy radio play and he decided to ride on the new wave that was blowing. Shatta Wale has enjoyed commercial and critical success, drawing on a large fan base that are mainly in the lower rungs of soceity. He has managed to present himself as one of them and has their interest at heart. He has presented himself as a champion of their cause and the rasion d'etre for his presence in music. His style of music brings together local hiplife, Afro Pop and Jamaiaca dancehall, employing risque themes. He is also a comedian, which talent fits quite well into the Shatta Wale persona he has created. Spectacularization of the brand calls for a certain presumed empowerment of Shatta fans who drive the demand for his music and other acts.

The "Shatta Movement" (SM) has become a cult, with followers who are ever present on social media and elsewhere to defend their icon from any kind of attack—physical, spiritual and psychological. Picking a fight with Shatta Wale, then, is a fight with the Movement. The members of the movement closest to Shatta Wale are called Militants, that included five musicians who were featured routinely in Shatta's songs and videos. They were Addi Self, Captan, Joint 77, Natty Lee and Pope Skinny. In an interview with the journalist Delay in November 2017, three of the militants (Captan, Addi Self and Joint 77) mentioned that the Shatta Movement is for life, and people should consider carefully the SM offer before joining. Their most popular collaborations with Shatta include "Taking Over", "Forgetti" and "Thunder Fire", all songs of war against imaginary enemies who seek the downfall of Shatta.

In several media appearances (including in the Shatta Story documentary), his father Capo Shatta stresses the fact that Shatta Wale has always been musically-inclined and was destined for greatness in the music industry. He quotes bible verses to support his claims and concludes that all who seek to thwart this effort will fail.

Other stategies for specularizing the Shatta brand is captured in the media exchanges in May 2020 when Shatta Wale fired his militants, mentioning specifically Addi Self, Joint 77 and Natty Lee. He mentioned Pope Skinny in passing and clearly instructed his fans to drop his militants except Captan. Following the firing and the comments on social media that the fired militants wrote, Shatta published a video response. His response was over 75 minutes long and was intended to give his fans the story behind the firing. The fan comments on this video indicates audience perception of Shatta Wale as "real". We will come back to this later.

Spectacularizing Shatta

The economics of spectatorship that underlie spectacularization invites transformation of public content into proprietary property demanded by audiences (Debord, 2011). Shatta Wale has indicted in several interviews that he dreams of his picture being displayed in Times Square as a global artiste—he wants to see his name in lights! This means a certain level of global popularity that can be made possible only by consumers of his music and other acts. Over numerous interviews, Shatta Wale has also noted repeatedly his conscious attempts to shape the brand in efforts to change the nature of Ghana's music industry and to make himself extremely wealthy along the way. To boost the demand for his act, Shatta Wale has adopted highly unorthodox methods, breaking a lot of social and cultural rules, encouraging fans particpation by courting controversy towards crafting a particular impression of himself.

Courting Controversy

In almost every interview, Shatta Wale indicates that he likes controversy. In this effort, he has gotten himself into all kinds of it, sometimes creating trouble where none existed through "beefs". A "beef" is a major disagreement with another; in the music industry, it is often used to indicate relationship problems between artistes. In the case of Shatta Wale, it is often used to disagree with anyone who does not believe that Shatta Wale is the biggest artiste in Africa. Shatta Wale has used "beefs" quite effectively, targeting some of the most popular artistes in the country, including Reggie Rockstone (revered as the father of contemporary HipLife that merged local and global music), Samini, Sarkodie, Stonebwoy and Yaa Pono, among many others. In most of his arguments with these artistes, Shatta Wale references his talent and wealth, noting that these folks were in the industry before him but he has more money than them. That fans like the beef means that it gives Shatta Wale and the cooperating other artistes a lot of media attention, that fuels a certain sense of bad blood between artistes that may not be the real case. It is all business.

For instance in an interview with Abeiku Santana, Shatta Wale noted that he had engaged in a beef with Samini for purposes of boosting business, but Samini did not take the bait and may have not realized that it was all business.

> I have invited Samini for a collaboration. I think he did not get the business side because I heard him say that I had insulted and disrespected him publicly. I do not think he recognizes the business side of it….I was always laughing and I was like, ah, this guy does not see the business side…Yes, I have insulted him, but I have never hit him, have I?...[Samini] should have taken advantage of this at the time…now, [our beef] has become dull. It will not be news now.

Shatta Wale and his acolytes have argued that he was the one who turned the music industry in Ghana into a business and raised the bar on how much artistes can charge for performance. They, therefore, suggested that any artiste who received payment of more that GHs 50,000 (about US$12,000) for any performance should pay a fee to Shatta Wale. Asked about this in a Hitz FM interview in September 2018, Stonebwoy reacted quite angrily, asking which bar Shatta had raised "chop bar" or "beer bar". Stonebwoy also expressed his anger and disgust at Shatta Wale bringing Stonebwoy's mother into their public spectacle, including suggesting that he (Stonebwoy) was responsible for his mother's death in 2015.

Numeriq Media (https://pan-african-music.com/en/stonebwoy-shatta-wale-beef/) reported:

> Following the rather jejune narrative of 'there can't be two kings in a kingdom', these artistes have had to publicly and shamelessly mark their territory. Most of the blame is apportioned to Shatta Wale who, in character, has dragged Stonebwoy and Samini into the mud in the past. His song 'Dancehall King' which helped him win 'Artiste of the Year' in the 2014… pushed this trope. The braggadocio-laced song was no doubt an infectious number which played on the naturalistic idea for self-confidence. Name dropping Bob Marley even, Shatta Wale goes on to sing the following lines:

> "*Dancehall a mi ting wi nuh watch biter*
> *No say mi is a nite rider*
> *So wi never wanna roll wif some fool faker*"

> All through this, Stonebwoy kept his cool, maybe making subliminal references to his industry rival...Digging even deeper, one finds out that the duo has had contact since ...a dancehall competition held on the Tawala Beach in Accra. The "Battle Days" event was reportedly dominated by Stonebwoy which might have led to the heightened sense of rivalry years later when the duo would become direct competitors for the biggest dancehall awards in the country and indeed the continent.
>
> Although both artistes have sought out peace in the past, it's been a tipsy turvy relationship for two of Ghana's biggest artistes. In March 2018 Shatta Wale released 'No Mercy For The Cripple' a song which, as most listeners rightly conjectured, was about Stonebwoy who has a knee condition that makes him walk with a slight limp.

The beef came to a head when Stonebwoy won the 2019 Dancehall Artiste of the year and was on stage to receive his award. Shatta Wale and his crew approached the stage, apparently to congratulate Stonebwoy. Stonebwoy interpreted the gesture differently, perceiving it as an attack by Shatta Wale. He pulled a gun on stage, in apparent self-defence. Both men ended up in court over the incident and were barred from participation in the awards event. But in September 2020, the two came together to perform in an event organized by Assaase Radio—the CLASH as the event was dubbed.

Sarkodie, meanwhile released "My Advice" admonishing Shatta Wale. At one point, Yaa Pono responded to Shatta Wale with a song "Gbe Naabu" that was a real insult to the physical attributes of Shatta Wale, essentially describing him as ugly. He extended the beef to Shatta Wale's wife at the time (Shatta Michy), calling her a slut who sleeps around and advised Wale to check the DNA of his children to be sure they are his. Shatta took real offence to this and responded emotionally with his own insults. In late 2018, Sarkodie release "Oofeetsɔ", essentially saying he has had enough and will not listen to Shatta again (https://www.youtube.com/watch?v=tbC-gCHMIdY). The second verse ends with the word "Sheege", meaning "fuck off". The lyrics suggest that this is the last word from Sarkodie on the Shatta beef. However, Shatta carried the beef into the era of coronavirus, calling other artistes names for failing to recognize the pandemic as a priority over "beef".

The core representation therefore are ones of (1) Spirituality laced to appeal to the African's incurably religious sentiments, (2) each individual for himself (even though Yaa Pono and Sarkodie teamed up against Shatta Wale, (3) the anti-establishment Shatta Wale was infact in conflict with the other artiste when in fact they are in cahoots. This was implied by Shatta Wale in his interview with Rev Erskine in January 2021, when he indicated that the fights do not necessarily mean they hate each other. He indicated that his next album will include tracks from Sarkodie and Stonebwoy. The Shatta spectacle seems to have succeeded in painting him as a bad boy even when he is one of the most disciplined business men in the industry. He has significant respect for time, and is dedicated to his craft. His work ethic is exemplary and that is what makes him not suffer fools lightly—like the militants who expected him to do their work for them.

Managing Impressions

In economies of audiences, brands seek enhanced rents by growing the size of audiences and expanding the network of sponsors. In line with the cultural branding approach (Holt, 2004), creating and circulating mythic stories that strengthen associations between the brand offer and the cultural tensions may be a good starting point to implement the amplification strategy. Reaching distant audiences requires production of less coherent narratives that introduce new themes and representations that obscure the original content. Indeed, contradictory messages my be presented to each target group as needed.

Shatta Wale has made it his vision in music to change the Ghana music industry and make himself very wealth in so doing. Toward these ends, the Shatta spectacle is shaped in part by the successful impression among fans that he represents the truth; one who is "real", speaking his mind, without consideration for political correctness. The controversies he courts gives him room to shift the narrative over a spectrum of representative realities. It sometimes draws new audiences, some who remain neutral through the beef. Nonetheless, they follow the relevant artistes allowing them to harness and valorize the audiences interests.

Revelations in his video deposition in an attempt to explain the firing of his militants is telling indeed, suggesting that a major part of the public image of Shatta Wale is contrived for business benefits. For instance, he admits that his father is very wealthy and took very good care of him growing up. He says he is not a street kid per se, but he likes the street life because the street offers "smarts" that are not availabele elsewhere. He mentioned that even in secondary school, he would wear wretched clothes to create the impression that he came from a poor home. Throughout the 75-minute rant, he emphasized the fact that he has a business to run and so his actions are all designed to support the business. Thus, he had to fire his militants because (1) they are not loyal enough and (2) they are not ready for the hard work that goes into crafting and maintinaing the Shatta brand. While music in Ghana has always had a very broad appeal, contemporary dancehall music has been more popular with the poor and the youth. Disclosing that he was never poor, may buy him some ssentiments from the new and growing middle class that prefers traditional highlife and such music.

The rant also reaffirmed the Shatta Wale spectacle that includes his "bad boy" image in the Ghana music, modelling himself along the likes of American musicians Lil Wayne and Snoop Doggy Dogg—in terms of being unconventional—and JayZ in terms of wealth. He is able to get away with a lot of publicity stunts, and is often able to convert both real and traumatizing experiences into financial value, by way of his bad boy image. For instance, when he was arrested for statutory rape for intimacy with a girl he thought was 18, Shatta was quiet about it for a while but now talks about it to indicate his frailties as a human being. The story may be news to some who are hearing it for the first time and his solemn appraoch to it is likely to win him sympathies from some of these new audiences.

By close of the year 2020, there was no doubt that the Shatta brand was one of the most influential in Ghana, with appeal across a wide range of demographics. The controversial life of Shatta Wale may seem like a series of life accidents that derive from his bad boy character. Indeed, in an interview with media journalist Abeiku Santana in 2018, Shatta noted that "I think sometimes people get the wrong impression about me. They feel that the way they see me on stage is really what I am. No". He presents a certain image of himself that includes a disrespect for authority and others, in his path towards money. In his song, *For the Money*, Shatta sings "Everything I do is for the money; Everything, Everything I say is for the money". Several other songs express the same sentiments, that the pursuit of money as his primary goal and that he needs to demonstrate that he has made a lot of it. With his contrived story of having grown up in the slums of Accra, he will offer hope to many in those areas, expanding his musical kingdom. In his interview with Abeiku and also with Rev Erskine, Shatta Wale identified with wealthy objects (his US$60,000 Rolex, his top of the line Range Rover, Mercedes Benz, Porsche Canyon etc.) and his million dollar homes in Accra. He mentioned some of his neighbours to include Osei Kwame Despite, one of the wealthiest businessmen in the country. His song, "Forgeti" features lines that reaffirm his seeming wealth: "If ibi dough forgetti" [If it is about money, forget the competition]…"Money, money I get plenty" [I have plenty of money].

This public image of Shatta Wale being all about money, regardless of casualties along the way is not consistent with his true self. He is constantly in his old neighbourhood helping the poor. Apparently, he is a very humble person who is in touch with his roots; one of the few celebrities in Ghana who feels very comfortable in the slums of Accra. Videos of him interacting with the poor and engaging poor communities are not uncommon. He has become some kind of a Robin Hood, spending a chunk of his wealth to support the poor in the communities where he grew up. That is to say that behind the public façade of a ruthless money maker is the compassionate Shatta who supports over 57 families by way of monthly salaries over the years. He cares but that will not facilitate creating large audiences. He should be a bad boy for some and not so bad for others.

Shatta Wale tries to manage his divergent public personae through his activities. For intance, constrast his argument for firing his "militants" with his "Faith Concert" in Arpil 2020 in support of Covid-19 relief in

Ghana. In the firing, he presented them as lazy individuals who were not contributing to the expansion of the brand. Thus, they have violated the growth imperative of the Shatta Movement and had to be sent away. This toughness is often represented in his beefs or public challenges, as in the CLASH with Stonebwoy. In his Faith Concert, he is presented as a calm, cultured gentleman with a heart for humankind. Both presentations were designed to appeal to specific audiences but was also intended to invite new soldiers into the Shatta Movement.

Discussion/Conclusion

I have presented Shatta Wale as a brand that takes advantage of its local milieu, blends its with global socio-cultural elements towards engaging fans not merely as spectators but as active participants in shaping the brand. Boyle (2003) notes that such an economy produces profits by commodifying its unique features in a manner that encourages fans and sponsors to buy. A cursory look at Shatta Wale and his brand would make them seem, especially by reason of his public foul-mouthed dealings with other artistes and sometimes his sponsors and fans. It seems illogical that his fans would condone his acts and actively seek to endorse his public rhetorical fights. Indeed, they feed the spectacle of the Shatta Wale machine, in all its incoherence. This is especially because for Shatta Wale and his fans, their only focus is to make money. Shatta Wale himself mentions this at every opportunity and comments from fans on his interview videos indicate support for this.

According to Debord (2011), in the age of integrated spectacle, the spectacular encourages fans to voluntarily reject the safety and security in multiple regions of life (religion, politics, work, consumption), while embracing risks to mind, body and bank account. Our observation of the Shatta Wale brand lead us to disagree with this conclusion. Shatta Wale always drew his audience's attention to his religious practices, encouraging them to read the bible as defense against the enemy. He emphasizes the value of hard work for success when he cited laziness as the reason for firing his militants and plays hard—as he repeatedly said. Thus, he has encouraged the integration of religion, politics and other spheres of life into his spectacle. In an enterprise culture where the individual is deemed responsible for his life, Shatta Wale exploits the seemingly incurable religious affinity of the African to build his fan base. Within his seemingly hedonistic brand spaces [e.g., sex, drugs], he employs religious imagery and activities in conformity with fan expectations, offering hope of heaven on earth, without risk to eschatological salvation as preached by contemporary Ghanaian pastors (Appau & Bonsu, 2020; Bonsu & Belk, 2010).

The Shatta Wale brand spectacle embody a diversity of characters that may seem incompatible. Enterprise culture's offer for the individual to be an entrepreneur of the self allows for any combination of good and bad behaviour around a spectacle (Krier & Swart, 2016). For instance, the brand connotes a disreputable character as acceptable so long as related musings and actions yield financial results. The brand represents character unbecoming of a traditional artiste (foul-mouthed, boastful), virtues that would not be sustained by traditional employment. The bad character appeals to a fan base that focuses on the money and aspire to be like Shatta. Then in his "Faith Concert" and certain interviews, Shatta Wale displays a calm and collected behaviour, showing sides of him that are inconsistent with his bad boy image. Here, he appeals to another set of audiences who may understand that the popular Shatta personae is only an act of business. He engages in active maintenance, management, and reinvestments to ensure continued profits to the brand. This is perhaps what the militants—and the fans—do not see: that the Shatta spectacle is a business that requires constant strategizing to keep going.

The Shatta Wale brand has exploited the global enterprise culture to build a brand spectacle that has produced significant profits. The brand is shaped mainly by economic desires, even if other ideological motifs are engaged for this purpose. We observe the successful presence of a postmodern concept in an environment that was never modern, noting the ability to leapfrog cultural and technological differences, especially in the Internet era. Following our observation of the Shatta spectacle, we agree with brand culturalist who suggest that

> brands derive their value from how well the myths they embody respond to tensions between peoples' lives and society's prevailing ideology. Brands

> become icons not because they offer distinctive benefits but because they deliver cultural expressions that meet the ideological needs of their target consumers…the key challenges for marketers are to develop an understanding of cultural tensions; to compose a cultural expression that bears the right ideological, mythical, and cultural content; and to reinvent their brand in the face of social disruptions….. Managing demands from plural logics entails not only resolving tensions between logics but also strengthening and creating linkages between logics that collaborate with each other (Ertimur & Coskuner-Balli, 2015, p. 57)

That this conclusion evokes skepticism, given the active deference of the strategy to an assemblage of value-laden Western rationalities and bodies of knowledge that are articulated through a specific set of techniques (Bonsu & Polsa, 2011), globalization and its McDonaldization processes (Ritzer, 2004) facilitate active blending of the local and global even as instruments of exploitation. In Shatta Wale, I observe an analytical businessman who sees value and money in embracing Western instruments of brutality (e.g., self-entrepreneurship) to develop a financial empire. Can we blame him for securing this path to material success? No, because there are so few alternatives besides sleeping with the enemy, and Shatta Wale will tell you: It is all about the money.

References

Aaker, D. A. (1991). *Managing brand equity—Capitalizing on the value of a brand name*. The Free Press.

Akgun, A., Kocoglu, I., & Imamoglu, S. (2013). An emerging consumer experience: Emotional branding. *Procedia: Social and Behavioral Sciences, 99*, 503–538.

Appau, S., & Bonsu, S. K. (2020). The spiritual marketplace in contemporary Ghana. In H. R. Chaudhuri & R. W. Belk (Eds.), *Marketization: Theory & evidence from emerging economies* (pp. 165–191). Springer Nature.

Arvidsson, A. (2005). Brands: A critical perspective. *Journal of Consumer Culture, 5*(2), 325–358.

Bonsu, S. K., & Polsa, P. E. (2011). Governmentality at the base-of-the-pyramid. *Journal of Macromarketing, 31*(3), 236–244.
Bonsu, S. K., Darmody, A., & Parmentier, M.-A. (2010). Arrested emotions in reality television. *Consumption Markets & Culture, 13*(1), 91–107.
Bonsu, S. K., & Belk, R. W. (2010, November), Marketing a new African god: Religion and material salvation in Ghana. *International Journal of Nonprofit and Voluntary Sector Marketing, 15*(4), 305–323
Boyle, J. (2003). The second enclosure movement and the construction of the public domain. *Law and Contemporary Problems, 66*(1/2), 33–74.
Choonara, J. (2020). The precarious concept of precarity. *Review of Radical Political Economics, 52*(3), 427–446.
Debord, G. (1977), *The society of the spectacle.* Black and Red.
Debord, G. (2011). *Comments on the society of the spectacle*. Verso.
Ertimur, B., & Coskuner-Balli, G. (2015, March). Navigating the institutional logics of markets: Implications for strategic brand management. *Journal of Marketing, 79*(2), 40–61.
Foucault, M. (2010). *The birth of biopolitics: Lectures at the Collège de France, 1978–1979* (M. Sellenart, Ed.). Palgrave.
Goldman, R. (1992). *Reading ads socially*. New York: Routledge.
Goldman, R., & Papson, S. (2006). Capital's brandscapes. *Journal of Consumer Culture, 6*(3), 327–353.
Haughton, L. (2005, August 16). The rising tide of customer defection. *Small Business Trends.* www.smallbiztrends.com/2005/08/rising-tide-of-customer-defection. Accessed 23 December 2020.
Hearn, A. (2008). 'Meat, mask, burden' probing the contours of the branded 'self.' *Journal of Consumer Culture, 8*(2), 197–217.
Holt, D. B. (2004). *How brands become icons: The principles of cultural branding*. Harvard Business School Publishing Corporation.
Krier, D., & Swart, W. (2016). The commodification of spectacle: Spectators, sponsors and the outlaw biker diegesis at Sturgis. *Critical Sociology, 42*(1), 11–32.
Levitt, T. (1983, May/June) The globalization of markets. *Harvard Business Review*, 92–102.
Martin, J., Feldman, M. S., Hatch, M., & Sitkin, S. B. (1983). The uniqueness paradox in organizational stories. *Administrative Science Quarterly, 28*(3), 438–453.
McNay, L. (2009). Self as enterprise: Dilemmas of control and resistance in Foucault's The Birth of Biopolitics. *Theory, Culture & Society, 26*(6), 55–77.

Moor, E. (2003). Branded spaces: The scope of new marketing. *Journal of Consumer Culture, 3*(1), 39–60.

Newman, J. I., & Giardina, M. D. (2011). *Sport, spectacle, and NASCAR nation: consumption and the cultural politics of neoliberalism.* New York, NY: Palgrave Macmillan.

Peters, T. (1994). *The pursuit of wow! Every person's guide to topsy-turvy times.* Vintage.

Peters, T. (1997). The brand called you. *Fast Company.* http://www.fastcompany.com/28905/brand-called-you.

Peters, T. (1999). *The brand you 50: Or: Fifty ways to transform yourself from an "employee" into a brand that shouts distinction, commitment, and passion*! Alfred Knopf.

Pike, A. (2013). Economic geographies of brands and branding. *Economic Geography, 89*(4), 317–339.

Ritzer, G. (2004). *The McDonaldization of society* (4th ed.). Pine Forge Press.

Standing, G. (2011). *The precariat: The new dangerous class.* Bloomsbury Academic.

Thompson, C. J. (1997, November). Interpreting consumers: A hermeneutical framework for deriving marketing insights from the texts of consumer's consumption stories. *Journal of Marketing Research, 34*, 438–455.

Vallas, S. P., & Cummins, E. R. (2015). Personal branding and identity norms in the popular business press: Enterprise culture in an age of precarity. *Organization Studies, 36*(3), 293–319.

Yoo, C., & MacInnis, D. (2005). The brand attitude formation process of emotional and informational ads. *Journal of Business Research, 58*, 1397–1406

Zwick, D., Bonsu, S., & Darmody, A. (2008). Putting consumers to work: "Co-creation" and new marketing govern-mentality. *Journal of Consumer Culture, 8*(2), 163–197.

9

Using Local Culture in Brand Positioning and Communication

Marian Makkar

Introduction

Branding is nothing more than commercial storytelling. But why do brands need an interesting story to tell? More specifically, why do global brands benefit from a story being locally relevant for it to be satisfying and appealing? Since the beginning of the twenty-first century where everything is for sale, everything can also be branded (Klein, 2000). This means that brands will struggle to create a point of difference in a world of brands. As James Twitchell (2004a) explains in his book, *Branded Nation: The Marketing of Megachurch, Inc., and Museumworld*, brands infuse culture with meaning through stories attached to products or services. Brands can be understood as communicative objects that translate these meanings. They are given a name, symbol, logo or icon that identifies them, and a tagline to differentiate them from others in

M. Makkar (✉)
RMIT University, Melbourne, VIC, Australia
e-mail: marian.makkar@rmit.edu.au

S. Appau (ed.), *Marketing Brands in Africa*, Palgrave Studies of Marketing in Emerging Economies,
https://doi.org/10.1007/978-3-030-77204-8_9

the category (Einstein, 2007). They consist of emotions that consumers can recall or experience when they think of the brand (Simeon, 2006). Branding also occurs through stories or myths as fictional accounts surrounding the brand with a plot, storyline, story climax, and characters imagined or real, and told for other's entertainment (Twitchell, 2004b).

And while you can brand anything from cars to religion, it is harder to differentiate them as many offer the same end benefit. To stand out, brands rely on the services provided as an added value, or they rely on symbols that designate them, including a brand's story. Competitors, therefore, cannot easily replicate the myths and stories embedded in the brands. These stories are conveyed through marketing and advertising efforts that are meant to position the brand in the minds of consumers (Einstein, 2007). Think of two American department stores positioned as low cost—Target and Walmart—yet they are perceived by consumers differently. That is branding. In other words, the goal of branding is to "attract and keep customers by promoting value, image, prestige, or lifestyle" (Rooney, 1995, p. 48). It must convey information, minimise risk or increase trust (Knox, 2004), help identify key factors or values and differentiate itself from the competition (Palumbo & Herbig, 2000). Over time, consumers should not have to intentionally think about the brand's attributes. When the name or logo appears, every meaning and aspect associated with that brand should come to mind. These almost unconscious ideas about a brand allow for split-second load of information to be transmitted amidst a cluttered commercial media environment (Einstein, 2007). Consider the Nike swoosh. The symbol alone would mean nothing but with the associated meanings attached to the swoosh created over time and embedded in the consumer's mind, it can stand alone with meaning and representation.

With meanings attached, brands can have personalities (Aaker, 1997), are perceived as icons (Holt, 2004), represent the self (Belk, 1988) or reference groups (Escalas & Bettman, 2005), anchor nostalgia (Holbrook & Schindler, 2003), and become romantic partners (Aaker et al., 2004). Brands can be the basis for community (Mūniz & O'Guinn, 2001) and individuality (Erdem & Swait, 2004). They tell stories about consumers (Levy, 1959), and consumers tell stories about them (Roehm & Brady, 2007).

But how did we get to this moment where brands are purposed for more than just distinguishing between products and services? After major cultural shifts in the nineteenth century, companies caught on to the power of stories, and moved away from early conceptions that solely served a functional purpose. The Industrial Revolution gave rise to more products being made, as well as people wanting more things to fulfil those imagined desires. Campbell (1987) draws the connection between modern Romanticism and how consumers stopped rationalising and started dreaming and imagining new possibilities through consumption. Businesses started not only making things, but giving those things meaning.

However, Twitchell (2004b) believes that people do not necessarily know what they want. Thus, brands told remarkable stories that communicated cultural properties such as meanings, dreams, ideals, and desirable selves to inspire more interest in their product/service. Such cultural properties can be carried through to the extent of creating brand communities, where some might be more cult-like than others (e.g., Star Trek fans). Brands with strong stories can create fetishized adoration, with some brands succeeding in being sacralised like religion (McAlexander et al., 2002; Mūniz & Schau, 2005). It is clear that brands (and brand consumers) create stories that appeal to consumers' desires to experience satisfaction in material things by providing cultural narratives that are necessary to form loyalty and a brand following.

This chapter examines how businesses can leverage culture and storytelling to develop their brand positioning and communication. Unlike brands in Western contexts whose adoption of market logics leads to their success (Twitchell, 2004a), in Africa market logics are heavily intertwined with nonmarket, informal economies that are deeply engrained in culture. This chapter includes branding cases from international and national companies in a North African country (Egypt) as examples to demonstrate different ways of utilising local culture in branding. The cases presented help demonstrate how local culture employed in commercial storytelling can work for brands.

What Is (Local) Culture?

Culture is a broad and varied phenomenon where multiple cultural groups overlap and produce complexity in interaction, action and meaning (Arnould & Thompson, 2005). It encompasses the system of shared signs, codes, meanings, activities, relationships and ways of organising groups of people. These symbolise the cultural content that relays mass-cultural expressions which are well-established historically in the society's culture. On one hand, culture is based on ethnic groups, nations or regions, and involves the "customs, values, and rule systems of a social group" (Ziff & Rao, 1997, p. 2). It is expressed in the material, spiritual and cultural representations of a group that identifies as a culture (Hart, 1997). Attached cultural markers include the group's language, religion, customs, rituals, history and activities performed by them, which form their cultural identity (Kennedy & Makkar, 2021). On the other hand, consumer culture specifically looks at the symbolic character of consumption and marketing, which are both essential to the understanding of how to create meaningful brands.

McCracken (1986) describes the significance of consumer goods as they rest largely in their ability to carry and communicate cultural meaning. He suggests that the ultimate role of brands is to carry and communicate cultural meaning that is emotional, informative, relatable and transformational in character. However, it is a challenge for brands to communicate cultural meaning that is relatable to all consumer cultures when global marketplaces are fuelled and being fed by mass consumption orientations (Featherstone, 1991; Joy & Wallendorf, 1996).

Local culture is not the same as a global culture. A global culture signifies non-local signs and symbols that are assumed to be understood by consumers around the world (Alden et al., 1999), and gives a sense of a 'global village'. Indeed, many global brands create a somewhat homogenous cultural theme around the "good life" using desirable characteristics in all societies. For example, companies can relate to where something is made such as Japanese products that are regarded as state-of-the-art, modern, high quality and therefore more desirable in global markets (Ger, 1999). However, consumer cultures are not homogenous; historical and economic local conditions interact to shape consumers' consumption patterns and perceptions in each locality (Ger, 1999). Yet consumer researchers have pointed out local appropriations that take place (Appadurai, 1996; Ritzer, 2007). With cultural meanings crossing borders, what may be considered global culture actually assumes local meanings, and vice versa (Ritzer, 2007). Nevertheless, this notion is created by global brands with a more Western view of the world; these cultural meanings and practices are not always accepted by all.

Consumers are more curious and exploratory in their search for unique consumption experiences and meanings. Consumers are interested in foreign cultures, cuisines, art and spirituality and want to discover the unexpected (Firat & Venkatesh, 1995). The intrinsic value of brands instilling local culture is their ability to provide a "local" identity, which eventually presents an 'authentic' local brand equity. Ger (1999) explains the potential for mingling local with global product attributes to fulfil the diversity in demand and interest in local resources. However, branding practices need to be managed carefully as brands have great power in society. Brands help consumers construct and communicate an identity, relate to others, mark social differences and pursue emotional and aesthetic gratifications in unique and exciting ways (Campbell, 1987).

Scholars have argued that any local culture should be viewed in terms of the global cultural flows of which it is part of (Appadurai, 1990; Urry, 1995). Indeed, these flows are fuelled by what Goff (2007) calls, cultural industries (e.g., radio and television, books, blogs, social media), in which they carry "sociocultural value" (p. 4). As "vectors of culture and identity" (Goff, 2007, p. 169), these cultural products, can influence a whole community. But what is important to note is that culture is a moving target, dynamic and constantly changing as it participates in the ongoing promotion of collective and individual identities.

Cultural Branding

The phenomenon of branding has been previously conceptualised as an outcome of advanced economic development. By drawing on the genealogy of a brand defined as a mode of connectivity and relationships between producers and consumers (Drescher, 1992; Lury, 2004), it is surprising that we have not been studying brands with a cultural lens this entire time. Brands took on this role during the ancient empires and the Industrial Revolution when trade expansion and economies of scale demanded better management between producers and consumers (e.g., Wengrow, 2008; Wilk, 2006). How this connectivity was performed and achieved has evolved with time due to the technological as well as political–economic and socio-cultural environments. As a result, new perspectives on brands have emerged (Holt, 2006; Kapferer, 1992; Levy, 1959).

One such perspective includes the notion of cultural brands, which scholars associate with conditions of late-industrial economy (Baudrillard, 1998; Holt, 2004). Hirschman (2010) argues that we need to look at brands differently and as part of innate human drives towards differentiating and melding social groups. This involves studying brands as cultural products that fuel and direct society. Brands are starting to be viewed as symbolic articulators of production and consumption where "all brands are representational texts, and are socially, not merely managerially, constructed" (O'Reilly, 2005, p. 585). Cultural brands do not simply identify a product or the producer, rather they are symbolic as they represent the dominant ideals, ideas and values in a society (Holt, 2004).

Holt (2004) defines cultural branding as "the set of axioms and strategic principles that guide the building of brands into cultural icons" (p. 11). He explains how brands become iconic when they perform identity myths. These are simple fictions that address cultural anxieties that consumers experience in their everyday lives. These iconic brands become aspirational identities and imaginative rather than literal. The idea of 'brands as badges' has great meaning here. For instance, when you see someone drinking Johnnie Walker at the bar, you might automatically drum up images of the sophisticated connoisseur attending a gentleman's club. The same idea translates to cars and fragrances, which allows us to communicate to others who we are by the brands we consume as ways for identity creation.

As Ricoeur (1996) explains, people receive a narrative identity from the stories that are told to them, and those they tell themselves, and this identity is mixed with that of others to become "literally entangled in stories" (p. 6). Holt (2004) further elaborates that these identity myths are important fabrications for people as they stitch back together what are otherwise damaged tears in the cultural fabric of society. These tears are what create personal anxieties and tensions that people negotiate through their consumption. These myths, as Holt (2004) finds in his analysis of six American iconic brands, help people "create purpose in their lives and cement their desired identity in place when it is under stress" (p. 8).

Not only are brands involved in giving purpose to personal (or historical) identities, but they can shape collective identities as well. When thinking about using local culture in branding, one must consider the strong linkages brands could have with social groups. Brand communities and subcultures come together as they share a common identity (Mūniz & O'Guinn, 2001). Brands that possess archetypal (Fournier, 1998) or iconic (Holt, 2004) status within a society or subculture evolve in their meanings depending on their adoption into specific groups (Hirschman, 2002). While all cultures have specific myths, deities, villains and warriors, these are particular to their communities (Campbell, 1987). Similarly, cultures also create brand affiliations and brand admiration which Hirschman (2010) argues are other forms of symbolism and metaphors that help a collective make social and personal meaning and connections.

Hence, mass production of products or standardising brand meanings in the pursuit of gaining greater market share is no longer sufficient when we live in a world full of brands at war battling to win the affections of the consumer. One must be sure that consumption not only has economic and in-use value but also identity value. Holt (2004) redefines this as 'cultural value'—an imaginative resource that people use to build their identity. It can be used as a marker of social and cultural difference (Veblen, 1899) as well as ways of appropriation and resistance as consumers create an identity for themselves in opposition to dominant culture (Hebdige, 1979). Hence, brands have an important role in creating meaning for individual identities and collective group identities.

The issue with branding lies with global companies entering new local markets with their standardised (mostly westernised) messaging and advertising campaigns as their way of developing a global brand image and gaining greater market share (Porter, 1986). The mistake falls on global brands misrepresenting—sometimes completely ignoring—the national, social, ethnic, and cultural values and rituals of the local market and what matters most to them. As consumers make seemingly utilitarian choices, they still imbue brands with affective values and ideals that transcend their own use values (Miller, 1998). Cultural branding can add a strategic perspective for organisational goals by developing new business, gaining market share and stronger market positioning, and steady profit.

In Africa, utilising local cultural knowledge is necessary to create a better understanding of their markets, as their consumption is highly driven by culture (Appau & Churchill, 2019). People in this region retain their fundamental values (Bhatia & Bhargava, 2008) where their frame of reference is culturally restricted and "home-grown". Egypt has a unique identity that combines a modern consumer product with a conservative culture whose values, I argue, impact the ways consumers experience brands, local or global. As the third most populous country in Africa (approximately 103,392,211 people living in Egypt at the time of writing this chapter) and home to one of the oldest civilisations in the world (Plecher, 2019), Egypt provides fertile ground to revealing the extent to which an understanding of local culture is important for brands.

Consumer culture in Egypt is still influenced by a Marxist ideology. In the 1970s, Egypt witnessed a growing policing and segregation of public opinion and production, which coincided with the growth of Islamism, and the 1990s witnessed a growing availability of such reshaped meanings and a new age of mixing of norms and tastes (Abaza, 2001). Yet a study shows that 32.5% of people (32 million) in Egypt are poor in 2018, with a steady increase in income poverty rates from 1999 to 2018 (Armanious, 2020). Nevertheless, the incorporation of Egypt into the world economy and its greater contact with the West since the nineteenth century had a great influence on Egypt's patterns of consumption and the consumption of imported versus locally made products (Russell, 2004).

I use three different yet popular brands in Egypt to explain four directions to support brands in incorporating local cultural narratives successfully in their branding initiatives: Birell (a local non-alcoholic beer company), Vodafone Egypt (formerly Click GSM (a national company), and currently acquired by the global network-mobile provider, Vodafone), Orange Egypt (formerly Egypt's national telecommunications company, Mobinil, and currently acquired by the global network-mobile provider, Orange) and Coca-Cola (a global beverage company).

Four Cultural Directions for Branding in Egypt

People value the "right" cultural expressions because they play an important role in where we see ourselves in society, how we understand our place in the world, and what is meaningful, moral, and humane (Holt, 2012). Holt (2012) explains that a brand's cultural expressions is the outcome of a product's ideology when staged through myths and cultural codes. Brands with a distinctive local cultural expression with relevance to the times are more successful in creating customer value.

While traditional sources of cultural expression come from religion, arts, educational social institutions and the state, mass media and commerce have come to the fore riding the tail end of changes in culture. Egypt is proof of that with the success of the political movement and mass protests in 2011 which began through the social medium, Twitter. Egypt spearheaded the Arab Spring revolution using key values of nationalism and social consciousnesses—of sociocultural relevance—in order to lead the masses over Twitter messages to protest and oust the former President Hosni Mubarak. This created a strong emotive brand around the revolution (Meraz & Paracharissi, 2013). These efforts eventually led to a wave of uprisings across the Middle East and North Africa that witnessed major demonstrations and political changes. And while companies in Egypt have not necessarily led the way with political and cultural activism like the USA (Vredenburg et al., 2020), they have tagged on to what Holt (2012) explains to be a compelling brand ideology—a point of view that is widely shared yet taken for granted as a 'truth'. Brand narratives are therefore considered fundamentally critical in how we structure and make sense of our lives (Shankar et al., 2001) and a means by which our experiences are made meaningful (Polkinghorne, 1988). What is interesting is how the story highlights the importance of locally relevant narratives in experiencing and sensemaking of brands. The following four directions to using cultural narratives elaborate on how to interrogate ideologies using myths and cultural codes successfully in a North African context.

Embrace a Local Brand Identity

Brands generally interact with culture as they become communicative objects for brand managers to get consumers' buy-in to the symbolic world that is defined by the brand's identity (Lury, 2004). The meanings that consumers ascribe to brands are the result of a projected brand identity (Schroeder & Salzer-Mörling, 2006). That is, a unique set of brand associations that is created with symbols used to help people identify with the brand (Aaker, 1997).

A personality is one key aspect of a brand's identity. As a positioning strategy, Aaker (1997) defines a brand personality as "the set of human characteristics associated with a brand" (p. 347). Hence, human's personality traits associated with the brand are transferred to the brand itself (McCracken, 1986) to give it meaning and relevance. Brand managers can create an emotional response by giving the brand a personality because it can be easily deciphered by consumers. Aaker (1997) uncovered five basic dimensions of people that, according to Keller (2003), seem to have captured the perceptual space of brands. These include: sincerity, excitement, competence, sophistication, and ruggedness. To include a more culturally diverse perspective to personalities, Geuens et al. (2009) distinguish five globally-fitting dimensions (responsibility, activity, aggressiveness, simplicity, and emotion) for brand personalities.

However, it can be argued that these scales assume a homogenous consumer culture which, as we know, is far from true when considering diversity in groups, communities, and subcultures. Contrary to these static notions of personality traits, brands can actually evolve with their consumers. This idea is reflected in Twitchell's (2004a) basic premise that much of our shared knowledge about who we are and where we stand in the world comes to us through branding, which requires a mass media agent to transmit this knowledge. So as products gradually transition from messages with more utilitarian provisions of information regarding the quality and production origin (i.e., transactional), they can deliver on more complex brand characteristics involving image-building, and eventually develop a brand personality (i.e., transformational; Moore & Reid, 2008).

One approach brands might take is to assume a stable, enduring and innate identity. Yet that would be at odds with notions of an individual's identity in much of the current social thought. Current contemporary identities of consumers are dynamic, reflexive, complicated and multi-faceted. As social identities are fluid and changing, Csaba and Bengtsson (2006) suggest that brands can be flexible and adaptive in order to stay relevant and connected with consumers, engaging in the negotiations of cultural identity. Companies that fail to engage in the wider conversations of culture and enter debates of identity categorisation might find themselves under attack by consumers wanting them to take a stand (a point to be discussed later).

On the other hand, brands can completely ignore cultural conversations and ideas on brand personalities or brand relationships. However, they run the risk of finding themselves irrelevant in a society such as Egypt where consumer cultures are transforming to meet the demands of globalisation and the "folklorisation of culture" (Abaza, 2007, p. 282).

A good example of a strong brand identity in Egypt is the formerly known telecommunications brand, Mobinil, which was acquired by France's global network provider, Orange. Mobinil, as the first and oldest provider in Egypt was known for their patriotic and sentimental messaging that echoed popular culture. Orange took over Mobinil and coincidently both brand logo colours are orange, with somewhat similar typesets. Mobinil's earlier campaigns entitled "Communicate without Talking", and "Always Together" came after the 2011 revolution. Mobinil promoted a message of hope to the Egyptian community for a better future that brings people together, keeps the peace, showcases minority groups and rural and urban areas around Egypt and equalises social classes. Orange took on similar sentiments with their rebranding to Orange Egypt. This is especially true in their 2020 advertisements that came in parallel with COVID-19 social distancing and travel restrictions. Their recent messaging revolves around "The Circle of Life" also imbues sentiments of togetherness despite the distance. The outcome is a perception of raising hope and boosting optimism during the challenging times of the 2020 pandemic.

From an economic perspective, there would be several differences between a globally run company and a local one. However, from a consumer's perspective, the differences are minute. The key to an effective brand identity overhaul is maintaining the core brand identity (characteristics) and local culture that consumers are familiar with while interjecting it with a fresh feel. In other words, maintaining brand consistency whilst respecting the local nuances, meanings, and symbols relevant to the culture.

Tell a Compelling Story

Humans often make up stories about themselves and the groups they relate to as ways of togetherness and creating interest (McAdams, 1993). Storytelling is a tool for sharing, transmitting and interpreting knowledge or experiences through a story, script, plot or episodes to deliver a complicated idea, concept, or relationships in easy and often entertaining ways (Lee & Shin, 2015). An attractive story, account, tale or description can draw the attention of an audience through immersion and narrative transportation, a phenomenon where consumers can enter the world the story presents (van Laer et al., 2014).

We cannot think of life without stories: whether it involves listening, watching, reading, or telling them (Gergen & Gergen, 1988). From childhood, our parents begin telling us stories, therefore we become socially and culturally conditioned into understanding the narrative form of storytelling. In essence, life too exhibits basic feature of all narratives—a beginning, middle and an end. Stories make our lives and ourselves intelligible to us and to others (Gergen & Gergen, 1988). Storytelling is pervasive to human nature at an individual, social and cultural level.

The basis for a good story is it should include a guiding reason for which the story is formed (i.e., a story goal), important events that relate to this story goal, and putting the events in a sensible order (Gergen & Gergen, 1988). Frye (1957) suggests four basic plots for a good story: comedy, tragedy, romance and satire. For instance, romantic plots often "consist of a series of episodes in which the major protagonist experiences challenges or threats and through a series of struggles emerges victorious" (Gergen & Gergen, 1988, p. 23).

Stories can be told differently using folklore, legend or myth. Myth—one element of cultural expressions that brands often use—is an instructive story that imparts ideology (Holt, 2004). Myths can dramatise ideologies by conveying a specific type of subculture that becomes comprehensible, instinctively felt and resonates with people only because it is embedded in myth (Holt, 2012). Myths convey meaning, transfer values, the history and the culture to future generations.

Storytelling is pivotal to modern marketing because it can improve the product or service when used effectively. On an individual level, stories become a powerful device to frame a storyteller's experience and influence their likelihood of repeating the narrated experience (Shankar et al., 2001; Thompson, 1997). Storytelling can make information memorable, meaningful and understandable. On a market level, consumer and branding research provide examples of how companies-as-storytellers can benefit by telling stories to their current and prospective customers (Holt, 2012; Papadatos, 2006). It is an effective technique to shape brands and create an emotional investment in a product or service.

A story told through branding can be channelled through a multitude of communication tools (e.g., stories, social media, videos, reviews and word of mouth) that give life to brands and drive market change (Fog et al., 2005). Through different forms of popular culture, consumers are offered a ready-made story they can use as a resource for sensemaking aspects of their life (Ritson & Elliott, 1999). In other words, branding is the commercial process of storytelling (Twitchell, 2004a). The success of a business, when introducing new products or negotiating its way through market changes can be, in part, attributed to how well they narrate their own story.

Generally, the purpose of stories is to generate certain emotional responses or sensations from the audience. Great stories are also memorable while lousy stories have no punch, lack centre or focus (Twitchell, 2004b). Hence, great brands are those that tell emotive and compelling stories that may reinforce or challenge cultural norms and practices (Holt, 2004). These stories carry cultural meanings as they teach us how to think and feel by hearing them.

Even more so, consumer audiences can co-construct parts of the story to maximise the story's explanatory power. The power of storytelling, compared to straight facts, is demonstrated in McCloskey's (1994) Rhetorical Tetrad that simply explains how facts and logic (an impersonal human argument) can be supplanted by stories and metaphors (with more personal relevance), making this a more persuasive tool for brand management.

One strategy that brands often use in Egypt is leveraging brand associations. These associations can include memories of past events (Keller, 1993). Brands may draw upon consumers' personal and communal associations in culture, specifically those that endow emotional connections such as nostalgia. Nostalgia, a branding communication strategy, is often conceptualised as the preference to consume goods and experiences related to the past (Holbrook & Schindler, 2003). It comes with ideas that things from the past are good. Nostalgic ideas may also include a desire to consume patriotically for ethnocentric reasons.

Coca-Cola in Egypt uses nostalgia as a branding strategy to engender and typify virtues highly valued in the society. Nostalgia in Egypt is a reminder for many older-generations as well as the youth of the idealised 'olden days' for refined taste (Abaza, 2007), solidarity, perseverance, equality and resilience. Since Coca-Cola first started selling in Egypt in 1942 and was nationalised in 1952 after the first Egyptian revolution against the then-monarchy, Coca-Cola worked hard to build a story around their nationalism and support of local businesses. The story is not so different from their global mission to offer support to communities. Coca-Cola tells a compelling story with the punch line "Search for the best flavour", which they are referring to Egypt's local (not global chain) restaurants and small businesses. And as a global brand, they have been working effortlessly to show their support of local culture. Their advertising messages present Egypt's many informal sectors and labour forces (coffee houses, restaurants, beggars, small grocery shops), with iconic street foods and dishes all around Egyptian governates that both the rich and poor patronise. They use images, music, identifiable Egyptian men and women as the main characters, cultural idioms, and sayings and expressions in their advertising that is familiar and comfortable. These are reflective of thick and deeply-seated cultural codes. The stories told through the Coca-Cola brand provide audiences an ability to be transported through the imagined (real but 'better') life and a reminder of peaceful times, which eventually incite sentimental and heart-warming emotions (van Laer et al., 2014).

Integrate Symbolic (Identity) Markers

As social groups tell their own stories, inscribing their treasured qualities, codes, virtues and values, products can have the same effect. Symbolic interactionists (Mead, 1934) theorised that meanings behind a symbolic gesture, such as the use of a brand, is a social product of a consumer's reaction to it. These meanings are dynamic and socially constructed.

The idea that a brand's identity meanings are general knowledge is important in the use of brands as identity markers. This means that consumers not only have to interpret the brand's identity meanings for themselves, but they must know that other people in their social networks will interpret them in the same way (Avery, 2012). Groups, tribes and communities use symbolic markers to distinguish themselves from others and create group boundaries (Richerson & Boyd, 2005).

Symbolic markers comprise a set of important props to create compelling stories. Employing these symbolic markers when branding is critical not only for brands to signal to consumers what they are all about, but for consumers to signal to other consumers their affiliations or interests. These markers "may label the individual or group as adventurous, dominant, rare, generous, or creative" (Hirschman, 2010,

p. 579). Brands can also enact people's understanding of their relationships with their peers, society and state; becoming loci of objectification of desired identities and social relations. 'Symbolically dense' brands that focus on shared meanings, signs and ideas that iconic goods come to represent (Arvidsson, 2001; Holt, 2004) can deliver a message about the brand and serve as a foundation of consumer markets.

While the deployment of such symbolic and metaphorical markers (i.e., a brand's meaning) within a culture is based on their linkages with social groups, there are far too many brands competing in the cultural war to win consumers' affections. Brands that work on embedding socially 'visible' and meaningful identity markers within their cultural stories can stand out. Markers may be tangible (e.g., headcover, apparel) or intangible (e.g., masculinity, family values), but they simply must reflect the local culture where the brand performs a supporting role. And while ideologies can convey meaning, it is the markers and cultural codes that provide consumers short-hand information that allow them to easily understand and experience the intended meanings (Holt, 2012).

Consider Birell, a national non-alcoholic beer company (currently bought out by the Heineken Group), as a good example of a brand that deploys strong symbolic markers. Birell competes on one main construct—masculinity. Despite it being non-alcoholic, Birell consistently tries to reflect a cultural ideology as being aggressive and strong while painting these ideals in direct opposition to 'femininity', perceived as the 'gentler gender'. While their branding is positioned in oppositional intersectional ways, stereotyping men and women, and portraying a hegemonic masculine oppression of femininity, this require a deeper discussion outside the bounds of this chapter. Here, my focus is on the use of the symbolic markers Birell uses as a reflection of the Egyptian culture.

The brand employs comedy as their basic plot, and calls itself "the masculine brand… that requires competence to handle its bitterness" (Al Ahram Beverages, n.d.). In a world they reflect in their messaging between men and women (oppositional), their "Be a Man" and "Man up" campaigns that started as early as 2009 express the pressures of men being caretakers and protectors of women and their struggles in daily life. Drinking Birell will give men the energy (due to the benefits of plain malt) they need to help them to stand up to 'women's complaints and incessant needs'. That physiological effect is transferred into a cultural idea where drinking Birell meant being a man, and showing masculinity often in violent ways that Egypt and Egyptian men have increasingly idealised. This perspective represents a historical ideology of the masculine man as hard-working and strong, helping Egypt gain its freedom from colonisation since the 1952 revolution (Ghannam, 2013). Brands like Birell that express a reactionary masculinity utilise symbolic markers that are understood by men as well as women in Egypt. Their campaigns involve objectification of women in their television advertisements, such as the use of cat-calling and staring, showcasing a woman's figure, or insinuating ideas that women constantly nag, and that "being a man is not easy" as per their advertising messages. While these are extremely problematic identity markers (i.e., promoting toxic masculinity) in society, these are all cultural expressions that the Egyptian man can relate to. A study conducted by UN Women disturbingly found that 99.3% of Egyptian women and young girls surveyed have been sexually harassed more than once (El-Deeb, 2013). However, the brand uses a comedic plot, thus making it supposedly acceptable for Birell to use such cultural ideologies in their communication.

Mobilising Key Local Institutional Players

Egypt, as with many countries in Africa, runs primarily around systems of *religion* and *government* (viewed here together rather than separate institutions). In principle, the institution of society that a nation is built on confers meanings of what happens inside the society and how that society relates to the 'outside' world. These are systems that become culturally important pillars or institutional forces shaping the marketplace and consumers (Arnould & Thompson, 2005). Research shows how consumers are organised by institutional structures to gain social legitimacy and social inclusion, access identity resources, or influence the marketplace (Dolbec & Fischer, 2015; Scaraboto & Fischer, 2013). Thus, brands should understand these institutional structures and their boundaries in order for the brand's identity to reflect what people find important in society and what they resonate with.

Religion is an aspect of culture, and an integral one. There has never been a society without religion (Burkert, 1996). Durkheim (1965) notes that religiosity cannot be separated from the socio-cultural environment in which they exist. With a monotheistic perspective in mind, the mark of a religion is that it has a canonical text with authoritative interpretations, officials that preserve the faith, a legal structure, and ethical norms that are put in place to regulate individuals and communities (Raday, 2003). This makes religion an institutionalised aspect of culture that can influence and be influenced by ideological and social culture.

Extant scholarship has recognised the significance of religion in shaping political and public life. And while the Church and State might be legally separate in many Western countries (Medhurst, 2004), that is not the case when it comes to religion and the government or public policy in many North African countries such as Egypt. The role of Islam and 'shariah (Islamic) laws' can be seen impacting freedom of speech, such as the use of 'blasphemy law' in Egypt that prosecutes harshly against any public or private insult of religion—mainly Islam (Barsoum, 2016).

Religiosity as a social institution has been found to shape individual's tastes and consumption decisions through beliefs, rituals, values and a common faith that its members subscribe to (Mathras et al., 2016). As narratives are often built on or from myths (Bhattacharyya, 1997) which are powerful meaning-providers (Lévi-Strauss, 1979), brands can include historical elements, and linguistic and material cues to a given religious and ritual values in order to appeal to the society already indoctrinated into religious culture and its practices in their everyday lives.

As the state religion of Egypt, Islam makes up the majority of the population (approximately 90%; 10% are Christians). Important markers of religious identity in Egypt may involve cultural events such as fasting for the holy month of Ramadan and breaking fast, preparing halal meat (Islamic slaughter rituals), wearing of the hijab (headcover) by many Muslim women to maintain their modesty, privacy and avoid men's gaze, or the spoken and unspoken rules on public displays of affection between romantic couples. With the influence of religion in Egypt, it is no surprise that the grand imam of Al-Azhar (Islamic authority) is heavily involved in the Egyptian constitution as a main source for legislation. Even though the government is a military-dominated regime that significantly increased their involvement in laws and procedures that stifles people's freedom (especially since the 2011 revolution), religion/shariah and the government work together and are heavily embedded in the Egyptian constitution.

Brands may mobilise these institutions for their own benefit and to represent the status quo or changes in society. With Ramadan as a peek season for advertisers' marketing spend, the likes of Coca-Cola and Orange Egypt are found positioning themselves as sentimental/emotional brands that bring people together in celebration of this holy month. Vodafone Egypt (global mobile-network provider) utilises key pillars and institutions in their campaigns but in a different way. Their campaign around "Our Power" with accompanying tagline "We didn't send people to the streets, we didn't start the revolution ... We only reminded Egyptians how powerful they are", that came after the 2011 revolution alongside images of the Tahir Square protests and people praying in mosques for their freedom. Their communications strongly implied that Vodafone was responsible for the Egyptian revolution, which insinuated Vodafone's strong socio-political involvement in Egypt that supposedly inspired people to take back their "power" to the streets. The irony that also demonstrates Vodafone's stance with Egyptian institutions is that during the early days of the Tahrir Square demonstrations, Vodafone sent out to their subscribers pro-Mubarak (ousted President) text messages. The alleged allegations that Vodafone collaborated with the Egyptian government's effort to block Internet and mobile phone access (as ways of silencing protestors) is yet to be known. While Vodafone's intentions may have been pure and patriotic, their message incited rage amongst Egyptian revolutionaries that took to social media arguing that the company ignored years of activism and police brutality to eventually take credit for the revolution.

Does Local Cultural Branding Always Work?

Based on the previous examples and literature reviewed, we can see that brands adapt and repurpose cultural resources to take advantage of ideological opportunities. They may focus their efforts on cultural source materials such as consumer subcultures (i.e., groups or places that cohere around an ideology, myths and cultural codes) and media myths (i.e., mass media often borrow from subcultures in order to spread new cultural expressions, packaging them in cultural products such as news) (Holt, 2012). These cultural expressions can be antithetic to a cultural orthodoxy of a category. Utilising cultural materials can provide great credibility for brands because they attest that the subcultural ideology actually exists in the world and provides value for its participants.

Yet using culture blindly without understanding what these codes and myths mean to stakeholders, whether they are accepted or align with general ethical and moral standards, is inexcusable. Even the most apt ideology packaged in a powerful myth can backfire if it is composed of culturally insensitive and illiterate codes. Holt and Cameron (2010) recommend that the right cultural expression requires a bearing of the "right ideology, and dramatised through the right myth, expressed with the right cultural code" (p. 176). Thus, the precise codes used must work together and be well tested in the market, rather than taken-for-granted facts about the marketplace culture.

Consider the example of Birell. While masculinity may have worked with brands like Jack Daniel's, Marlboro cigarettes or Harley Davidson motorcycles, Birell is a controversial beer brand that professes to make 'sissy' boys 'men'. While hegemonic masculinity as a subcultural ideology does indeed exist in Egypt, the buck stops there when mass media rejected what the brand stands for. Egyptian feminists, journalists and bloggers argued against Birell's message as it amplifies and diffuses this ideology from the margins to the masses as a "parasitic" brand (Holt, 2006), arguing that it promotes a culture of sexism, gender discrimination and toxicity (e.g., Khairat, 2015). Culture source materials must be carefully studied and tested prior to communicating it to the public. If anything, brands should be doing more good in the world (or staying neutral), rather than harm.

Branding with Cultural Intention and Activism

Positioning and communicating brands in a compelling and unique manner require brand managers to use appropriate cultural resources that build iconic brands that take a central role in culture. Brands have become so woven immanently into our daily lives, that they become "saturated with sensibilities of a particular time to the point of embodying them" (Kravets & Örge, 2010, p. 220). Brands can also reproduce and proliferate their existence in the world. This means that they should not simply be vehicles for shared meanings, but they can reflect and stand for a culture, endowed with agency towards positive change. They can do that by communicating a sociopolitical stance on issues of importance.

There is a growing stream of literature researching brand activism in the market. Moorman (2020) defines brand political activism as "public speech or actions focused on partisan issues made by or on behalf of a company using its corporate or individual brand name" (p. 388). This research interest in societal-level debates accelerated when global brands took a stand, with Nike supporting specific events such as Colin Kaepernick's protest to support the #BlackLivesMatter movement, Apple's protection of civil liberties related to privacy, or broader conversations on toxic masculinity that Gillette's viral ad tackled recently. Companies are finally seeing that doing nothing is a form of complicity and is no longer an option.

As demonstrated earlier, brands can have a lot of cultural power to incite change, as brands themselves are powerful social actors that embody ideas and meanings critical to society (Holt, 2012). Some consumers might even argue that brands have a duty and responsibility to act on this position of power. Thus, the more engaged brands are in culture—having cultural authority—as a desirable position and iconic, the more that is expected of them by varied stakeholders (e.g., employees, partners, consumers, policy makers, etc.). Some of these stakeholders may wish to maintain the status quo on these issues and others will seek a changed world. As a result, brands would need to pick a side. And while it is impossible not to offend 'the Other' or stir controversy, a deeper knowledge of cultural symbols, tensions and public debates will serve these companies best (Csaba & Bengtsson, 2006).

Brands may showcase their activism by advocating for/against climate change initiatives, transgender rights, racial justice or gender issues. However, that cause must be supported and accepted first, by the subculture in mind, and second, by the company itself. Moorman (2020) recommends brand managers to look inwards first and understand the company's own beliefs and perceptions of the brand and politics as these must align with the sociopolitical issue in mind.

While activism literature suggests that there is a growing acceptance of brands getting involved in societal issues (Milfeld & Flint, 2020), they are studying brands that exist in Western countries where freedom of speech and opinions allow for this. Brands in North Africa, particularly conservative and Islamic countries like Egypt, are constituted by shariah laws and a grand imam (Islamic authority involved in Egyptian constitution) as main sources of legislation. As the majority population in Egypt is Muslim (with several Islamic extremists), supporting a social or political cause can be very controversial. For example, the Egyptian Consumer Protection Agency (CPA) bans advertisements that are considered "immoral" to society which must be subjected to applications of Islamic principles. Hence, social issues such as discrimination against minority religions (e.g., Coptic Christians), repression of transgender rights and their prosecution, or discussions on female genital mutilation (Human Rights Watch, 2020)—to name only a few of Egypt's systemic issues—would certainly not be tolerated by the legal/shariah systems. We are also reminded that the riskier the changes brands choose to take, the higher the chances that consumers might have polarised reactions to socially-charged narratives (Milfeld & Flint, 2020), given how taboo these discussions are perceived by the Egyptian public.

One way around this would be for brands to engage in what Vredenburg et al. (2020) call 'silent brand activism' where brands can embrace sociopolitical causes as part of their strategic focus, yet they operate behind the scenes with low marketing messaging of their activism (e.g., funding charities that support women suffering domestic violence like Beit Hawa (a 'women's refuge' in Cairo)). These brands are considered ones with the least to lose.

Another solution would be for brands to listen in to mass sentiments and cultural narratives. Given the public's existing support for these efforts, brands' actions would be no longer viewed as political—meaning socially divisive. For example, brands that want to show their support of the Egyptian revolution can do so now by reminding consumers of Egypt's transition and inciting hope for a better future.

A final word of caution relates to brands that detach their activist messages from their core values and practices, leading to inauthentic brand activism known as "woke washing" (Sobande, 2020). This practice has the potential of misleading consumers with their claims, which can eventually damage the brand's image and the cause itself. Brands are urged to survey their identity that encompasses their brand purpose, values and practices, and consider carefully whether these align with sociopolitical movements, or whether they are only engaging with these out of a sense of urgency and market response (Georgallis, 2017). If the brand's executives believe in this cause and what is important in society, they are encouraged to revisit the company's activities and decision making, including making changes to products and services.

Conclusions

Companies have for long competed to profit from their rich source of economic value, where their brands have become the main commercial vehicles for positioning and communicating that value. Holt (2012) argues that we need to perceive brands as not located in market spaces but they are embedded in cultural marketplaces. Brands are able to market these cultural expressions and ride on the tail end of changes in culture.

Consumers view a brand's communication outputs through the lens of a story. In this case, marketers not only need to consider their brand's identity to resonate with consumers' individual and collective identities—a local perspective nontheless—but they must also consider their marketing strategy developments as a narrative as well. Brands, products and experiences become central characters in their story, and brand managers (including marketers, advertising and communications agencies) assume the role of the author to retell that story in a compelling way. To appeal to consumers, the stories they tell should have cultural relevance in the market, and involve symbolic identity markers as cultural codes that consumers can understand and eventually experience its intended meanings. Yet it would also be remiss to ignore the key pillars in society, specifically when we talk about North African brands where culture is heavily intertwined in religion, moral and political governance and a deep history involving revolutions, wars and colonisation. Similar to consumer culture researchers studying non-western markets (Karababa, 2012), several historical trajectories in Egypt and their evolving institutions are able to shape modern consumer culture(s).

The time is ripe for brands to redefine their marketing as narrative projects. Marketing research's role would be to identify stories based on cultural ideologies that can be created with cultural expressions and turned into rhetorical metaphors of persuasive power (Holt, 2012; Shankar et al., 2001). With a small subset of cultural expressions activated at any one time, brands can engage in topics that are considered credible and accepted by consumers. The cultural codes and myths in society all depends on how the product, benefits, uses and its consumers are represented in the mass media. This exercise would appeal to consumers in search of the 'ideal story', where studies show that strong emotions are generated when consumers sense a match between an actual or potential story, and an idealised one (e.g., Sternberg, 1998). However, telling a compelling story with expressions of subculture's ideology is not enough and may not always lead to positive outcomes as demonstrated with the Birell and Vodafone examples. Sociocultural narratives, including brand activism narratives, may provoke polarising responses from stakeholders. Thus, brands, global and national, are urged to tread these waters with caution because with every story, there is a deep-seated and delicate meaning sitting within a culture that is a moving target, dynamic and constantly evolving in society.

References

Aaker, J. L. (1997). Dimensions of brand personality. *Journal of Marketing Research, 34*(3), 347–356.

Aaker, J., Fournier, S., & Brasel, S. A. (2004). When good brands do bad. *Journal of Consumer Research, 31*, 1–16.

Abaza, M. (2001). Shopping malls, consumer culture and the reshaping of public space in Egypt. *Theory, Culture & Society, 18*(5), 97–122.

Abaza, M. (2007). Shifting landscapes of fashion in contemporary Egypt. *Fashion Theory, 11*(2–3), 281–297.

Al Ahram Beverages, .n.d. *Birell*. https://www.alahrambeverages.com/brands/birell/

Alden, D. L., Steenkamp, J.-B., & Batra, R. (1999). Brand positioning through advertising in Asia, North America, and Europe: The role of global consumer culture. *Journal of Marketing, 63*, 75–87.

Appau, S., & Churchill, A. S. (2019). Bridging cultural categories of consumption through indeterminacy: A consumer culture perspective on the rise of African Pentecostal-Charismatic Christianity. *Journal of Consumer Culture, 19*(1), 125–145.

Appadurai, A. (1990). Disjuncture and difference in the global cultural economy. *Theory, Culture & Society, 7*(2–3), 295–310.

Appadurai, A. (1996). *Modernity at large: Cultural dimensions of globalization.* University of Minnesota Press.

Armanious, D. (2020). Accelerating global actions for a world without poverty: Egypt experiences. *United Nations Report*. https://www.un.org/development/desa/dspd/wp-content/uploads/sites/22/2020/03/Armanious-Paper-World-without-poverty-Egypt.pdf

Arnould, E. J., & Thompson, C. J. (2005). Consumer culture theory (CCT): Twenty years of research. *Journal of Consumer Research, 31*(4), 868–882.

Arvidsson, A. (2001). From counter culture to consumer culture: Vespa and the Italian youth market, 1958–78. *Journal of Consumer Culture, 1*(1), 47–71.

Avery, J. (2012). Defending the markers of masculinity: Consumer resistance to brand gender-bending. *International Journal of Research in Marketing, 29*(4), 322–336.

Barsoum, M. (2016). *Egypt's anti-blasphemy law: Defence of religion or tool for persecution?* Al Ahram (Online). http://english.ahram.org.eg/NewsContent/1/151/216896/Egypt/Features/Egypts-antiblasphemy-law-Defence-of-religion-or-to.aspx

Baudrillard, J. (1998). *The consumer society: Myths & structures*. Sage.
Belk, R. W. (1988). Possessions and the extended self. *Journal of Consumer Research, 15*, 139–168.
Bhatia, T. K., & Bhargava, M. (2008). Reaching unreachable resolving globalization/ localization paradox. *Journal of Creative Communication, 3*(2), 209–230.
Bhattacharyya, A. (1997). Historical backdrop. In K. N. Dwivedi (Ed.), *The therapeutic use of stories* (pp. 1–18). Routledge.
Burkert, W. (1996). *Creation of the sacred: Tracks of biology in the early religions*. Harvard University Press.
Campbell, C. (1987). *The romantic ethic and the spirit of modern consumerism*. Blackwell.
Csaba, F. F., & Bengtsson, A. (2006). Rethinking identity in brand management. In J. E. Schroeder & M. Salzer-Mörling (Eds.), *Brand culture* (pp. 118–135). Routledge.
Dolbec, P.-Y., & Fischer, E. (2015). Refashioning a field? Connected consumers and institutional dynamics in markets. *Journal of Consumer Research, 41*(6), 1447–1468.
Drescher, T. D. (1992). The transformation and evolution of trademarks: From signals to symbols to myths. *Trademark Reporter, 82*, 301–340.
Durkheim, E. (1965). *The elementary forms of the religious life*. Free Press.
El Deeb, B. (2013). Study on ways and methods to eliminate sexual harassment in Egypt. *United Nations Women*. https://web.archive.org/web/20170721*f*200450/http:/www.dgvn.de/fileadmin/user_upload/DOKUMENTE/English_Documents/Sexual-Harassment-Study-Egypt-Final-EN.pdf
Einstein, M. (2007). *Brands of faith: Marketing religion in a commercial age*. Routledge.
Erdem, T., & Swait, J. (2004). Brand credibility, brand consideration and choice. *Journal of Consumer Research, 31*, 191–198.
Escalas, J., & Bettman, J. R. (2005). Self-construal, brand meaning and reference groups. *Journal of Consumer Research, 32*, 378–389.
Featherstone, M. (1991). *Consumer culture and postmodernism*. Sage.
Firat, A. F., & Venkatesh, A. (1995). Liberatory postmodernism and the reenchantment of consumption. *Journal of Consumer Research, 22*(3), 239–267.
Frye, N. (1957). *Anatomy of criticism*. Princeton University Press.
Fog, K., Budtz, C., & Yakaboylu, B. (2005). Branding through storytelling. In K. Fog, C. Budtz, P. Munch, & S. Blanchette (Eds.), *Storytelling: Branding in Practice* (pp. 12–25). Springer.

Fournier, S. (1998). Consumers and their brands: Developing relationship theory in consumer research. *Journal of Consumer Research, 24*, 343–373.

Georgallis, P. (2017). The link between social movements and corporate social initiatives: Toward a multi-level theory. *Journal of Business Ethics, 142*(4), 735–751.

Ger, G. (1999). Localizing in the global village: Local firms competing in global markets. *California Management Review, 41*(4), 64–83.

Gergen, K. J., & Gergen, M. M. (1988). Narrative and the self as relationship. In L. Berkowitz (Ed.), *Advances in Experimental Social Psychology, 21* (pp. 17–56). Academic Press.

Geuens, M., Weijters, B., & De Wulf, K. (2009). A new measure of brand personality. *International Journal of Research in Marketing, 26*(2), 97–107.

Ghannam, F. (2013). *Live and die like a man: Gender dynamics in urban Egypt*. Stanford University Press.

Goff, P. M. (2007). *Limits to liberalization: Local culture in a global marketplace*. Cornell University Press.

Hart, J. (1997). Translating and resisting empire: Cultural appropriation and postcolonial studies. In B. Ziff & P. V. Rao (Eds.), *Borrowed Power: Essays on Cultural Appropriation* (pp. 1–27). Rutgers University Press.

Hebdige, D. (1979). *Subculture: The meaning of style.* Routledge.

Hirschman, E. C. (2002). Metaphors, archetypes and the biological origins of semiotics. *Semiotica, 142*, 315–349.

Hirschman, E. C. (2010). Evolutionary branding. *Psychology & Marketing, 27*(6), 568–583.

Holbrook, M. B., & Schindler, R. M. (2003). Nostalgic bonding: Exploring the role of nostalgia in the consumption experience. *Journal of Consumer Behavior, 3*, 107–127.

Holt, D. B. (2004). *How brands become icons: The principles of cultural branding*. Harvard Business School Press.

Holt, D. B. (2006). Jack Daniel's America: Iconic brands as ideological parasites and proselytizers. *Journal of Consumer Culture, 6*(3), 355–377.

Holt, D. B. (2012). Cultural brand strategy. In V. Shankar & G. S. Carpenter (Eds.), *Handbook of marketing strategy* (pp. 306–317). Edward Elgar Publishing.

Holt, D. B., & Cameron, D. (2010). *Cultural strategy: Using innovative ideologies to build breakthrough brands.* Oxford University Press.

Human Rights Watch. (2020). Egypt events of 2019. *World report 2020.* https://www.hrw.org/world-report/2020/country-chapters/egypt

Joy, A., & Wallendorf, M. (1996). The development of consumer culture in the Third World: Theories of globalism and localism. *Consumption & Marketing: Macro Dimensions*, 104–142.

Karababa, E. (2012). Approaching non-western consumer cultures from a historical perspective: The case of early modern Ottoman consumer culture. *Marketing Theory, 12*(1), 13–25.

Kapferer, J. N. (1992) *Strategic brand management*. The Free Press.

Keller, K. L. (2003). Brand synthesis: The multidimensionality of brand knowledge. *Journal of Consumer Research, 29*(4), 595–600.

Kennedy, A. M., & Makkar, M. (2021). Cultural appropriation. In L. Eagle, S. Dahl, P. D. Pelsmacker, & C. R. Taylor (Eds.), *The SAGE Handbook of Marketing Ethics* (pp. 155–168). Sage.

Khairat, M. (2015). The beer company promoting sexism and sexual harassment in Egypt. *Egyptian Streets*. https://egyptianstreets.com/2015/03/27/the-beer-company-promoting-sexism-and-sexual-harassment-in-egypt/

Klein, N. (2000). *No Logo*. Flamingo.

Knox, S. (2004). Positioning and branding your organization. *Journal of Product & Brand Management, 13*(2), 105–115.

Kravets, O., & Örge, Ö. (2010). Iconic brands: A socio-material story. *Journal of Material Culture, 15*(2), 205–232.

Lee, Y., & Shin, W. (2015). Marketing tradition-bound product through storytelling: A case study of a Japanese sake brewery. *Service Business, 9*(2), 281–295.

Lévi-Strauss, C. (1979). *Myth and meaning: Cracking the code of culture*. Schocken.

Levy, S. J. (1959). Symbols for sale. *Harvard Business Review, 37*, 117–124.

Lury, C. (2004). *Brands: The logos of the global economy*. Routledge.

Mathras, D., Cohen, A. B., Mandel, N., & Mick, D. G. (2016). The effects of religion on consumer behavior: A conceptual framework and research agenda. *Journal of Consumer Psychology, 26*(2), 298–311.

McAdams, D. P. (1993). *The stories we live by: Personal myths and the making of the self.* Guilford Press.

McAlexander, J. H., Schouten, J. W., & Koenig, H. F. (2002). Building brand community. *Journal of Marketing, 66*(1), 38–54.

McCloskey, D. (1994). *Knowledge and Persuasion in Economics*. Cambridge University Press.

McCracken, G. (1986). Culture and consumption: A theoretical account of the structure and movement of the cultural meaning of consumer goods. *Journal of Consumer Research, 13*(1), 71–84.

Mead, G. H. (1934). *Mind, self, and society*. University of Chicago Press.

Medhurst, M. J. (2004). Religious belief and scholarship: A complex relationship. *Journal of Communication and Religion, 27*, 41.

Meraz, S., & Papacharissi, Z. (2013). Networked Gatekeeping and networked framing on #Egypt. *International Journal of Press/politics, 18*(2), 138–166.

Milfeld, T., & Flint, D. J. (2020). When brands take a stand: The nature of consumers' polarized reactions to social narrative videos. *Journal of Product & Brand Management*. https://doi.org/10.1108/JPBM-10-2019-2606

Miller, D. (1998). *Theory of shopping*. Cornell University Press.

Moore, K., & Reid, S. (2008). The birth of brand: 4000 years of branding. *Business History, 50*(4), 419–432.

Moorman, C. (2020). Commentary: Brand activism in a Political World. *Journal of Public Policy & Marketing, 39*(4), 388–392.

Mūniz, A. M., & O'Guinn, T. C. (2001). Brand community. *Journal of Consumer Research, 27*, 412–432.

Mūniz, A. M., & Schau, H. J. (2005). Religiosity and the abandoned Apple Newton community. *Journal of Consumer Research, 31*, 737–747.

O'Reilly, D. (2005). Cultural brands/branding cultures. *Journal of Marketing Management, 21*(5–6), 573–588.

Palumbo, F., & Herbig, P. (2000). The multicultural context of brand loyalty. *European Journal of Marketing, 3*(3), 116–124.

Papadatos, C. (2006). The art of storytelling: How loyalty marketers can build emotional connections to their brands. *Journal of Consumer Marketing, 23*(7), 382–384.

Pletcher, H. (2019). *Egypt—Statistics & Facts, Statista*. https://www.statista.com/topics/2510/egypt/

Polkinghorne, D. E. (1988). *Narrative knowing and the human sciences*. SUNY Press.

Porter, M. E. (1986). *Competition in global industries*. Harvard Business Press.

Raday, F. (2003). Culture, religion, and gender. *International Journal of Constitutional Law, 1*(4), 663–715.

Richerson, P. J., & Boyd, R. (2005). *Not by genes alone*. University of Chicago Press.

Ricoeur, P. (1996). Reflections on a new ethos for Europe. In R. Kearney (Ed.), *The Hermeneutics of action* (pp. 3–14). Sage.

Ritson, M., & Elliott, R. (1999). The social uses of advertising: An ethnographic study of adolescent advertising audiences. *Journal of Consumer Research, 26*(3), 260–277.

Ritzer, G. (2007). *The globalization of nothing 2*. Sage.

Roehm, M. L., & Brady, M. K. (2007). Consumer responses to performance failures by high equity brands. *Journal of Consumer Research, 34*, 537–545.
Rooney, J. A. (1995). Branding: A trend for today and tomorrow. *Journal of Product & Brand Management, 4*(4), 48–55.
Russell, M. L. (2004). Advertising and consumer culture in Egypt: Creating al-Sayyida al-Istihlakiyya. In M. L. Russell (Ed.), *Creating the New Egyptian Woman* (pp. 49–78). Palgrave Macmillan.
Scaraboto, D., & Fischer, E. (2013). Frustrated fatshionistas: An institutional theory perspective on consumer quests for greater choice in mainstream markets. *Journal of Consumer Research, 39*, 1234–1257.
Schroeder, J., & Salzer-Mörling, M. (2006). Introduction: The cultural codes of branding. In J. Schroeder & M. Salzer-Mörling (Eds.), *Brand culture* (pp. 16–26). Routledge.
Shankar, A., Elliott, R., & Goulding, C. (2001). Understanding consumption: Contributions from a narrative perspective. *Journal of Marketing Management, 17*(3–4), 429–453.
Simeon, R. (2006). A conceptual model linking brand building strategies and Japanese popular culture. *Marketing Intelligence & Planning, 24*(5), 463–476.
Sobande, F. (2020). Woke-Washing: "Intersectional" femvertising and branding "woke" bravery. *European Journal of Marketing, 54*(11), 2723–2745.
Sternberg, R. (1998). *Love is a story: A new theory of relationships*. Oxford University Press.
Thompson, C. J. (1997). Interpreting consumers: A hermeneutical framework for deriving marketing insights from the texts of consumers' consumption stories. *Journal of Marketing Research, 34*(4), 438–455.
Twitchell, J. (2004a). *Branded nation: The marketing of a Megachurch, College Inc., and Museumworld.* Simon & Schuster.
Twitchell, J. B. (2004b). An English teacher looks at branding. *Journal of Consumer Research, 31*(2), 484–489.
Urry, J. (1995). *Consuming places*. Psychology Press.
Van Laer, T., De Ruyter, K., Visconti, L. M., & Wetzels, M. (2014). The extended transportation-imagery model: A meta-analysis of the antecedents and consequences of consumers' narrative transportation. *Journal of Consumer Research, 40*(5), 797–817.
Veblen, T. (1899). *The theory of the leisure class*. New American Library.
Vredenburg, J., Kapitan, S., Spry, A., & Kemper, J. A. (2020). Brands taking a stand: Authentic brand activism or woke washing? *Journal of Public Policy & Marketing, 39*(4), 444–460.

Wengrow, D. (2008). Prehistories of commodity branding. *Current Anthropology, 49*(1), 7–34.

Wilk, R. (2006). *Home cooking in the global village: Caribbean food from buccaneers to ecotourists.* Berg.

Ziff, B. H., & Rao, P. V. (1997). *Borrowed power: Essays on cultural appropriation.* Rutgers University Press.

10

Unbranded: The Challenges of Branding for Africa's Informal Economy

Tendai Chikweche

Introduction

Marketing researchers and practitioners' research on branding in Africa has primarily been focused on replicating western based studies which investigate common or familiar issues. These include African consumers' preferences of local versus international brands, assumed importance of branding to these consumers and opportunities for adaptation of strategies. Marketers' primary brand focus in Africa has been on accommodating local tastes to become glocal in their approach. Whilst these issues address pertinent marketing issues on branding, they do not address an important contextual variable that is predominant in the livelihoods and interaction of most African consumers. This relates to the impact of the informal economy, which is a key economic and

T. Chikweche (✉)
Western Sydney University, Sydney, NSW, Australia
e-mail: t.chikweche@westernsydney.edu.au

S. Appau (ed.), *Marketing Brands in Africa*, Palgrave Studies of Marketing in Emerging Economies,
https://doi.org/10.1007/978-3-030-77204-8_10

social space that shapes African consumers' day to day lives and interactions amongst themselves, with the government, with entrepreneurs and private sector at large and other external actors such as non-governmental organizations (ILO, 2020a; Medina et al., 2017).

By definition, the informal economy encompasses the diverse economic activities by small enterprises, workers, and economic units, that are in law or in practice not covered or insufficiently covered by formal arrangements or the state (Benjamin & Mbaye, 2012; ILO, 2020a). Any initiative to understand or explore the importance of branding in Africa cannot be complete without a reflection of the challenges and opportunities that are posed by the informal economy. The informal economy's importance in Africa is reflected by its significant contribution to the national economies of countries across the continent where informality is more of the norm than the exception with prospects for increased share in total employment in the post COVID-19 crisis (ILO, 2020b).

The general discourse on branding has primarily focused on western developed markets where the origins of branding can be traced to ancient civilisation of Greeks and Romans (Keller, 2003; Sarkar & Singh, 2005). The phenomenon has evolved over various epochs resulting in different eras of focus. For example, the era of national manufacturer brands of the 1860s–1914 to the establishment of brand management standards from 1946 to the 1980s (Low & Fullerton, 1994). The American Marketing Association's (AMA) defines a brand as a name, term, sign, symbol, or design, or a combination of them which is intended to identify the goods or services of one seller or a group of sellers and to differentiate them from those of competitors (Keller, 2003). The definition has evolved and changed over time in response to developments such as growth of digital marketing (AMA, 1960, 2007).

The informal economy's strategic positioning in Africa's economic and social landscape creates a unique opportunity for marketers to explore the challenges and opportunities for brand building in this complex context. The purpose of this chapter is to expand the discussion on brand building in Africa from the vantage point of the informal economy to identify challenges and benefits and missed opportunities and prospects. A roadmap that can be used to accelerate and improve brand building in the informal marketing is then outlined. In so doing the chapter raises the following pertinent question: Could the informal economy be the key for marketers to unlock potential opportunities for tapping on the proverbial low hanging fruit for brand building among the often-ignored majority consumers in Africa?

The Informal Economy in Africa

The role and importance of the informal economy in Africa is underpinned by its connection to the livelihoods of most citizens on the continent. These consumers rely on the informal economy for diverse social and economic activities of which self-employment is the main one. Any reflection of the informal economy must acknowledge its complexity that is shaped by diverse external environmental variables. This complexity partially explains why the informal economy in Africa has received less systematic attention from marketing scholars and practioners compared to other regions such as Latin America. Africa's informal economy has diverse co-existence of small enterprises usually individually operated, street-vendors, non-governmental organizations and sophisticated social networks that link these actors (ILO, 2020a).

The International Labour Organization (ILO) has been the key institutional custodian of monitoring developments in the informal economy and regularly provides updates on trends in various regions in the world. In Africa's case, the ILO has consistently reported that informal employment in the informal economy is the main source of livelihoods for at least 85.8% of African men and women (ILO, 2020). Table 10.1 is a summary of the key indicators on the size and composition of the informal economy in the different regions of Africa.

Central and Western Africa have the largest proportions of informal employment for both males and females compared to Southern and Northern Africa. Women's participation in the informal sector is higher in all the regions apart from Northern Africa. These variations can be attributed to the different individual characteristics of the different actors in the informal economy and the nature of the institutional environment that is in place in countries in these regions. The different actors refer

Table 10.1 Key Indicators on the Size and composition of Informal Employment (2016–18) in Africa

Males	Females
82.7%—share of informal employment	89.7%—share of informal employment
% share of informal employment in total employment	% share of informal employment in total employment
Central—89.2%	Central—93.6%
Eastern—74.8%	Eastern—92.8%
Southern—54%	Southern—57.3%
Western—84.7%	Western—90.2%
Northern—68.6%	Northern—62%
Aged between 15 and 65–84.9%	Aged between 15 and 65–90.1%

Source ILO Brief (2020a)

to the workers, enterprises, public institutions, and other stakeholders such as the non-government organizations and private sector. The institutional environment refers to the diverse economic and social contexts, weak or inadequate regulatory framework, corruption, lack of enforcement mechanisms for laws, hostility to governance systems due to lack of transparency and accountability. This environment then becomes an enabler for increased informality in countries in the regions.

Characterising the Informal Economy in Africa

A key characteristic of the informal economy in Africa is its complexity and heterogeneity across the continent largely because informality cannot be measured by one criterion. The criteria that are used to conceptualise the informal economy includes the size of the business, registration with the government, and maintenance of honesty and complete accounts (Brutton et al., 2012; ILO, 2020a). Informal economy activities in Africa cover diverse sectors such as carpentry, craftwork, construction, foreign currency and import trade, restaurants, street vending, urban transportation, wholesale and retail trade and waste management (Arosanyin, 2010; Plooy et al., 2012).

A key economic space that has emerged in the informal economy is the mobile phone payment platform sector. Mobile phone companies have created various self-employment opportunities in distribution of mobile phone products that are central to their payment platforms. This has been particularly important in enhancing financial inclusion in the informal economy where formal banking services are difficult for consumers to access. The integration of payment systems using the mobile telephony networks across the continent has enabled the previously unbanked consumers to access some form of formal financial transacting services. Although the informal economy in Africa is heterogenous, there are some common features which have been identified in extant literature (Islam et al., 2017). These are outlined in Fig. 10.1.

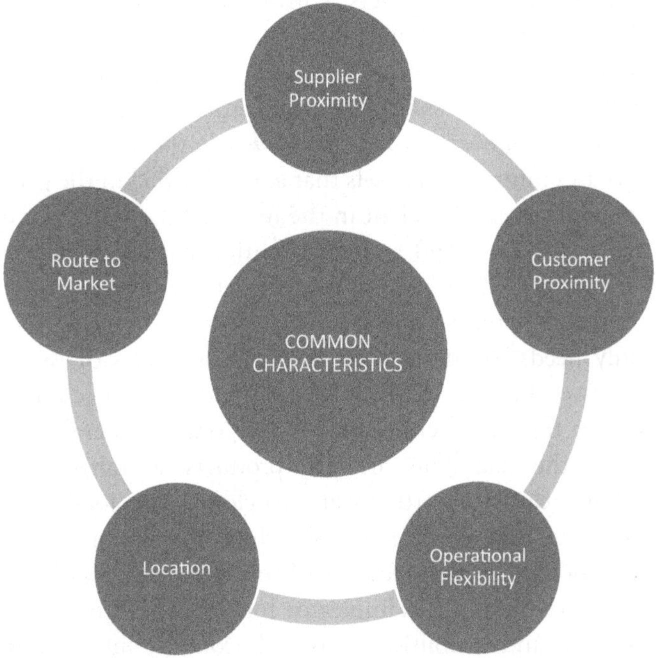

Fig. 10.1 Common Characteristics of the Informal Economy (*Source* Adapted from Islam 2017)

Enterprises and self-employed people in the informal economy have high levels of operational ***flexibility*** due to sole ownership and absence of legal registration which in turn minimises complex decision making. This flexibility also enhances ***customer proximity***. This proximity has potential implications for brand building because of the relationship and trust the enterprises and the self-employed create with customers which can influence product development and communication strategies. ***Proximity to suppliers*** is also key in the informal economy because of its implications on cost-effective strategies of serving the market, reliability of supplies and flexibility of supply terms given the constraints that are faced by enterprises delivering the variety of products and services. ***Location*** is a key differentiator in the informal economy. Actors such as small enterprises and the self-employed look for strategic high traffic locations from which to conduct their businesses. Key considerations include proximity to customers and suppliers, convenience (close to their homes), and flexibility to move without much cost. The diverse nature of business activities at play in the informal economy often require the need for mobility to do business hence consideration for the flexibility to be mobile. ***Access to market or route to market*** in the informal economy is diverse and uses informal channels that are embedded in the general flexible operational system prevalent in the informal economy. For example, proximity to customers and strategic location enables small enterprises and the self-employed to be able to deliver their products and services from various touchpoints.

One only needs to take a walk in the busy streets of Accra, Cairo, Dakar, Lagos or Luanda to see how men and women sell all kinds of products from the streets either on vending stalls or literally walking in the middle of the road. The variety of products can range from mobile phone recharge cards to bottled water to clothes and food items. Thus, there is a direct route to the market where interaction is direct with customers. The nature and structure of route to market varies across the continent where there are examples of higher concentration of mobile flexible markets and established informal economy market hubs where traders and the self-employed ply their trade. In Nairobi, Kenya there is a fledging informal market where customers can buy various household products in the Kibera slum area which is similar to the sprawling

Mbare Home Industry informal market in Harare, Zimbabwe where one can visit stalls selling diverse products such as building material and motor vehicle parts. In South Africa, migrant entrepreneurs from Somalia, Congo and Nigeria are the dominant actors in the informal retail grocery neighbourhood shops known as spazas which fill an important retail gap where formal large retail supermarkets are not available. In Kinshasa in the Democratic Republic of Congo there are more than 400 markets and over 1 million traders serving the city of more than 10 million with various products. In Cairo, Egypt the Talaat Harb Street markets are flourishing markets strategically located in a busy neighbourhood whilst in Rabat and Casablanca in Morocco, informal markets are strategically located around tourist hubs that sell products ranging from clothes to craftwork targeting tourists. In Luanda, Angola, at least 42% of families rely on the various informal markets for supply of their day-to-day provisions and other needs. High foot traffic is a common factor in all the examples identified above.

Across Africa, there are various informal market hubs where economic activities such as retail, wholesale and various services are provided making these hubs key sources of livelihoods. A list of some of these markets is outlined in Table 10.2.

Key Actors/Stakeholders in the Informal Economy

An understanding of the key actors and stakeholders of the informal economy is important in creating a foundation for innovative brand building. There are various actors in the informal economy but the main ones who are central to how the space functions are discussed here.

The Bottom of Pyramid Citizens. The major actors in the informal economy are the bottom of pyramid (BOP) consumers who survive on less than $2.50per day and represent over 2.7 billion people in the world (Hammond et al., 2007; Hart, 2002; Prahalad & Hammond, 2002). These citizens are active in the informal economy via various roles, namely as consumers of products and services that are generated in the economy and as self-employed owners of small enterprises that operate in the various economic activities in the informal economy. An

Table 10.2 Examples of Key Informal Market Hubs in Africa

Country-City	Market
Abidjan-Cote Divoire	Grande Marche De Treichville
Accra-Ghana	Accra Streets Informal traders Kantamanto Market Kumasi Central Market
Addis Ababa-Ethiopia	Merketo
Algiers-Algeria	Cub 1 Local Market
Bamako-Mali	Bamako Market Bamako Pink Market
Cairo-Egypt	Cairo Bazaar Markets
Dar es Salaam-Tanzania	Kariakoo Market Msasani Area Market
Harare-Zimbabwe	Mbare Siyaso Market Budiriro Home Markets
Johannesburg-South Africa	CBD Informal traders
Kampala	Owino Markets Kampala Street MArkets
Khartoum-Sudan	Ombudurman Market
Kigali-Rwanda	Kimironko Market
Kinshasa-DR Congo	Central Market Gambela Market Wood markets
Lagos-Nigeria	Eko Farmers market Oyingbo Makoko Mile 12
Luanda-Angola	Luanda CBD informal traders
Lusaka-Zambia	City Markets Roadside Chongwe Markets
Maputo-Mozambique	Central Market
Marrakech-Morocco	Marrakech Market
Nairobi-Kenya	Kibera Markets Maasai Markets Marikiti Markets
Tunis-Tunisia	Tunis Market
Yaounde-Cameroon	Buea Central Market Mokolo Market

important characteristic of the BOP which is pertinent to brand building in the informal economy which is not well covered by extant literature is its heterogeneity.

The BOP in the different African countries is comprised of various intra-country heterogeneity even though the whole group is conceptualised or defined by the globally and contentious daily income threshold. Common heterogeneous groups of the BOP that are prevalent in Africa are the urban based group and rural based group. The urban group is made up of citizens who are based in urban areas and are likely to be residing in high density residential areas such as Kibera in Nairobi, Dansoman in Accra Ghana or Soweto in Johannesburg or Makoko in Lagos. Residents in these areas are a mixture of those born in these areas and those who have migrated from other areas—mostly smaller towns and rural areas in search of opportunities for better livelihood. They are likely to find themselves resorting to the informal sector through self-employment or working for the informal enterprises that operate in this space.

The rural based BOP is made up of those who are permanently residing in the rural areas and are active in various activities mostly related to small-scale agriculture. This group is also a key supplier of agriculture produce to the informal businesses located in urban areas. The BOP is a key point of contact for any formal businesses that interact with the informal sector via the different roles such as distribution which in turn creates opportunities for innovative brand building strategies. A key group in both the urban and rural based BOP groups is the youthful groups of millennials and Generation Z. These two groups have different product tastes and relationship with brands compared to older generations and provide an opportunity for marketers to re-think their brand building approaches in the informal economy to reach out to these groups.

Business Enterprises. Small informal business enterprises are the key forms of business enterprises that are active in the informal economy in Africa. These cover diverse areas of business activities that have been mentioned earlier in the chapter. These include wholesale and retail, distribution and trade areas such as carpentry, construction and various repair services. These enterprises provide employment and income for the BOP citizens who are active in the informal economy.

An important role that is played by these enterprises is in facilitating interaction between members of the informal economy and other formal large and small business enterprises. Multinationals like Nestle and Unilever have effectively used these enterprises and individuals as a key distribution channels for their products to the BOP. Iconic brands such as Milo, Nido, Maggi, Surf and Omo are available from the swathe of informal markets across the continent in Accra, Lagos, Doula, Dar es Salaam, Lusaka, Addis Ababa and Maputo. The same applies to domestic multinationals such as MTN and Safaricom in mobile phone services. By default, formal enterprises are effectively finding themselves dealing with questions on how to effectively build their brands in this space because of its proximity to key target segments of the BOP. This further reinforces the need for a more deliberate discussion on the need for a roadmap for brand building in the informal economy which is the overarching objective of this chapter. The dynamic and complex context of the informal economy challenges formal enterprises to constantly review their brand building strategies in the informal economy.

Networks. The complexity of informality in the informal economy creates opportunities for developing various coping mechanisms for the enterprises and self-employed. A key coping mechanism is the different formal and informal social networks that are common in the informal economy. These networks facilitate information exchange, access to capital and interaction with supplier-firms. Members of the informal economy form social networks such as informal familial ethnic groups in their different areas of residence and operations. These are often based on ethnic kinship and links to one's rural connection in the case of those urban based BOP who would have migrated to urban areas. Other formal social networks that are active in this space include self-help groups such as savings clubs which are then used to provide access to capital for the members. Others are structured around the various areas of business specialisation, for example carpenters and furniture makers might create a network group that can be useful in securing bulk procurement of raw materials. Extant BOP literature covers this area of study indicating the strength of these social networks in creating bonds and trust among the members who have to deal with constraints of informality (Casson et al., 2009; Chikweche, 2013; Fafchamps, 2004). In Francophone West Africa, there are kinship driven informal trading networks that are used to facilitate cross-border trade amongst groups such as the Yourba in Nigeria, Benin and Togo and the Mourides in Senegal and The Gambia (Benjamin & Mbaye, 2012). These networks become key supply chains to the various informal markets in these countries and their strength is in the unwritten rules and commitment that is cemented by the strong kinship bonds.

Other External Actors. Non-governmental organizations (NGOs) and social enterprises are examples of other external actors that often tap into the informal economy in Africa for several reasons. These range from philanthropic initiatives such as helping out marginalised groups among women and youths to set up their own enterprises in the informal economy to private sector partnerships that seek to reduce levels of informality by converting informal businesses to formal businesses. In some cases, these NGOs operate as alliance partners with formal established enterprises such as multinationals to exploit opportunities in the informal economy (Webb et al., 2010).

The Contextual Challenges of the Informal Economy

It is important to recognise the contextual constraints that are prevalent in the informal economy in Africa because these can impact on marketers' branding strategies. The primary drivers of informality in Africa are linked to several linked macro and micro variables. The core ones are related to the economic, political, regulatory and policy limitations that are prevalent in most African countries. Combined with micro -level constraints such as limited access to education, entrepreneurial business services, capital and general high levels of poverty, informality levels tend to be high in Africa. Poor investment in technical and vocational training together with weak alignment to the labour market's needs results in Africa's youth being excluded from the limited formal employment market. The general lack of investment in public infrastructure and technology by African countries coupled with unattractive investment climate has resulted in acceleration of informality. This leaves the informal economy as the only source of livelihood for most African citizens. Rapid and often uncontrolled urbanization across mega cities such as Cairo, Kinshasa, Lagos and Nairobi has also accelerated the growth of the informal economy bringing pressure on already under pressure infrastructure.

These shortcomings are amplified by the general weak governance and institutional support systems indicative of aspects of state failure across the continent (Ishengoma & Kappel, 2006; Kanbur, 2009; Perry et al., 2007). This can be reflected in infrastructure-related challenges and disruptions such as lack of utilities (water, electricity, telephone) or where they are available, they are either inconsistent or unreliable or expensive thereby causing disruptions to any forms of businesses. Unlike the formal often large enterprises, informal businesses do not have the resources to invest in coping mechanisms such as generators or boreholes.

The onset of the COVID-19 pandemic disruption had significant implications on the informal economy across Africa. The ramifications in the post-COVID era have the potential to influence how marketers develop branding strategies in the informal economy. The containment and mitigation strategies that were put in place by African countries essentially amounted to shutting down the informal economy. The contextual structural challenges of the informal economy meant that the actors were incapacitated from using coping mechanisms used by the formal sector such as capacity to operate virtually and leveraging e-commerce. For example, the lockdown measures in urban settings literally closed business in the informal economy due to the high concentration of human traffic and the potential for these spaces to be super-spreaders. For example, in areas such as Kibera in Nairobi, or Dansoman in Accra or Mbare in Harare or Msasani in Dar es Salaam, these measures essentially eliminated the source of livelihoods for the self-employed and small enterprises in the informal economy (ILO, 2020b; World Bank, 2020). Considering the scope of actors in the informal economy, various opportunities for branding strategies can be identified by marketers for future proofing in the event of other disruptions emerging. Any branding strategy initiatives considerations for the informal economy must be framed in the context of the possibility of different forms of disruptions.

Firms' Interaction with the Informal Economy-Branding Perspectives

There are very few studies in marketing that focus on branding in the informal economy with the exception of studies that focus on branding to the base of pyramid and by extension make some reference to the informal economy (Biswas & Alam, 2015; Chikweche & Fletcher, 2011a, 2011b; Rajagopal, 2009). Branding is generally associated with the formal large businesses and not necessarily actors in the informal economy. However as noted earlier in the chapter, the interactions that take place between the different actors in the informal economy provide insights on potential branding implications. Earlier in the chapter reference was made to how multinationals use the informal economy as a route to market their products to the BOP customers thereby requiring clear brand strategies. NGOs and social enterprises also enter alliances with these firms to leverage their brands in the informal economy. However, there is no definitive roadmap on how these interactions can be consolidated into a framework that can be used for enhancing branding in the informal economy. Interactions that occur between the consumers in the informal economy and a variety of brands create a basis for an in-depth understanding of what this means in the big picture of how these brands develop strategies that can be effective in developing loyalty and brand equity in the informal economy. At an enterprise level, the informal enterprises operating in the informal economy that act as distribution channels for established brands adapt various branding strategies in the different stages of their life cycle which have to be reflective of the formal enterprises' brand strategy.

Therefore, a complementary interaction that formal enterprises must undertake involves interacting with the informal enterprises in the informal economy that are a gateway for their route to market in the informal economy. This places more importance on the relationships that exist between these actors because the formal enterprises must have confidence and trust in the custodianship of these brands by the informal enterprises. But whether these enterprises are effectively integrating this consideration in their branding strategy for the informal economy is an area that can form a basis for outlining a potential roadmap for brand building in the informal economy. The interactions between the formal firms and the informal economy are also influenced by the contextual constraints that have been discussed.

The contextual challenges and drivers of informality and interactions of firms with the informal economy create a foundation for marketers to reflect on the potential benefits and missed opportunities from the informal economy. Thus, a discussion or introspection on some of the benefits of the informal economy is useful in justifying the reason for marketers to consider developing branding strategies that are responsive to the nuances of this environment. The informal economy is at the centre of provision of livelihoods for most consumers in Africa, thereby creating a market for a variety of products and services targeting a wide profile of customers. This is a clear benefit of growth in markets for formal established business such as multi-nationals and domestic businesses. The general discussion on the informal economy currently focuses on the informality and lack of direct tax payments to governments. This argument misses the all-important contribution this sector makes to livelihoods through self-employment and entrepreneurship and consumption of products and services. These can cumulatively have an overall impact on these countries' growth in various ways such as economic growth and social cohesion.

Informal enterprises in the informal economy create new customers and engage with their communities in ways that have created opportunities for firms that interact with these enterprises to develop new products and scale up their operations. With the continued growth in urbanization across Africa and the youthful population that is forecasted to continue to grow (African Union Commission, 2019), the informal economy has the potential to continue to create more jobs and directly and indirectly contribute to economic growth. The informal economy's concentration in diverse sectors such as retail and wholesale and non-tradeable services sector enhances its prospects for providing opportunities for marketers to develop innovative branding strategies.

Although the COVID-19 pandemic disrupted the informal economy disproportionately compared to the formal economy, there are potential positives in terms of opportunities that could emerge for marketers to re-think their branding strategies in that space. The pandemic challenged marketers to re-think how they could empathise with consumers and informal business enterprises in the informal economy. This reflection can form the basis for developing post-COVID branding strategies drawing on lessons learnt from the pandemic. Central to this process is the need for brands to re-think how they engage with the stakeholders in the informal economy ecosystem in a way that can bring them closer to understanding and responding to the nuances and complexities that are prevalent in this sector. Local African brands' proximity to the informal economy places them in a vantage point to shape or influence how brands can engage the informal economy in a more engaged approach in the post pandemic era. Informal businesses face the same challenge of growth and sustainability just like the formal enterprises and with that comes challenges for branding or opportunities for leveraging their role in supporting formal established brands. This together with other prospects is an area of opportunity that marketers could explore in the broad conversation on the benefits of the informal economy.

A Roadmap for Innovative Brand Strategies/Building in the Informal Economy

The synopsis and reflections of the informal economy confirms the diversity and heterogenous nature of the sector highlighting current contextual challenges, nature of interaction between stakeholders in the sector, benefits, and opportunities for marketers to revisit branding strategies in this sector. A key starting point in addition to what has already been outlined in this chapter such as the benefits and identification of stakeholders is the need to identify trends and enablers that are shifting the paradigm for branding in the informal economy.

Trends That Are Shifting the Paradigm Towards Branding in the Informal Economy

Fragmented but Connected Consumers. Urbanization and expansion of the informal economy in a new digitalized world has created a mass of final consumers who are mobile and are bound to be found in various locations across African cities and rural growth points. This segment is a major growth area for marketers given the sheer numbers of BOP consumers who rely on the informal sector for their livelihoods. This in turn requires marketers to re-think their engagement of this audience in innovative ways that can entrench brand visibility and loyalty within the complex context of the informal economy.

A More Empowered and Discerning Audience. Digital technologies have expanded the realm of potential touchpoints for brands' connection with an increasingly more informed, discerning audience who have more options in terms of choice. These consumers are likely to engage in more screening of brands in their space and their loyalty cannot be taken for granted. This poses challenges for brands to re-frame their approach and narrative about what their value proposition is to engage this audience.

Pressure for Accountability in Face of Informality. The nuances and complexities of informality have been a traditional obstacle to marketers developing a clear branding framework for the informal economy. However, the continued growth of the sector and participation by key demographics such as the youth means marketers cannot ignore the informal economy neither can they have a haphazard unstructured branding approach in the sector. Pressure for accountability for return on investment in branding strategies has increased with the acceleration of interaction with the sector. The diverse customer journeys in the interaction with brands in the informal economy puts pressure on marketers to develop different metrics for measuring brand success in the informal economy that might be different to metrics used in formal markets.

The Enablers

Digital Transformation. The World Bank highlights opportunities for Africa arising from the digital revolution, which has seen increased demand and support for digital technology and led to growth in the digital economy (Lewis et al., 2017; Ndemo & Weiss, 2017b; World Bank, 2020). The bank and the Africa Union see this as a key potential source of benefits such as inclusive growth, innovation, job creation, service delivery, and poverty-reduction in Africa. Stakeholders in the informal economy are key actors in this digital revolution. The growth of mobile telephony in Africa has reconfigured the informal and formal economy in various ways. For the informal sector, mobile phones have improved access to telecommunication given the limitations of the dilapidated fixed telephone network system which has excluded the informal enterprises and self-employed from access to telecommunications. The key transformation that has emerged from mobile cellular growth is the introduction of payment platforms which has changed the way the informal economy conducts transactions and move money in the system.

Informal enterprises and BOP consumers in the informal economy have traditionally been excluded from formal banking systems due to their informality. This gap has been addressed by mobile money services such as SafariCom's Mpesa in Eastern Africa, South Africa's MTN services and Zimbabwe's Ecocash whose payment plans have enhanced digital financial inclusion. This is in the form of access to financial services such as transfers, savings, credit, and remittances from overseas relatives. These platforms now account for billons worth of dollars of transactions in both the formal and informal economy although the informal economy is the main domain for these platforms. The main beneficiaries of this digital financial inclusion have been youths, women, traders, and farmers who have managed to establish a variety of entrepreneurial entities primarily in the informal sector. Take for example Econet's Ecocash money transfer service that has not only enhanced financial inclusion in Zimbabwe but has also become the main source of payment considering the country's shortages of cash in the last decade.

These local brands have emerged to be leading brands in some of these African countries. For example Econet in Zimbabwe was the only local brand that was in spot number one in the last Africa top brands survey whilst Safaricom in Kenya and MTN from South Africa featured in the top ten of lists that were dominated by international brands (African Branding, 2020). This digital transformation has posed new challenges for marketers to re-evaluate their branding strategies considering the important role the informal economy now plays in their business models. However, despite this digital transformation, marketers have a limited understanding of the extent to which these digital technologies have shaped branding in the informal economy. The transformation of the digital economy raises several pertinent key questions for marketers' branding strategies in the informal economy. For example, what is the impact of these digital technologies on the nature of interaction between formal brands and the informal economy? Is there scope to define their role in enabling development of a branding roadmap for the informal economy which is inclusive of all the stakeholders in the informal economy. These are questions that are important in developing a framework for branding strategies in the informal economy.

Social Media-Disruption/Explosion. Although Africa currently has low internet penetration levels compared to other continents, this has not stopped its citizens from accessing the various forms of social media. Moreover, its real potential lies in the increased future prospects of a growing young population which is forecasted to become a quarter of the global population by 2025 with improved access to digital technology. There is also a direct correlation between the growth in mobile cellular telephony and increase in social media especially among the youths who are dominant actors in the informal economy.

All the major cellular networks like Econet, SafariCom, Airtel and MTN have a variety of pay as you go product bundles that give consumers options to use their airtime for popular social media applications such as Facebook WhatsApp, Instagram and Twitter. In fact, networks such as Econet have gone on to develop their own home-grown social media applications—like the Sasai application which competes with WhatsApp. Social media has assumed an important role in the informal economy through its use in communication and creating virtual marketplaces for informal economy stakeholders and acting as a catalyst for interaction between brands and the informal economy. Hence, any framework for branding in the informal economy must recognise the important role of the growth of social media use.

Towards a Framework for Brand-Building in the Informal Economy

Any effort by marketers to revisit the conversation on the importance of branding in the informal economy requires re-thinking the mindset and approach to branding. This must be embedded in acknowledging the nuances and complexities of the informal economy such as the contextual challenges represented by the informality drivers and enablers. These have the potential to influence the nature and scope of branding in the informal economy as outlined in Fig. 10.2.

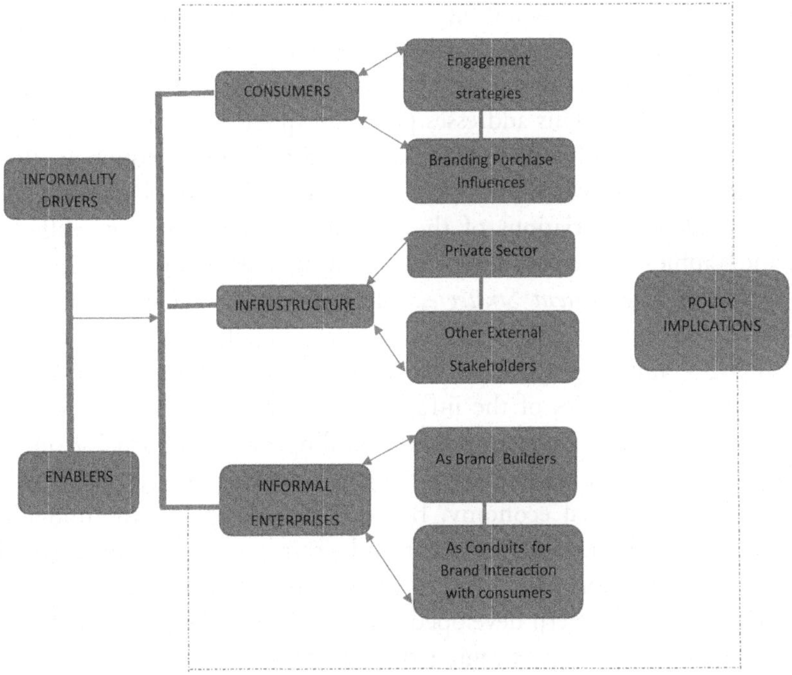

Fig. 10.2 A Framework for brand building in the informal economy

The framework outlined in Fig. 10.2 is an important starting point for developing a reference point for branding that can be used by marketers to integrate branding in the informal economy ecosystem in Africa. Hence the framework is inclusive in terms of identifying the roles of the different actors in this ecosystem including consideration of implications on policy given the potential role of the government in creating an environment that addresses some of the contextual challenges and promote brand building in the informal economy.

Consumers and Branding

The BOP consumers in the informal economy are the key consumers of products and services generated in this space by the informal enterprises and those that are provided by formal enterprises such as multinationals and SMEs. Marketers must develop innovative branding strategies that demonstrate an understanding of the nuances and complexities which these consumers deal with. Furthermore, marketers need to have an in-depth understanding of the perceptions and attitudes of these consumers towards branding. This addresses pertinent questions which will inform marketers on whether brands are an important consideration in these consumers' lives, what motivates them to make brand choices, and if there are any variations of these considerations across the different demographics of the consumers in the informal economy.

Inclusive Engagement Strategies. The contextual challenges of informality and subsequent enablers such as digitalization pose distinct challenges and opportunities for marketers to reframe their overall engagement strategies of the informal economy. This entails a context responsive or relevant approach to branding in the informal economy which is not necessarily one size fits all because of the diversity of the African informal economy. But one that recognises the underling nuances and complexities prevalent in the sector and whose focus should not be a replication of marketers' branding approaches used in formal economies and Western developed markets. There is scope for enhancement of a mindset of engaging the informal economy and its actors as equal partners who have a clear contribution to branding initiatives of formal enterprises that currently engage the informal economy at an arm's length pre-dominantly driven by third part facilitators.

When one looks at global multinationals of fast moving consumer goods such as Nestle and Unilever, one can note their recognition of the consumption potential of the informal market of their products as is evident in the presence of their brands across the informal markets in Africa. This engagement has been pre-dominantly through third part arrangements of distributors in the informal economy and in some cases creativity by both self-employed BOP and informal enterprises who bulk buy products and sell them at their stores. However, these actors do not necessarily have a direct relationship or interaction with manufacturers of these products and services even though they are indirect custodians of the brand in the market. As part of the inclusive engagement process, marketers will need to improve and introduce new approaches to their brand building strategies working with actors in the informal economy. This process should recognise strengths and limitations of some of the current strategies being used and look for opportunities to improve them and establish a clear more engaged relationship with the actors. Below are some of the potential initiatives that could form part of this re-thinking.

(a) Dedicated Internal Resources: A key element of this new approach to engaging the informal economy should entail re-visiting the approach to resource allocation for brand building purposes by firms. Part of the reasons for the lack of a structured and focused approach to brand building in the informal economy is due to lack of internal resources that are specifically dedicated to brand building initiatives in the informal economy. Marketers in Africa must avoid the cosmetic approach of allocating minimal resources to brand building initiatives in the informal economy. Concerns on difficulties of measuring return on investment in brand building in the informal sector are not entirely justified given the established fact that most of the BOP consumers are both consumers and entrepreneurs in the informal economy who constitute a key market for brands. Therefore, measurability challenges of return on investment assume a similar importance as in the formal economy and nuances of the informal economy can be mitigated by having dedicated resources to serve the sector. Current initiatives vary across industries and countries, but common ones include appointments of channel managers and in some cases business development managers. However, these roles do not have the same resources in terms of marketing budgets, supporting processes and systems which their counterparts who serve formal economy segments receive. Re-framing this important aspect of brand building is an important enabler for enhanced brand building in the informal sector in Africa.

(b) New Product Idea Generation and Co-Creation: The current focus of firms providing products and services to the informal economy is centered on the firms serving existing products to these consumers. This approach misses out on the opportunity of involving these consumers in new product idea generation which will result in development of products that are relevant to these consumers. This should be extended to involving the consumers in co-creation of these products. This has the potential of developing brand loyalty to these brands because of the investment the consumers will have in the brands. Formal enterprises already have a foundation from which to extend this strategy in areas where they are already involving consumers in the informal markets in brand building. This can include product testing and promotion using social networks such as women's clubs and other self-help networks. This is evident for food brands such as Maggi that have gone on to introduce small store keeping unit packages targeting the informal sector. But the initiative must extend beyond just limited initiatives such as the packaging issue.

(c) Re-Imagining Experiential Marketing Based Brand Building: As an extension of the co-creation approach, there is scope to expand the use of experiential marketing in the informal economy considering the nuances of the consumers. Real life focused brand building strategies are likely to be more effective in the informal economy because of the premium that is placed on word-of-mouth communication and the desire by consumers to feel and try products before purchase. This is likely to enhance brands' positioning in the consideration set of consumers when it comes to purchase decision making. Trust and creating bonds in relationship building is important in the informal sector because of the absence of enforcement tools that are common in the formal economy. There is a need for marketers to enhance authenticity of their engagement of consumers in the informal economy by expanding current scope of experiential brand building activities. For example, more focus on direct marketing activities such as roadshows in informal market hubs where consumers get to taste products at idea generation stage as co-creators is important. This can then be extended and integrated in marketing communication activities such as drama skits and storytelling of brands that capture how these consumers use these products. A key element of this process should be the integration of informal economy consumers in these initiatives whereby the actors and storytellers actually belong to these informal economy hubs. The actors should be involved in the actual design and execution of the campaigns. This will reinforce the authenticity of the message which the brands will be delivering. Across Africa's informal economy hubs, consumers (especially the youths) develop variations of catchy slang which becomes part of the lingo that is trendy and used and seen as part of their identify. This can be integrated in the messaging of the experiential marketing activities which in turn can create trust and connection for the brands that will be featured in these campaigns.

(d) Leveraging Integrated Digital Platforms in the new Gig Economy: The digital economy in Africa provides opportunities for marketers to leverage the increasing influence of digital platforms in the informal economy to enhance brand building initiatives. Marketers can harness the other engagement strategies such as allocation of dedicated resources to expand the scope of their brand building initiatives using digital platforms. Digital platforms are a key component of the enablers of brand building in Africa as evident from earlier discussions in this chapter. Technology is the next frontier of 'hanging fruits' for marketers in the informal economy especially when interacting with the youths in this sector who are already interacting with digital platforms in their operations in the informal economy. Therefore, engagement strategies for brand building in the informal economy must tap into this enabler to enhance brand visibility and equity.

Moreover, technology is creating new opportunities in the gig economy which serve the informal economy thereby creating opportunities for collaboration in brand building initiatives. For example, the growth of mobile money payment platforms, ride sharing, and e-commerce has expanded the scope of business activities that actors in the informal economy can participate in or serve their counterparts in the informal economy. The mobile money payment sector in Africa best demonstrates this synergy. African mobile phone networks such as Airtel, MTN, Orange and SafariCom have established thousands of formal small-scale distributors of their products who in turn sub-contract their business to millions of informal economy self-employed distributors. These distributors become brand custodians of these iconic brands. In the e-commerce space, Jumia the prominent platform employs more than 3000 people across Africa, but has extended its business through the more than 100,000 affiliates who overlap into the informal economy and play an important role in the platform's market penetration. The development of African social media platforms such as Sasai provide marketers with opportunities for enhancing digital word of mouth in the informal economy considering the already high usage of these platforms by both consumers and enterprises in this space.

Branding Purchase Influence

Extant literature has covered the importance of branding in contexts such as bottom of pyramid and general developing markets and by extension these studies have reinforced branding's importance in the informal economy (Chikweche & Fletcher, 2011a; Rajagopaul, 2009). However, there is gap in understanding what motivates consumers in the informal economy to buy brands, what are the drivers of their decision-making process and how is this shaped by the contextual challenges of informality? An understanding of these variables is an important component of re-imagining a framework for brand building in the informal economy. A study of African consumers by the Liberty Institute of Strategic Marketing indicated how consumers in the informal market considered brand origin, affordability and durability as core drivers that influenced their decision to purchase brands.

Income limitations and other contextual constraints inevitably make affordability of brands a key issue for consumers in the informal economy. This places an added challenge for providers of products and services to be creative in making their brands affordable. There is room to integrate the other engagement strategies discussed earlier to providing a framework for improving affordability of brands in the informal economy beyond current limited initiatives. For example, use of small store keeping disposable product formats such as sachets because this is not possible for the diverse products and services consumed in the informal economy.

More importantly the Liberty Institute of Strategic Marketing study demystified the assertion that consumers in the informal sector did not place importance on branding. Beyond the generic preference of branded products versus non-branded products, the origin of the brand was deemed a core driver for preferences and purchase. There was a definitive separation of preferences of international brands versus local brands with international brands featuring dominantly on the top for preferred brands. These findings are like those from the Africa branding report where the top ten brands were all foreign brands.

The common variable defining durability is related to the perception that branded products especially international ones could be used over a long period of time compared to non-branded products. Contrary to general perceptions, aesthetic appeal of brands is a variable that consumers in the informal economy also consider; although it might not be a core driver there is still a preference of branded products, given a choice. Informal economy consumers hold a general notion that manufacturers of branded products have invested more resources in enhancing the appearance of their brands which made them a standout from non-branded products. International brands were generally regarded to be more aesthetically appealing than local brands. The history and heritage of brands in the market is also a key consideration for consumers in the informal economy. This in some ways explains loyalty to traditional old iconic brands such as Omo, Surf, Maggi or Ricoffy. However, the youths are more likely to be open to trying out new emerging brands and their loyalty is not driven by the heritage factor as much as the older consumers. A framework for re-thinking brand building in the informal economy requires an extension of consumer knowledge on how the complex and ever-changing dynamics of the informal economy potentially influences these brand drivers since this will influence the strategies that will be used.

Infrastructure

The contextual challenges and drivers of informality that have been outlined clearly indicate the impact of weak public infrastructure in Africa which in some ways has contributed to the expansion of the informal economy. This limitation has implications on brand building in the informal economy. The private sector and other stakeholders have an important role to address this gap and by extension enhance branding in the informal economy.

Private Sector Role. The private sector represents the formal enterprises such as multi-national corporations, domestic conglomerates, retailers, and wholesalers and SMES. All these organizations interact with the informal economy in various ways. Key of which is through indirect distribution of products through the retailers and wholesalers and distributors active in the informal economy. Examples of brand supporting infrastructure includes reliable road networks, regular supply of water and sanitation, reliable power, and premises from which the informal economy actors operate. Whilst it remains the responsibility of the various forms of government to ensure that this infrastructure is available, the reality in Africa is that governments have limited resources and, in some cases, do not prioritise investment in these infrastructures.

This then poses challenges for the private sector to consider investing in these infrastructures. Why should Coca Cola,cNestle or Uniliver or MTN or SafariCom invest in public infrastructure, why is this important for their branding? By investing in reliable roads or power these brands will be enhancing access of their brands by the informal economy consumers. Products that require a cold chain will have prospects for longer shelf life if there is power which will enable refrigeration to be used by informal economy distributors. Good roads will enable quicker distribution of products in the informal sector. Electricity can create opportunities for more innovative marketing communications options, for example in outdoor advertising.

Africa has witnessed massive growth in the use of various formats of outdoor advertising by regional multinationals such as Alliance Media who have a presence in many African countries and are pioneering innovative formats of outdoor advertising in the informal marketing. But some of these formats such as illuminated street and market signs, and mobile billboards require reliable electricity. Informal economy hubs in cities like Accra, Lagos, Kinshasa and Nairobi operate on a 24-hours basis thereby creating an opportunity for brands to promote their products the whole day but this is limited by the lack of supporting infrastructure. Lack of clean water can impact on opportunities for experiential marketing through wet sampling or demonstration of product use in the case of food related products, yet this is a key mechanism for engaging consumers in the informal economy. Thus, it is in the interest of private sector actors to consider partnering with governments and other stakeholders in investing in infrastructure in the informal economy which can enhance their brand building initiatives.

Other Stakeholders. Non -governmental organizations and social enterprises are examples of other key stakeholders that are active in the informal economy. These actors need to re-visit their current role of facilitating interaction between the informal economy and the formal economy. For example, both groups are active in working with various forms of social networks in the informal economy linking them to various marketing activities of formal enterprises such as research and in some cases advancing self-employment among youths and women. Critics of this model highlight ‘the cannibalization ’nature of this intervention whereby the NGOs focus more on leveraging the benefits of these networks for their purpose rather than improving the whole ecosystem of the informal sector. For example, they could contribute towards consolidating private-public sector partnerships in improving infrastructure in the informal economy which will then enhance win-win situations for brands and the informal economy. Social enterprises could play an important role in enabling the capacities of informal enterprises to build their own brands that are relevant to the needs and preferences of the informal economy.

Informal Enterprises

The informal economy in Africa has thousands of informal enterprises that are active in diverse business activities that have been mapped out in this chapter. These form the backbone of the informal economy because this is where the self-employment primarily occurs. Thus, they assume a very important role in any framework for building brands in the informal economy from two perspectives. First in their role as conduits for facilitating access to brands from the formal economy and second in their own potential to develop local brands in their various business activities.

As Conduits for Facilitating Interactionbetween Formal Brands and Consumers. The established but non-recognised role of informal enterprises is how they are conduits for facilitating access of brands from formal enterprises into the informal markets thereby indirectly becoming custodians of these brands by default. Across various sectors, manufacturers distribute their products in the informal economy through self-employed individuals and informal enterprises. An effective framework for brand building in the informal economy needs to harness the important role of the informal enterprises beyond just using them as ad hoc/silent partners but integrating them into the brands' systems and structure. This will create a foundation for the brands to train these enterprises on their branding strategies, provide them with support and resources that can enhance the formal brands' capacity to grow their brands and to measure the impact of their engagement of the informal markets. Informal enterprises can be an important cog in formal brands' experiential marketing strategies in the informal economy given their proximity to the consumers and their in-depth knowledge of these consumers and nuances of the informal economy.

Brand Building Role. Informal enterprises in Africa can change the branding landscape by extending their role beyond just being conduits or facilitators of interaction between formal enterprises and the informal economy to that of establishing locally relevant domestic brands. These enterprises already engage in small scale development of their own products with some limited investment in branding but there is scope for these enterprises to begin to look for opportunities to leverage their local knowledge of the nuances and opportunities present in the informal economy. Informal enterprises have the potential to play a leading role in frugal innovation given their experience in this space. In fact, the informal enterprises do not get credit for influencing formal enterprises' innovations of bulk breaking products to develop small affordable units such as sachets targeting BOP consumers. These are adaptations that have been made by formal enterprises literally copying what they see informal enterprises doing.

Informal enterprises in Africa could play a key role in branding in the informal economy by entering win-win partnerships with formal enterprises to develop new products and brands whose identity and soul will be associated with the informal economy. Whilst research on brand preferences by consumers in Africa indicates a bias of preference for international brands, this does not diminish the potential of local brands if they are durable and affordable. These enterprises should leverage their current engagement with formal enterprises to develop their skills in building winning brands in their sector that are home grown and involve co-creation by the consumers in the informal economy with a distinctive African narrative. This can contribute towards how marketers re-imagine what brands stand for and represent in the context of the informal economy.

Role of Government

Debates on the role of the government in the informal economy is on-going and permanent in areas such as economics. Whilst there is some consensus on the contribution of the informal economy, there is no consensus on other policy implications that can support the sector.

This is no different for branding, which is why the suggested framework for a roadmap for branding in the informal economy recognises the importance of a conducive policy environment as an enabler for the strategies that have been outlined in the framework. The suggested interventions in the framework clearly require policymakers to engage the stakeholders and create a conducive environment that will support branding initiatives in the informal economy. This could cover areas such as facilitating private-public sector partnerships that will promote investment in supporting infrastructure such as power, water and roads which have been highlighted as being important for brand building.

The government is the custodian of laws that guide the informal economy in Africa and by extension influence the drivers of informality. Therefore, it is important for government to consistently review the regulatory environment in order to minimise disruptions to the informal economy and to mitigate some of the impact of informality which could affect branding initiatives in the informal economy. The same applies to enablers such as the digital economy; this is a grey area which governments are getting used to and revisiting their regulatory framework in this space. Considering the important role of digitalization, policymakers need to continuously review laws in the space and create opportunities for the informal sector not to be constrained by laws in their effort to support brands leveraging digitisation. Support for the informal economy by governments should not be limited to the traditional formalization route because that is not a practical one size fits all approach, given the complexities of the sector and its embedded important role in many African economies. Any initiatives to support the informal economy's capacity to enhance brand building should be undertaken from a holistic approach which addresses other established gaps such as lack of infrastructure and general improvement of supporting institutions and governance framework in Africa.

Glossary Terms

AMA American Marketing Association
BOP Bottom of Pyramid
ILO International Labour Organization

Bibliography

African Business. (2020, June). A challenging decade for brands, No.474.

African Development Bank. (2011, April). *The middle of the pyramid: Dynamics of the middle class in Africa* (Market Brief). African Development Bank.

African Union Commission. (2019, September). *Africa's Future: Youth and the Data Defining their lives* (Policy Brief). African Union Commission, Addis Ababa, Ethiopia.

American Marketing Association. (1960). *Marketing definitions: A glossary of marketing terms.*

American Marketing Association. (2007). *Definition of brand* (AMA's online dictionary). https://marketing-dictionary.org/b/brand/

Arosanyin, G. T. (2010). Earnings from commercial motorcycle operations in Ilorin, Nigeria: A study on determinants. *Ghana Journal of Development Studies, 7*, 53–66.

Benjamin, N., & Mbaye, A. A. (2012). *The informal economy in Francophone West Africa,Firm Size, Productivity, and Institutions.* Agence Française de Developement and the World Bank.

Biswas, K., & Alam, M. S. (2015). A case approach to test the potentials of transformation from informal into formal sector: A snapshot from Dhaka Metropolis. *Contemporary Issues in Business Research, 1*, 61–72.

Bruton, G. D., Ireland, R. D., & Ketchen, D. J., Jr. (2012). Toward a research agenda on the informal economy. *The Academy of Management Perspectives, 26*(3), 1–11. https://doi.org/10.5465/amp.2012.0079

Casson, M. C., Marina, D. G., & Uma, S. K. (2009). Formal and informal institutions in development. *World Development, 38*(2), 137–141.

Chikweche, T. (2013). Revisiting the business environment at the Bottom of the Pyramid (BOP)—From theoretical considerations to practical realities. *Journal of Global Marketing, 26*(5), 239–257.

Chikweche, T., & Fletcher, R. (2011a). Branding at the base of pyramid: A Zimbabwean perspective. *Marketing Intelligence & Planning, 29*(3), 247–263.

Chikweche, T., & Fletcher, R. (2011b). Franchising at the Bottom of the Pyramid (BOP): An alternative distribution approach. *The International Review of Retail, Distribution and Consumer Research, 21*(4), 343–360.

Chikweche, T., & Fletcher, R. (2014). Marketing to the "middle of the pyramid" in emerging markets using a social network perspective. *International Journal of Emerging Markets, 9*(3), 400–423.

Deloitte. (2018). *Meaningful brands: connecting with the consumer in the new world of commerce.* https://www2.deloitte.com/content/dam/Deloitte/au/Documents/consumer-industrial-products/deloitte-au-cip-meaningful-brands-report-2018.pdf

Fafchamps, M. (2001). Networks, communities and markets in Sub-Saharan Africa: Implications for firm growth and Investment. *Journal of African Economies, 10*(2), 108–141.

Fafchamps, M. (2004). *Market Institutions in Sub-Saharan Africa.* MIT Press.

Ferman, P., & Ferman, L. (1973). The structural underpinning of the irregular economy. *Poverty and Human Resource Abstracts, 8*, 3–17.

Galdino, K. M., Kiggundu, M. N., Jones, C. D., & Ro, S. (2018). The informal economy in pan-Africa: Review of the literature, themes, questions, and directions for management research. *Africa Journal of Management, 4*(3), 225–258.

Hammond, A. L., Kramer, W. J., Katz, R. S., Tran, J. T., & Walker, C. (2007). *The next four billion.* World Resources Institute and International Finance Corporation.

Hart, S. H. (2002). *The world economic pyramid*. World Business Council for Sustainable Development.

Houston, J. (1987, September). The underground economy: A troubling issue for the policymakers. *Business Review*, 3–12.

ILO. (2020a, April 14). *The impact of the COVID-19 on the informal economy in Africa and the related policy responses* (ILO Brief).

ILO. (2020b). *COVID-19 crisis and the informal economy—Immediate responses and policy challenges.* ILO.

Ishengoma, E., & Kappel, R. (2006). *Economic growth and poverty: Does formalisation of informal enterprises matter?* (GIGA Working Paper 20). German Institute of Global and Area Studies.

Islam, T., Shahriar, S. H. B., & Alam, S. (2017). A transformation from informal to formal, where customer engagement is an issue: Case study on rise of Mr Burger (pp. 216–223). Paper presented at the second International Marketing Conference on Customer Engagement & Experience, IBS Mumbai.

Kanbur, R. (2009). *Conceptualizing informality: Regulation and enforcement* (Working Paper 09-11). Department of Applied Economics and Management, Cornell University.

Keller, K. L. (2003). Brand synthesis: The multidimensionality of brand knowledge. *Journal of Consumer Research, 29*(4), 595–600. https://doi.org/10.1086/346254

Lewis, R., Villasenor, J., & West, D. M. (2017). *The 2017 Brookings financial and digital inclusion project report: Building a secure and inclusive global financial ecosystem.* https://www.brookings.edu/wp-content/uploads/2017/08/fdip_20170831_project_report.pdf

Low, G. S., & Fullerton, R. A. (1994). Brands, brand management, and the brand manager system: A critical-historical evaluation. *Journal of Marketing Research, 31*(2), 173–190. https://doi.org/10.1177/002224379403100203

McGahan, A. M. (2012). Challenges of the informal economy for the field of management. *The Academy of Management Perspectives, 26*(3), 12–21. https://doi.org/10.5465/amp.2012.0104

Medina, L., Jonelis, A. W., & Cangul, M. (2017). *The informal economy in Sub-Saharan Africa: Size and determinants.* IMF.

Ncube, M. (2013, October 2). *The making of the middle class in Africa.* World Bank Blog. http://blogs.world-bank.org/futuredevelopment/ch/comment/84.

Ncube, M., Lufumpa, C., & Kayizzi-Mugerwa, S. (2011). *The Middle of the Pyramid: Dynamics of the Middle Class in Africa.* Africa Development Bank.

Ndemo, B., & Weiss, T. (2017). Making sense of Africa's emerging digital transformation and its many futures. *Africa Journal of Management, 3*(3–4), 328–347. https://doi.org/10.1080/23322373.2017

Perry, G. E., Maloney, W. F., Omar, S. A., Fajnzylber, P., Mason, A., & Saavedra-Chanduvi, J. (2007). *Informality: Exit and exclusion.* World Bank.

Plooy, A. T., de Jager, J. W., & van Zyl, D. (2012). Drivers of perceived service quality in selected informal grocery retail stores in Gauteng, South Africa. *Southern African Business Review, 16*, 94–121.

Prahalad, C. K. & Hammond, A. (2002). Serving the world's poor, profitably. *Harvard Business Review, 80*(9), 48–57.

Rajagopal. (2009). Branding paradigm for the bottom of the pyramid markets. *Measuring Business Excellence, 13*(4), 58–68.

Sarkar, A. N. & Singh, J. (2005). New paradigm in evolving brand management strategy. *Journal of Management Research, 5*(2), 80–90.

Shahriar, S. H. B., Sayed, A., & Sayeed, A. M. (2019). Branding in informal sector: Qualitative analysis from a developing country Perspective. *Sedme. Small Enterprises Development, Management and Extension Journal, 46*(3), 161–170.

Webb, J. W., Kistruck, G. M., Ireland, R. D., & Ketchen, D. J. (2010). The entrepreneurship process in base of the pyramid markets: The case of multinational enterprise/nongovernment organization alliances. *Entrepreneurship: Theory and Practice, 34*(3), 555–581.

Williams, C. C. (2006). *The hidden enterprise culture: Entrepreneurship in the underground economy*. Edward Elgar.

World Bank. (2020). *Assessing the economic impact of COVID-19 and policy responses in sub-Saharan Africa*. The World Bank.

11

Africa Is Not a Country: Rebranding and Repositioning Africa as a Continent

Emmanuel Mogaji

Introduction

What comes to mind when you hear about Africa? That's a question with diverse answers depending on your stake in the continent. Some may see it as a big country that always relies on aids and donations from developed countries, and some may consider it a third-world country. In contrast, many people may see it as a continent with diverse opportunities and prospects for growth. This answer is about the perception of the brand—Africa.

Aaker (2009) defined a brand as 'distinguishing name and /or symbol intended to identify the goods and services of one seller and to differentiate those goods and services from those of competitors.' Kotler & Keller (2016) further described a brand as a name, term, symbol, or design, or a combination of them, which is intended to signify the goods

E. Mogaji (✉)
University of Greenwich, London, UK
e-mail: e.o.mogaji@greenwich.ac.uk

S. Appau (ed.), *Marketing Brands in Africa*, Palgrave Studies of Marketing in Emerging Economies,
https://doi.org/10.1007/978-3-030-77204-8_11

or services of one seller or group of sellers and differentiate them from those of competitors. The American Marketing Association describes a brand as a name, term, design, symbol, or any other feature that identifies one seller's good or service as distinct from those of other sellers'; meanwhile, the Dictionary of Brand defines it as a person's perception of a product, service, experience, or organisation.' Also, Marty Neumeier, author of The Brand Gap, describes a brand as a person's gut feeling about a product, service, or organisation.' Jeff Bezos, the owner of Amazon marketplace, said, "Your brand is what other people say about you when you're not in the room."

While branding may be considered a distinguishing name and /or symbol intended to identify goods and services, there are possibilities to extend brands beyond products. Marketing researchers now agree that anything could be branded, including people, places and even a pandemic (Nguyen, 2020). Considering Africa is a place, place branding becomes relevant and applicable. Kemp et al. (2012, p. 508) positioned place branding on the "the principle that cities and regions can be branded" (Kemp et al., 2012) and Kerr (2006) defined it as 'the practice of applying brand strategy and other marketing techniques and disciplines to the economic, social, political and cultural developments of cities, regions and countries' (p. 278). Aitken and Campelo (2011) recognised that place branding is dependent on the relationships between the community, people and many other external stakeholders and recognise roles, responsibilities, relationships and rights as the 4Rs that shape place branding. While the discussion for place branding has shifted from tourism to business and marketing (Hanna & Rowley, 2008) and the need to create an attractive logo and a catchy slogan for a place (Kerr, 2006), this present study provides a different perspective. This is not an attempt towards destination branding of Africa or marketing the continent's assets or 'products', such as tourism, inward investment, culture and exports (Kerr, 2006) but to critically evaluate existing understanding and positioning of the Africa brand.

This chapter aims to discuss Africa's context as a brand and recognise the inherent challenges and the existing perception that has shaped the brand. The chapter seeks to theoretically position the different stakeholders and their impact on rebranding and repositioning the brand and

and to present relevant implications and recommendations for enhancing the Africa's brand value. This chapter contributes to existing knowledge on place branding, especially from a continent perspective, raises critical questions which challenge norms and suggest ideas for further research on the topic. Besides, it presents practical implications relevant for practitioners, policymakers and place branding researchers.

The rest of this paper is organised as follows. The next section presents Africa as a continent and highlights its historical context. Africa is subsequently presented as a brand, highlighting key distinct features. This section is followed by the stakeholders shaping the brand's perception. The prospects of Africa as a reputable brand are presented. This is followed by the critical implications and opportunities of the African brand and the concluding section.

Africa as a Continent

Settles (1996) posits that Africa's colonisation altered its history due to its influence on its political structure. As a result, modes of thought, ways of life, and cultural development patterns were negatively impacted. Africa is a diverse continent with different indigenous cultures, habits and religions overlain by the languages and political boundaries imposed by European colonialism (Freire, 2014). African economies were advancing before the colonial masters began exploiting the continent's economic, human, and physical resources solely for the colonising nation's benefit. In line with this, Africa's scramble and partition stifled the continent's economic system's natural development. The result was a technological and economic gap that continued to widen, the more the colonial masters exploited the region. In principle, Africa was reduced to a mere producer of raw materials and not an industrial capital. Due to this uneven distribution of proceeds and the increased vulnerabilities, Africa was ravaged by the consequences of underdevelopment due to lacking manufacturing capabilities (Settles, 1996). This was furthered by the slave trade that robbed the continent of the needed human capital to advance its economy. Hence, as the rest of the world progressed, Africa was locked in a stagnation state having had its resources exploited and its prospects of development hampered. Therefore, even as the individual countries acquired their independence, there was little that they could do to turn the economy around, at least not fast enough. As a result, a culture of reliance on the initial colonial masters was ingrained in African states, especially seeing that Africa had been isolated from the rest of the world.

As outlined by Papadopoulos and Hamzaoui-Essoussi (2015), this resulted in what is referred to as the continent effect whereby, products from other continents are perceived as being of superior quality compared to those produced on the continent. Collectively, this resulted in the perception of Africa as a poor and underdeveloped region. This reputation became characteristic of the continent and its countries for the larger part of its history until the recent past following the rise of the "African renaissance" characterised by systematic marketing efforts and development of the regions, especially regarding tourism, foreign investments, education, among others. As such, the dilapidation that has been most characteristic of Africa as a continent, as well as its member states, is a result of colonialism and its ills which locked Africa in a state of underdevelopment while the rest of the world continued to develop at a fast pace (Papadopoulos & Hamzaoui-Essoussi, 2015). However, as the individual countries began to stimulate the development of their local economies, Africa improved socially, economically, and politically. However, this development has been largely ignored by the same nations responsible for its dilapidation. But as Africa gets more control over its development and the overarching narrative over its state of development against that of the rest of the world, it is not only possible to right these wrongs, but it will result in the continent shedding its reputation as a poor and underdeveloped region and proving itself not only as a civilised region but also as the next major player in the world, both economically and politically.

Africa as a Brand

Consisting of 54 sovereign countries according to the United Nations, and with a median age of 19.7 years, Africa is the second most populous and second largest continent after Asia with over sixty officially recognised UNESCO World Heritage sites, such as the pyramids of Egypt, the city of Timbuktu, the slave castles of Ghana, the monolithic churches at Lalibela in Ethiopia and the continent's network of national parks (Freire, 2014). Most reports about the continent point to a great potential due to the existence of widespread factors of production, tourism prospects, and the relatively young and skilled population. However, most of what is known about Africa revolves around the issues that have historically plagued the continent: poverty, pestilence, war, corruption, and underdevelopment (Osei & Gbadamosi, 2011). International media has disproportionately focused on these factors because Africa is synonymous with these issues. As a testament to this, Western media channels such as CNN, the BBC, and the New York Times have been on the receiving end of backlash over negative reporting of the region. What is more, most Western media channels have perfected the art of generalising regional issues to the entire continent, which skews the world's perception of Africa. This is serious to the extent that many people in other regions worldwide perceive Africa as a single block oblivious that it is made up of several sovereign nations and that many times events in country do not necessarily translate to other nations.

The fact that Africa is not a country cannot be overemphasized—it is a continent with more than two thousand languages spoken according to UNESCO, making Africa the most multilingual continent in the world (Freire, 2014). Humans originated in Africa. Scientists have found that Homo sapiens evolved within a set of interlinked groups living across Africa (Scerri, et al., 2018); likewise, education has its root in Africa (Ndofirepi et al., 2020). According to Guinness World Records, the University of Al-Karaouine founded by Fatima al-Fihri in 859 AD in Fes, Morocco is considered as the "oldest existing, and continually operating educational institution in the world". The continent has also hosted global sporting events like the Football World Cup and Rugby World Cup.

The increased uptake and penetration of the Internet and smartphones in African states have also shaped the African brand. More information about the continent is being made available while its inhabitants are beginning to take back control by shaping perceptions of the region. What is more, the governments of the different countries are actively working to enhance their economic, social, and political standings and ultimately changing how Africa is perceived around the world. Hence, while the continent is not as primitive as the rest of the world has been led to believe for quite a while, there are still some challenges in transforming this perception to open the continent as a favourable destination for business opportunities. Reporting about Africa by other media channels, especially Western ones, has continually perpetuated the dominance/dependence relationship that historically characterised the region due to colonisation.

Therefore, regarding the prevalent perception about Africa, it does not accurately capture the continent's realities and the developments realised by different countries and the continent at large. Hence, in the interest of evaluating the challenges and opportunities in branding Africa, this section considers the continent's historical context and how it has influenced Africa's perception. In addition, the government's steps to improve the overall image of the continent will be evaluated as well as the influence of the Internet and social media in shaping the narrative about the continent. Hence, taking on a systems theory approach, this paper will evaluate how these factors have influenced branding efforts as well as the challenges and the opportunities for rebranding to ensure accurate representation both in the media and the minds of the world's population.

However, theoretical insights into branding Africa as a place is limited, and this chapter aims to contribute to the existing literature on this subject. Freire (2014) proposed a special issue inviting scholars and practitioners to submit articles to the *Place Branding and Public Diplomacy* journal, but the result was unfortunately disappointing as there was not enough quality submission to make the special issue. While the branding initiatives may be going on, it is essential to document these insights theoretically. Freire (2014) further argued that the concept of place branding is not as well grasped as one might expect in Africa. This presents a challenge for stakeholders to address this gap in knowledge and enhance our understanding of Africa's branding as a place.

Stakeholders in Shaping the African Brand

From the above evaluation, it is evident that branding Africa is complex. Historically, what has been known about the continent has come from Western media and scholars, which has disproportionately focused on the negative stories in the continent such as corruption, wars, and diseases. These factors have received widespread media attention with the positive ones being largely ignored. The result has been a significantly skewed perception of the continent. However, addressing this is not straightforward because of the introduced racialised dimensions that seek to present Africa as a primitive civilisation needing help. When this is coupled with the negative consequences of colonisation on the continent, especially access to resources and global markets, both the political and economic realities of the region have been negatively influenced. Though, since then, there have been significant governance and development gains that while they do not compare significantly against those of the rest of the world, when evaluated within the African context, are substantial improvements. In line with this, the biggest challenge for Africans has been regaining control over their lived experiences, including development and voicing their opinions on matters of interest to them. The essential role of stakeholder engagement in a place branding strategy cannot be ignored (Eugenio-Vela et al., 2020), suggesting the need to identify the stakeholders and how they can be engaged to enhance the brand. This section of the chapter highlights three key stakeholders in shaping the African brand.

Government

Marketing discourse describes branding as the process involved in creating a robust and positive perception of an entity (Aitken & Campelo, 2011). In line with this, while governments should tend to their population by enhancing their quality of life, they also have the mandate to strengthen their jurisdictions' social, environmental, and economic viability and sustainability. Poncian (2015) outlines that while Africa has been historically looked down upon by Western powers, Africans have also contributed to this progression. As such, how Africans perceive themselves before Westerners and how they seek to be perceived actively influences Westerners' views of Africa. Considering the importance of governance and economic policy on the development of a country, local and regional governments play a significant role in influencing how the individual countries and the continent are perceived by championing the activities that align with the intention. For instance, a country like Kenya has continually positioned itself with the digital transformation to the extent of earning the title "the African's Silicon Savannah" (Mallonee, 2018). This shows that a government has an inherent power and responsibility to improve peace and order and ensure good governance at the national level.

Therefore, based on the prevalent resources in a country, the local government should create an enabling environment that allows for utilising the prevalent resources while also marketing the country to the world in line with the competencies it holds. For instance, Libya and Nigeria are renowned as key oil producers, and Congo is known for minerals such as Cobalt, Nickel, and Gold. However, both countries' political climate is not stable due to the existing governance gaps. Therefore, it can be outlined that branding Africa will require consistent efforts by the governments not only to ensure law and order but also marketing a country based on its unique offerings which can either be its comparative or absolute advantage. Case in point, the Kenyan government through the Kenyan Tourism Board, launched the "Magical Kenya" initiative which aims to boost tourism in the country by not only describing the attractions in the country but also providing a database of safari operators and accommodation facility to make it easy for foreigners to travel and tour the country (Siele, 2020). What is more, the initiative is continually updated to ensure a comprehensive picture is painted on the expansivity of attractions through the creation of sub-brands such as "Kenya Coast" which is solely focused on attractions in the country's coast launched on October 29, 2020. On January 12, 2021, the English supermodel, Naomi Campbell, was appointed Magical Kenya's International Ambassador to promote the country as an ideal tourism and travel destination to the world (Njugunah, 2021; Siele, 2020).

Signe and Gurib-Fakim (2019) detailed a transformative period under which governments and other stakeholders ought to ensure the continent is better positioned to address both contemporary challenges whilst pursuing emergent opportunities. In line with this, governance is significantly linked to political stability which is a foundation for an enhanced economic climate. As outlined by *The Economist* (2020) governance and economic policy have contributed to the gap among the different countries in the continent with some getting richer and more democratic while others are locked in a perpetual state of poverty and do not have democratic systems of governance. Hence, individual African country governments are responsible for developing competencies and marketing these competencies to the rest of the world.

However, it is essential to note that these steps taken by the local governments are largely foundational. Hence, considering that Africa is mostly perceived as a block by the rest of the world, it is only fitting to have a body focused on selling Africa in its entirety by combining these national competencies to influence the prevalent narrative on the continent. This captures the role and responsibility of the African Union (AU), a pan-African organisation comprised of all African states. Its aim is political and economic integration to boost development, eradicate poverty, and enhance Africa's position in the global economy. Its role mirrors that of country governments with the only difference being the scope upon which it operates. Specifically, Kimenyi (2016) details that in addition to addressing the crises that have plagued African states, the AU is also supposed to coordinate continent-wide development agendas while also becoming the voice of Africans to the world on global governance matters. One of the ways this mandate should be fulfilled is the promotion and safeguarding of African common positions on issues of interest to the continent and its populace. This highlights the role of the AU in Africa's branding efforts of the continent since the perception and reputation of the continent and its member states is a key concern for the continent and its people as it influences the relationship between Africa and the rest of the world.

Nevertheless, it should be noted that the AU has not effectively met this mandate because of the collective laxity in taking action. However, it is important to note that the challenges faced by the AU in coordinating the different institutions and uniting Africans are twofold, that is, it required an in-depth understanding and appreciation of the diverse problems that face the continent, and having the requisite capacity to implement the needed policy and legal reforms (Kimenyi, 2016). Consequently, for the AU to promote and safeguard an accurate perception of Africa effectively, rebranding efforts should be informed by an extensive understanding of the problems that plague the continent. This should then be coupled with building the necessary competence to promote branding messages and actions as well as development efforts both within the continent and how this is manifested in the global relations between Africa and the rest of the world for which the AU is uniquely positioned to address.

Media

Isike and Omotoso (2017) assert that the role of the media in shaping perceptions of Africa to the world is tied to the role of communication in society as communication influences political and economic development. As such, by virtue of being involved in the handling and dissemination of information, the media has an innate power to influence political and economic development. Due to the information that is disseminated, the media controls what the public knows while also shaping their perceptions on the matter being reported.

In line with this, it is key to note how reporting about Africa has been covered in the media and its impact on Africa's perceptions. First, it is worth noting that comparatively, stories about Africa do not frequently appear on television in western countries' media stations (Norman Lear Center, 2018). When the stories about Africa are reported, if the overall message is not neutral, it has a higher likelihood to be negative. Even for scripted entertainment where Africa is mentioned, 35% were about crime. This shows that a typical viewer is more likely to see negative portrayals of Africa other than positive ones. What is more, 44% of scripted entertainment mentioned Africa without referring to a specific country (Norman Lear Center, 2018). When African nations are mentioned, roughly half of all mentions are of five countries: Egypt, Kenya, Seychelles, South Africa, and Congo. Therefore, while the content of media communication has been largely detrimental to the perception of people, especially perceptions Westerners have of Africa, it is key also to note that Africans have largely been robbed of the chance to control the narrative of the continent. In line with this, Adum et al. (2015) assert that negative narratives about Africa have been consistent with the interests of Western civilisations. Specifically, Western civilisation's key aim has been to create a culture of superiority whereby the media has been an instrument to present Africa as the opposite of their civilisations, hence the focus on negative coverage and representation of the continent. By making media coverage racialised, Western media present a supposed explanation that Africans' "backwardness" and "savagery" are biologically predetermined.

It is key to note that Western media's negative depictions have also resulted in the continent effect with these perceptions being generalised to all regions in Africa. These depictions negatively impact the lived experiences of Africans who live in Western countries since the opinions formed about the region and its inhabitants impact their future (Adekoya, 2013). An employer may be apprehensive about hiring an African because they believe they are not as skilled, or they are primitive. The same also impact Africa's shared perception in the global economy regarding its viability for foreign investments. While bad news sells, people feel much better about their lives if they believe they are leading better lives than others (Adekoya, 2013). However, the consistent negative reporting about the continent has resulted in the continent being perceived as unstable for foreign investments which has negatively influenced its development prospects especially considering the dilapidated state of most of these countries because of colonisation.

Nevertheless, it is not enough to blame all the prevalent opinions and thinking about Africa on negative reportage by Western media. It is also essential to evaluate the influence African media has had on this development. That is, to what degree they have enabled this or what they are doing to take back control of Africa's narrative. First, it is essential to note that due to the resultant dependence relationship between Africa and other continents, African media has had to capitalise on this relationship to enhance the chances of the continent getting foreign aid (Kwemo, 2017). As such, African media also disproportionately focuses on the challenges facing its countries and little time on the gains that have been made so far.

However, considering that bad news sells, and that Africans have little control over what Western media airs, it is only through African media that the continent and its member states can take back control over the continent's narrative. This is a sentiment shared by Adum et al. (2015). They declare it is essential for African journalists to practice development journalism by increasing their contribution in the coverage of developments by the continent, which is often not the focus of Western media. Tthe role of context cannot also be discounted. While Western media report about Africa from their perspectives, African journalists can document the prevalent conditions in the individual countries to offer the context based on which the rest of the world should evaluate the gains made by African countries while also informing the rest of the world on the key issues in Africa (Adum et al. 2015). This will result in a balanced discussion on African countries' strengths and weaknesses, resulting in a healthy debate on the degree of support the continent needs and ultimately transforming media into a tool for empowerment-based on social justice precepts.

The degree to which the media and communication environments are vibrant is vital for ensuring a developed and prosperous Africa. This is because, these can only be attained through a continuous political will and the establishment of a free and democratic society (Adum et al. 2015). The media is vital in attaining these ideals as it can influence the promotion of sustainable development, good governance, and fighting social ills such as corruption. Hence, Africa's negative narrative has primarily been a product of Western media with African media playing an enabling role. However, to change the prevalent opinion and thinking about Africa to the rest of the world, African media must regain control of the narrative by focusing more on the continent's positive and accurate reportage and its countries.

The role of the movie industry in shaping the narrative around the African brand cannot be overemphasised. African cinema and film industries engage in post-colonial mimicking of the West, with names mirroring Hollywood—there is Nollywood representing the Nigerian movie industry, Ghallywood in Ghana, Hillywood referring to films from Rwanda, Kannywood referring to the Hausa-language film industry of Northern Nigeria, based in Kano, Riverwood for films from Kenya. However, these film industries are also responsible for creating contents that are shaping the perspective of Africa. Onuzulike (2014) recognised the impact of Nollywood video film on African's culture and positioning. Endong (2018) also acknowledges that the film industry has become a transnational cinematic cardinal vector exporting African cultures to other parts of the world. The growing popularity of Netflix has further provided opportunities to shape the continent's narrative through various films and movies produced by Africans and shared on the streaming platform to many viewers around the world. Africans can now tell their stories and not rely on the west to create a different narrative.

Technology

According to Dwyer and Molony (2019), the Internet, specifically social media, has an inherent capacity to enhance access to information. By extension, this can influence politics within a region by expanding political participation. However, depending on how the narrative is phrased and who controls the dissemination of information, the Internet can either reinforce existing power structures and prevalent narratives or create new ones. Regarding branding Africa, Mkono (2018) asserts that the Internet presents diverse opportunities and avenues for Africans to change the African narrative since it offers them representational agency which is key in countering the prevalent negative stereotypes about Africa. Specifically, Africans capitalise on the blogosphere and social media to challenge the prevalent Afro-pessimism by creating new African narratives. In line with this, there is a collective move towards Afro-optimism which does not deny the continent's challenges but focuses on introducing multiple and complex images, stories, and narratives about the continent and its populace (Mkono, 2018). Due to the increased penetration of the Internet and supporting technologies such as smartphones, Africans are increasingly getting empowered to undermine the dark continent narrative. That is, by creating and distributing their self-representations, the Internet has become a democratising space whereby voices that were traditionally underrepresented now have an inexpensive and convenient channel for self-expression. By serving as a space to share routine experiences, ordinary persons are capturing positive human moments such as those of love, celebration, play, human interaction, and joy that media has not adequately focused on. By extension, this results in the creation of new narratives of Africa by resulting in some level of distancing from the pessimistic and stereotypical representation of Africa as a homogenous block characterised by lack of democracy, helplessness, disease, human rights abuses, and violence (Mkono, 2018).

Jamme (2011) who argues that Africans have historically needed an opportunity to engage and tell their own stories instead of letting someone else tell their stories or letting someone else tell them what to do. Through the different possibilities for self-expression such as blogs and social media, the Internet has presented a unique opportunity to engage and tell their stories themselves, which is enhanced by the increased access to computers, mobile devices, social networking sites, and internet connections (Jamme, 2011).

Africans are also using the Internet to hold different stakeholders accountable by ensuring transparency and consistency on how information about Africa and its member states is created and disseminated. Africans are beginning to hold their governments accountable for the adopted communication strategy they incorporate to promote Africa and its competencies. Local and regional alliances are not the only ones on the receiving end of this new-found self-expression. Western media have also been criticised over their negative reportage to ensure they stop perpetuating negative stereotypes about Africa. In 2015, through the hashtag #SomeoneTellCNN, Kenyans condemned CNN for referring to the country as a "hotbed of terror" before the visit by the then-president Barack Obama, despite US security officials confirming there was no security risk for the president (Dearden, 2015). Such examples show that social media is an avenue for self-expression and one to hold these media stations accountable and ensure accurate and transparent journalism. The hashtag #TheAfricaTheMediaNeverShowsYou has been used to highlight positive stories about the continent and its countries. Hence, through the young population's determination in controlling the narrative about Africa, and the alliance-forming capability of social networks, communities throughout Africa are taking action to influence the prevalent opinions and thinking about Africa (Mkono, 2018).

Therefore, the role of the Internet in rebranding Africa cannot be ignored. This is because, by supporting self-expression coupled with mass reporting, media channels are no longer the only source of information about the continent. Through the different opportunities offered by the Internet, notably social networking sites and blogs, Africans have taken charge of showcasing their countries and the continent at large to challenge negative reportage by most Western media channels and show the side of Africa that has been largely ignored. Moreover, since the Internet is increasing the interconnectedness of societies, it has made it easier to access information about Africa than was possible years ago. As such, the rest of the world can unlearn the negative stereotypes by acquiring more positive information about the continent, its countries, and people.

The Internet has also led to an increase in technology adoption and innovations in many emerging countries in Africa (Abdulquadri et al., 2021). To meet the growing need for Internet in this part of the world, the 2Africa subsea cable is being built around Africa, which will enhance connectivity across Africa and the rest of the world. At 37,000 km long, 2Africa will be one of the world's largest subsea cable projects. They will interconnect Europe (eastward via Egypt), the Middle East (via Saudi Arabia), and 21 landings in 16 countries in Africa (2Africa, 2021). There are growing investments in the technology landscape of Africa. Tech companies like Microsoft, Google and Facebook have offices across the continents and supporting the technology and innovation ecosystem. This has also opened an opportunity for global acquisition as seen with Stripe acquiring Nigeria's Paystack for $200M to expand into the African continent.

While the role of government, media, and technology has been identified in shaping this narrative around the African brand, many other stakeholders are worth mentioning. Education, Sports, Tourism and

Business organisations can also contribute to the enhanced brand. The dynamics in higher education and quest towards world domination in African higher education are recognised (Olaleye et al., 2020; Vasudevaz & Mogaji, 2020). Universities across Africa are striving towards building partnership with different universities across the world. International branch campuses are being opened in Africa to attract students from across the continent and meet the growing demands for quality higher education (Ndofirepi et al., 2020). Recognising the power of brands as a vector of the image, reputation, and competitiveness of nations, Brand Africa is also working on documenting strong brands emerging from Africa, promoting Africa's positive image, celebrating its diversity and driving its competitiveness (BrandAfrica, 2021). Many notable African sports personalities are making great exploits and contributing to shaping the narratives of the continent. The World Cup has been to Africa, the Basketball Africa League (BAL) is a brand collaboration with the U.S.'s National Basketball Association (NBA), and FIBA is Africa's premier men's basketball league.

Prospects of a Reputable African Brand

Enhancing the African brand has enormous prospects. Well managed brands are very valuable. They become significant assets for the owners. Branding adds value to what is branded, and the better the effort of brand management, the greater the value. Branding adds value to an asset, and it makes an ordinary brand becomes valuable, and people wants to associate with it (Mogaji, 2021). Rwanda, formerly Ruanda, officially the Republic of Rwanda, made a considerable effort to change people's perception in just over two decades following a devastating civil war. In 2018, the Rwanda Development Board, through their subsidiary, the Rwanda Convention Bureau, became the first official sleeve partner of English Premier League Arsenal Football Club as part of the country's drive to become a leading global tourist destination, using 'Visit Rwanda' messaging. This association (with Arsenal) support Rwanda's ambition to improve their county's brand value to build their tourism industry. "Before the partnership was signed, 71% of the millions of Arsenal fans worldwide did not consider Rwanda a tourist destination. At the end of the first year of the partnership, half of them considered Rwanda a destination to visit," said Belise Kariza, Head of RDB's tourism department. This shows that brand management helps a brand grow. It also endears a brand to users who might not ordinarily consider the brand in the first place.

Individual countries are bound to benefit from the right perception of the continent of Africa. There will be more private investment prospects with many investors willing to carry out business activities across different countries on the continent. There will be a more positive drive to explore bilateral economic agreement, especially when many other stakeholders outside Africa recognise what each country has to offer. When the right perception is crafted and delivered, the promotion and prospects for foreign direct investment (FDI) in Africa will be more enhanced, perhaps beyond what is presently offered by the Chinese (Donou-Adonsou & Lim, 2018).

While tourism is considered integral to economic activities in some Africa countries like South Africa, Kenya, Gambia and Egypt, an enhanced African brand is bound to ensure growth in the tourism sector. Other African countries will be better recognised and considered as a destination for tourism, to enjoy and explore nature, people and opportunities. This will ensure repeat tourism which presents a viable and steady income source for the host country (Van Dyk et al., 2019).

The educational sector can also benefit from the enhanced Africa brand. There will be prospects for international collaboration and exchange for staff and students. Perhaps this will curb the problematic presence of brain drain, which disrupts higher education and innovation in Africa (Ndofirepi et al., 2020). Researchers will be able to explore different opportunities that abound around the world without necessarily leaving their home countries. African universities can also benefit tremendously from strategic co-branding with academic and non-academic institutions worldwide (Kieu et al., 2020). African universities can also promote African programmes/initiatives/activities globally to attract an international audience and competition. There are, for example, enormous possibilities for an American student to come to

Africa to study Tropical Medicine, Yoruba language or Swahili, or any dominant African language that has been promoted globally.

Conclusion

The aim of this chapter was to evaluate the factors that have influenced the branding efforts, the challenges, and opportunities of rebranding in Africa. The chapter has discussed the rest of the world's negative perceptions about Africa that have resulted from the continent's (post)colonial racialised representations. To address this challenge will not be an easy feat and will require the responsible and conscious effort of many stakeholders to get this done. It will require ongoing efforts from the government, individuals, business organisations and even academic researchers, to create the narrative, effectively communicate, document action plans and evaluate progress. Every stakeholder must take the responsibility to lighten up their corner and as a whole change the perception about Africa.

In line with this, specific key opportunities arise regarding the role of national governments, the African Union, the media, and the Internet is challenging the negative stereotypes about the continent, its countries, and its people. The rebranding of Africa relies on Africans at different levels in society taking the initiative to ensure an accurate and consistent representation of the continent, its countries, and their people. As it can be inferred from the argument presented by Poncian (2015) on the enabling role that Africans have had in the perpetuation of these perceptions, there is a need for Africans at all levels to work actively to remedy the situation. Changing the perception of the African brand is not the sole responsibility of countries or the government. A holistic approach is expected; every stakeholder must recognize that things need to be improved and take responsibility for different actions.

Africans need to take control of the African narrative. This can be attained by capitalising on the self-expression opportunities presented by the Internet. People should continually capitalise on the power of the Internet by self-publishing stories that work to change Africa's narrative by presenting the positive stories of Africa. This should then be reinforced by African media focusing on the positive stories while both the local governments and the AU focus on ensuring social justice by improving the quality of life and social mobility for the people through effective governance and policy reforms. The AU should transform the political and economic realities throughout the continent and how other regions perceive Africa. Rebranding efforts should take a bottom-up approach to not result in the whitewashing of the challenges in Africa but ensure a balanced perception and debate about the social, environmental, and economic viability of the continent at large.

This chapter presents an effort to theoretically explore the Africa brand and highlights opportunities for future research. Following on from Freire (2014), future research needs to document place branding efforts conducted by different countries, regions and cities in Africa. The strategic marketing of destinations across Africa should also be empirically examined—to understand how different countries are positioning their place for investment, tourism and development. Furthermore, future research should examine the impact of education, tourism, sports, and entertainment on Africa's perception. The role that technology, growing access to the Internet, and social media iplay in changing attitudes towards the African brand should also be explored. Social media provides a unique opportunity for engagement and interaction (Gökerik et al., 2018); this understanding will contribute to the knowledge of different touchpoints that shapes the brand. Addressing these research gaps will ensure a more holistic understanding and preset practical implications for developing the Africa brand. More people must recognise the fact and must be continually reminded that Africa is not a country but a continent of many countries, each with its unique landscape, peoples, culture and values that are worth exploring and appreciating.

References

2Africa. (2021). *About.* [Online] https://www.2africacable.com/about. Accessed 2 February 2021.

Aaker, D. A. (2009). *Managing brand equity.* Simon and Schuster, New York.

Abdulquadri, A., Mogaji, E., Kieu, T. A., & Nguyen, N. P. (2021). Digital transformation in financial services provision: A Nigerian perspective to the adoption of chatbot. *Journal of Enterprising Communities: People and Places in the Global Economy, 15*(2), 258–281. https://doi.org/10.1108/JEC-06-2020-0126

Adekoya, R. (2013, November 28). *Why Africans worry about how Africa is portrayed in Western media.* Retrieved from The Guardian: https://www.theguardian.com/commentisfree/2013/nov/28/africans-worry-how-africa-portrayed-western-media

Adum, A. N., Emmanuel, N. M., & Ojiakor, O. E. (2015). Towards media of Africa by Africans and for Africans. *Journal of African Studies*, 1–9.

Aitken, R., & Campelo, A. (2011). The four Rs of place branding. *Journal of Marketing Management, 27*(9–10), 913–933.

BrandAfrica. 2021. *About Us.* [Online] https://www.brandafrica.net/AboutUs.aspx. Accessed 2 February 2021.

Dearden, L. (2015, July 23). *Kenyans ridicule US network CNN on Twitter for 'hotbed of terror' report*. Retrieved from Independent: https://www.independent.co.uk/news/world/africa/someonetellcnn-kenyans-ridicule-us-network-twitter-hotbed-terror-report-10410337.html

Donou-Adonsou, F., & Lim, S. (2018). On the importance of Chinese investment in Africa. *Review of Development Finance, 8*(1), 63–73.

Dwyer, M., & Molony, T. (2019, August 14). *Analysis across Africa shows how social media is changing politics*. Retrieved from The Conversation: https://theconversation.com/analysis-across-africa-shows-how-social-media-is-changing-politics-121577

Endong, F. (2018). Cinema Globalization and nation branding: An exploration of the impact of Nollywood on the Nigerian image crisis. *Journal of Globalization Studies, 9*(1), 77–90.

Eugenio-Vela, J., Ginesta, X., & Kavaratzis, M. (2020). The critical role of stakeholder engagement in a place branding strategy: A case study of the Empordà brand. *European Planning Studies, 28*(7), 1393–1412.

Freire, J. (2014). Place branding in Africa. *Place Branding and Public Diplomacy, 10*, 32–34.

Gökerik, M., et al. (2018). Surprise me with your ads! The impacts of guerrilla marketing in social media on brand image. *Asia Pacific Journal of Marketing and Logistics, 30*(5), 1222–1238.

Hanna, S., & Rowley, J. (2008). An analysis of terminology use in place branding. *Place Branding and Public Diplomacy, 4*(1), 61–75.

Isike, C., & Omotoso, S. A. (2017). Reporting Africa: The role of the media in (un)shaping democratic agenda. In A. Olukotun & S. A. Omotoso, *Political Communication in Africa* (pp. 209–227). Springer.

Jamme, M. (2011, June 17). *Africa's new generation is using social media to push for change*. Retrieved from The Guardian: https://www.theguardian.com/global-development/poverty-matters/2011/jun/17/social-media-transforming-communication-africa

Kemp, E., Childers, C., & Williams, K. (2012). Place branding: Creating self-brand connections and brand advocacy. *Journal of Product & Brand Management, 21*(7), 508–515.

Kerr, G. (2006). From destination brand to location brand. *Journal of Brand Management, 13*, 276–283.

Kieu, T., et al. (2020). Moving from research to practice: Marketing higher education in Africa. In E. Mogaji, F. Maringe, & R. Hinson (Eds.), *Strategic marketing of higher education in Africa.* Routledge.

Kimenyi, M. S. (2016). *An African Union for an Emerging Continent: Reforms to Increase Effectiveness.* Retrieved from Brookings: https://www.brookings.edu/wp-content/uploads/2016/07/african-union-kimenyi-2.pdf

Kotler, P., & Keller, K. (2016). *Marketing management*, (15th ed). Upper Saddle River, NJ, Pearson.

Kwemo, A. B. (2017, April 20). *Making Africa Great Again: Reducing aid dependency*. Retrieved from Brookings: https://www.brookings.edu/blog/africa-in-focus/2017/04/20/making-africa-great-again-reducing-aid-dependency/

Mallonee, L. (2018). *The Techies Turning Kenya Into a Silicon Savannah.* Retrieved from Wired: https://www.wired.com/story/kenya-silicon-savannah-photo-gallery/

Mkono, M. (2018, May 24). *Changing the African narrative through social media platforms.* Retrieved from The Conversation: https://theconversation.com/changing-the-african-narrative-through-social-media-platforms-97097

Mogaji, E. (2021). *Brand management: An introduction through storytelling.* Palgrave.

Ndofirepi, E., Farinloye, T., & Mogaji, E. (2020). Marketing mix in a heterogenous higher education market: A case of Africa. In E. Mogaji, F. Maringe, & R. E. Hinson (Eds.), *Understanding the Higher Education Market in Africa.* Routledge.

Nguyen, N. (2020). Can we brand a pandemic? Should we? The case for corona virus, COVID-19 or SARS-CoV-2. *Journal of Public Affairs,* e2546.

Njugunah, M. (2021, January 12). *British Model Naomi Campbell Appointed Magical Kenya International Ambassador*. Retrieved from Capital: https://www.capitalfm.co.ke/business/2021/01/british-model-naomi-campbell-appointed-magical-kenya-international-ambassador/
Norman Lear Center. (2018). *Africa in the Media*. Retrieved from Annenberg School for Communication and Journalism: https://www.mediaimpactproject.org/africa-in-media.html
Olaleye, S., Ukpabi, D., & Mogaji, E. (2020). Public vs private Universities in Nigeria: Market dynamics perspective. In E. Mogaji, F. Maringe, & R. E. Hinson (Eds.), *Understanding the higher education market in Africa*. Routledge.
Onuzulike, U. (2014). Nollywood video film's impact on Nigerian and other African environments and cultures. *Explorations in Media Ecology, 13*(3–4), 285–298.
Osei, C., & Gbadamosi, A. (2011). Re-branding Africa. *Marketing Intelligence & Planning*, 284–304.
Papadopoulos, N., & Hamzaoui-Essoussi, L. (2015). Place images and nation branding in the African context: Challenges, opportunities, and questions for policy and research. *Africa Journal of Management*, 1–24.
Poncian, J. (2015). The persistence of Western negative perceptions about Africa: Factoring in the role of Africans. *Journal of African Studies and Development*, 72–80.
Scerri, E., et al. (2018). Did our species evolve in subdivided populations across Africa, and why does it matter? *Trends in Ecology & Evolution, 33*(8), 582–594.
Settles, J. D. (1996). *The impact of colonialism on African economic development*. Retrieved from TRACE: Tennessee Research and Creative Exchange: https://trace.tennessee.edu/cgi/viewcontent.cgi?article=1182&context=utk_chanhonoproj#:~:text=The%20policies%20of%20colonialism%20forced,economic%20and%20technological%20position%20today
Siele, M. (2020, October 30). *Magical Kenya Launches New 'Kenya Coast' Brand, 7 Sub-Brands* [VIDEO]. Retrieved from Business Today: https://businesstoday.co.ke/magical-kenya-launches-new-kenya-coast-brand-7-sub-brands-video/#:~:text=The%20Kenya%20Tourism%20Board%20(KTB,%2C%20Diani%2C%20Watamu%20and%20Tsavo
Signe, L., & Gurib-Fakim, A. (2019, January 25). *Africa is an opportunity for the world: Overlooked progress in governance and human development*. Retrieved from Brookings: https://www.brookings.edu/blog/africa-in-focus/2019/01/25/africa-is-an-opportunity-for-the-world-overlooked-progress-in-governance-and-human-development/

The Economist. (2020). Why are some African countries improving and others not? Retrieved from The Economist: https://www.economist.com/special-report/2020/03/26/why-are-some-african-countries-improving-and-others-not

Van Dyk, A., Tkaczynski, A., & Slabbert, E. (2019). Repeat tourism, destination image and behavioural intentions: Implications for sustainable development in South Africa. *Tourism Recreation Research, 44*(3), 392–398.

Vasudeva, S., & Mogaji, E. (2020). Paving the way for World Domination: Analysis of African Universities' Mission Statement. In E. Mogaji, F. Maringe, & R. Hidson (Eds.), *Understanding the higher education market.* Routledge.

Index

S. Appau (ed.), *Marketing Brands in Africa*, Palgrave Studies of Marketing in Emerging Economies,
https://doi.org/10.1007/978-3-030-77204-8

The manufacturer's authorised representative in the EU is Springer Nature Customer Service Centre GmbH, Europaplatz 3, 69115 Heidelberg, Germany. If you have any concerns regarding our products, please contact ProductSafety@springernature.com

Printed and bound by CPI Group (UK) Ltd, Croydon, CR0 4YY

30/09/2026

02225455-0010